AF580157

Mrs Hobson's Album

M^RS HOBSON'S ALBUM

given to ELIZA HOBSON by her friends

when she returned to England in June 1843

as a remembrance of her time as wife to

NEW ZEALAND'S first GOVERNOR

Reproduced with Commentary and Catalogue by

ELSIE LOCKE & JANET PAUL

with notes on MAORI TEXTS and new translations by CHRISTINE TREMEWAN

Published by AUCKLAND UNIVERSITY PRESS for 1990

in association with the ALEXANDER TURNBULL LIBRARY

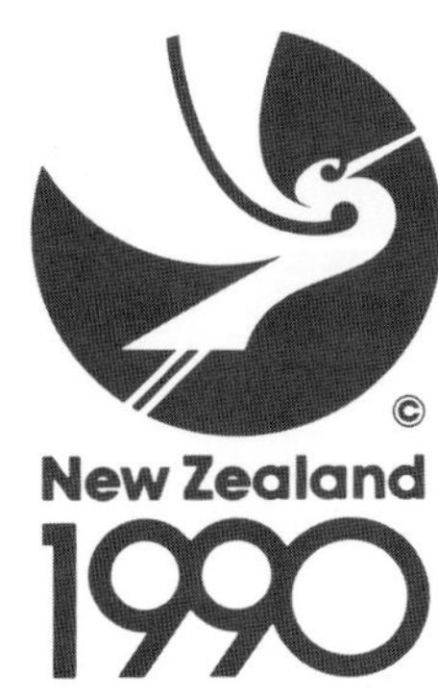

OFFICIAL PROJECT

THE RENDEL FAMILY
DESCENDANTS OF
ELIZA AND WILLIAM HOBSON
PRESENTED HER ALBUM
TO THE PEOPLE OF NEW ZEALAND
IN 1940.

This publication has been financially assisted by the NEW ZEALAND 1990 COMMISSION to commemorate New Zealand's 150th Anniversary in 1990.
Funding was made available by the Commission in recognition of the historical and social significance of the publication and in order that it may be accessible to a wide audience.
The Commission is not responsible for any statements made or opinions expressed herein. Responsibility for these rests with the authors.

The publishers also gratefully acknowledge the assistance of the Sir John Logan Campbell Residuary Estate Trust Board.

ISBN 1 86940 035 6

Typeset in Garamond by TYPESET GRAPHICS LTD, Auckland
Printed in Hong Kong by KINGS TIME PRINTING PRESS LTD
Designed by JANET PAUL

Contents

Acknowledgements

The Editors warmly acknowledge the assistance and co-operation of Mr J. E. Traue, Chief Librarian of the Alexander Turnbull Library, custodians of Mrs Hobson's Album, and of his research staff, especially the art librarians Moira Long and Marian Minson. We thank also Pamela Najar, formerly the conservator of works on paper of the Technical Services Branch of the National Library; and Dame Joan Metge for whose final comments we are particularly grateful.

The staffs of the following have been most helpful: Auckland Public Library, Auckland Institute and Museum Library, and the Auckland City Art Gallery; the Hocken Library, Dunedin; National Archives, Wellington; the National Library of Australia, Canberra; and the Mitchell and Dixson State Libraries of New South Wales, Sydney. We thank also the British Library for permission to use drawings from the album presented by Sir George Grey.

For some biographical details concerning Joseph Jenner Merrett we are indebted to members of the Gage and Merritt families (the spelling of the name has changed) and to Joy Tomlinson Phelan.

For contributing the detailed notes on Maori writings in the Album we thank Christine Tremewan of the Maori Studies Department, University of Canterbury. We are grateful for other information and advice concerning the Maori content to the following: Mary Barton-Donnell (Ngati Maniapoto); Robert Emery, kaumatua (elder) of Ngati Maniapoto; Stephen (Tipene) O'Regan; Hone Tuwhare; Mrs Rahera Ngeungeu Zister (Ngati Paoa); D. R. Simmons and Te Riria, Auckland Museum; Jim Mandeno of the Te Awamutu Historical Society; Margaret Orbell and Mervyn McLean.

In connection with the history of early New Zealand painting, Roger Blackley and Ron Brownson, of the Auckland City Art Gallery, have been most helpful. Ann Parsonson, Ian Wards, the late Ormond Wilson, Nancy Taylor, Dick Scott and J. O. C. Phillips have given advice on historical aspects, and W. D. Leadbeater has assisted with research. Many others have helped in a variety of ways.

Our deep appreciation goes to the Rendel family in England, descendants of Eliza and William Hobson, whose present members have given us every possible assistance.

J. P.
E. L.

Introduction

In January 1840, Governor Sir George Gipps of New South Wales, Australia, extended the boundaries of his colony to include any territory in New Zealand which might be brought under British sovereignty; and Captain William Hobson of the Royal Navy, already accredited as Consul, was sworn in as Lieutenant-Governor over those territories. On 21 May 1840 British sovereignty was proclaimed over all three islands. On 3 May 1841 the link with New South Wales was severed and, at a public ceremony, Captain Hobson was raised to the full dignity of Governor of New Zealand. Unfortunately, his term of office was marred by ill health and was ended by his death in Auckland on 10 September 1842.

His widow Eliza, with their five children, remained in Auckland for nine months longer. She was farewelled at a formal assembly with a 'loyal address' signed by 104 gentlemen and two ladies. More tangible was the gift of the unique and beautiful memento, Mrs Hobson's Album, which is reproduced here.

In its pristine state the volume was probably brought to New Zealand in the baggage of one of the artists. We have found no record of how it was compiled or presented. Most of the contributions were inserted, and this could have been done at any time; some material is dated later than Mrs Hobson's departure. But three items were written directly on to the pages of the Album: a poem, a poroporoaki (Maori farewell) addressed to her, and a message to be conveyed to Queen Victoria. That is evidence that she was given the book to take with her, though it is also possible that she left it to be supplemented and delivered later. Perhaps it was hoped in time to fill up the blank pages.

The known contributors to Mrs Hobson's Album are: Edward Ashworth, B. Connell, Wiremu Hoete Ririkakara, Dr John Johnson, William Mason, Felton Mathew, Joseph Jenner Merrett, John Guise Mitford, Edward Shortland, and Te Wherowhero (Potatau I).

After Mrs Hobson's death at Plymouth in 1876, the Album passed to the family of her daughter Eliza (Lila), Lady Rendel, the only one of her children whose descendants are now living. During the preparations for the centenary in 1940 of the founding of the colony, the New Zealand High Commissioner in London, Mr W. J. Jordan, was active in seeking the return of historical art and writings to their country of origin. The Rendel family responded by donating Mrs Hobson's Album and a number of letters to the Alexander Turnbull Library, Wellington.

In Maori custom a valuable taonga (treasure) was often presented to a visitor as a special tribute and honour, in the expectation that it would eventually be returned to mark some other significant occasion. The arrival of this taonga in Wellington, however, was overshadowed by the onset of war. Its publication now becomes a koha to all the people of the country of its creation.

It is a gift of friendship.

Elsie Locke
Janet Paul

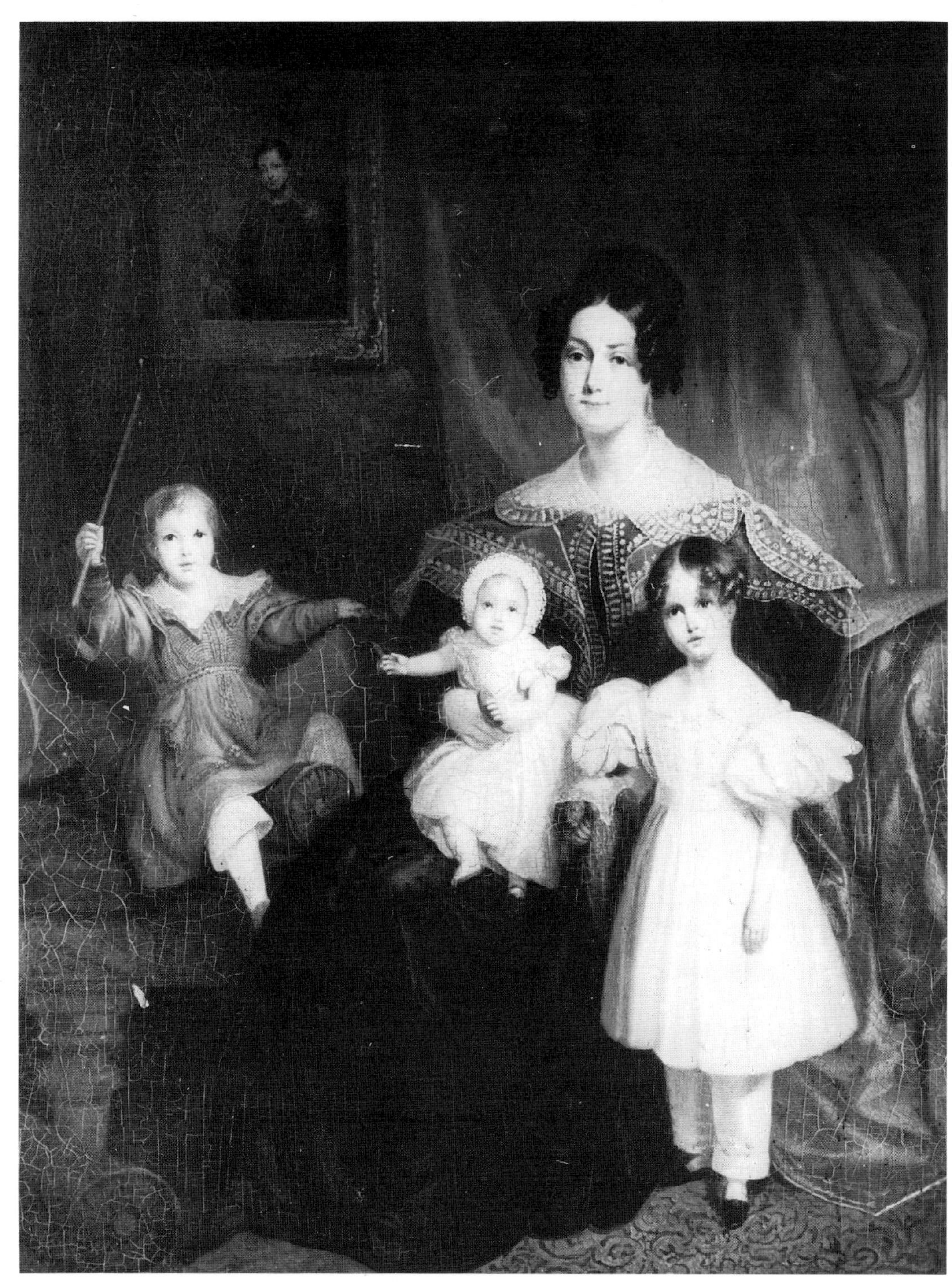

James Collins of Bath, *Mrs Hobson and her three children* [1835], 684 x 506 mm
National Library of Australia

The Hobsons in New Zealand

Elsie Locke

'My dearest Liz,' wrote William Hobson from HMS *Rattlesnake* in Sydney Harbour on 16 December 1836, 'Your letter and the accounts I have received of you so completely fill me with joy.... Rest assured, my treasure, that my greatest consolation since I left home has been derived from the Knowledge that you are placed beyond the reach of want, and I hope you believe I am sincere when I assure you that I so entirely and confidently rely on your discretion....'

And again the following day: 'The anniversary of our wedding, this blessed day nine years since we were united, not in form merely but in truth. Our sympathies, our loves and our wants, and nine years of the tenderest affection have cemented our union in bonds of natural confidence. What greater blessing can man look for on earth. One thing only is wanting to render our felicity complete.... When this reaches you the term of our separation will be reduced under a year, and with God's blessing it is to be hoped we will be in the enjoyment of each other's society within this period. Then indeed will our situation be enviable. How eagerly I look forward to it!'[1]

1. Hobson MS Papers 46, folder 1, ATL.

'My dearest Liz' was formerly Eliza Elliott, only daughter of a merchant in Nassau, Jamaica. William met her when he was a naval lieutenant combating piracy in the West Indies. They were married in 1827 when he was thirty-four and she only sixteen, and they went to England together at the conclusion of that tour of duty.

For over six years they lived in Plymouth where their children Lila, William, and Mary Esther were born. In 1834 William Hobson was given the command of HMS *Rattlesnake* and posted to the East India station, which included Australia. This appointment advanced his career and secured his livelihood (for Hobson had no private means), but kept the loving family divided for over three years.

While in Australia, the officers and crew of HMS *Rattlesnake* saw something of the settlers' lives around Sydney and made the first survey of Port Phillip as a forerunner to founding the colony of Victoria. Here Hobson went kangaroo-hunting in the company of aborigines, 'an inoffensive and rather an intelligent race of people'. Perhaps, he wrote to Liz, he might be appointed Governor of this new colony? 'These are fine castles dear — but don't be alarmed. I will not stir an inch without your full concurrence.'[2]

2. ibid., 20 December 1836.

The following year HMS *Rattlesnake* was ordered to New Zealand where a tribal conflict was causing alarm among Europeans at the Bay of Islands. Attempts at mediation were not wanted, so Hobson sailed as far south as Port Underwood with its whaling stations, and made observations at various points along the east coast. These six weeks (26 May to 4 July 1837) enabled Hobson to write a report for the New South Wales Governor, Sir Richard Bourke, with proposals for extending some control and protection to British citizens, short of annexing the country, which was not then the policy of Britain.[3]

3. *GBPP* 1837 [H.C. 122], pp.9-11.

To his Liz, William Hobson wrote with fresh enthusiasm about the attractions of New Zealand for an appointment ashore. He also shared his more serious thoughts: 'the day is not far distant when that country will be wholly occupied by white people' who already controlled trade and 'fisheries' and had purchased 'the most valuable districts'.[4]

4. Letter 28 August 1837, Hobson MS Papers 46, folder 1.

Within three years, British policy had adjusted to these rapidly changing conditions.[5] The *Rattlesnake* report and his experience in the colonies of Jamaica, India, and Australia meant that Hobson was drawn into official consultations, and his ambitions were realised. On 24 August 1839 he sailed from Plymouth, already appointed Consul, and prepared to be sworn in as Lieutenant-Governor under Sir George Gipps of New South Wales. With him travelled Eliza and the children, a few servants, the governess Ellery Short, and a friend and protégé, Lieutenant Willoughby Shortland. Eleven days before they reached Sydney, Eliza gave birth to another daughter, Emma.

5. See Peter Adams, *Fatal Necessity.*

Hobson had little time to cherish his new baby. Three weeks were absorbed in earnest discussions with Governor Gipps, in engaging his staff and in receiving businessmen with eyes on New Zealand opportunities. Eliza and the children remained in Sydney when he proceeded to the Bay of Islands. On his arrival on 29 January 1840, he read the proclamation extending the boundaries of New South Wales to any territory which would be acquired in New Zealand.

Hobson's instructions from the Secretary of State for the Colonies were explicit on principles, but often vague on their practical application. They were also inherently contradictory. He was to deal with the Maori people with mildness, sincerity, justice, and good faith, and to see that the Europeans did not 'repeat, unchecked, in that quarter of the globe, the same process of war and spoliation under which uncivilized tribes have almost invariably disappeared as often as they have been brought into the immediate vicinity of emigrants from the nations of Christendom'.[6] This view echoed the findings of the House of Commons Committee on Aborigines in British Settlements, two years earlier.[7] It reflected not merely the lobbying of missionary societies but also the extension of that humane concern which had so recently contributed to the outlawing of the slave trade in British ships. The veterans of the anti-slavery movement were active in founding the Aborigines Protection Society.

6. *GBPP* 1840 [H.C. 311], pp.37-42, Normanby to Hobson.
7. 26 June 1837. Extract in Bell and Morrell, *Select Documents on British Colonial Policy*, pp.545-8.

According to the 'Aborigines Report', no settler government could be entrusted with the care of indigenous peoples; but had not the Almighty himself endowed Great Britain with wealth, prosperity, and intellectual, moral and religious advantages? It followed that natives in due time would accept 'the opportunity of becoming partakers in that civilization, that innocent commerce, that knowledge and that faith with which it has pleased a gracious Providence to bless our country'.[8]

8. ibid.

Hobson therefore was to promote colonisation, in these islands possessed by 'a numerous and inoffensive people whose title to the soil and sovereignty . . . is indisputable'. It was taken for granted that they would willingly part with enough of that land which to them was 'of no actual use'.[9] The fact was that the Maori were in active occupation of the most desirable areas and had other values in land that the Colonial Office did not dream of. The conflict that must inevitably arise

9. *GBPP* 1840 [H.C. 311], pp.37-42, Normanby to Hobson.

between the need of the immigrants to acquire this land and the need of the Maori to retain it was obscured by the wish to serve both interests.

Captain Hobson was much more closely attuned to the current of thought behind these policies than were the ambitious Europeans he was sent out to govern; and he honestly attempted to carry out his instructions in circumstances where no man could have succeeded entirely. He must surely have longed for a little time to settle in at the Bay of Islands where he had been directed to make a start, where missionaries and merchants were concentrated and where the British 'Resident' James Busby had sponsored a grouping extravagantly called 'the United Tribes of New Zealand'. But Colonel William Wakefield had already made extensive land deals further south for the New Zealand Company, which was in the emigration business, and the first of its settlers were ashore in Wellington. The businessmen and intending land-buyers of Northland and later of Auckland had ambitions which Hobson could not satisfy; and when they discovered his sensitivity to criticism — he was a naval officer, accustomed to being obeyed without question — they needled him incessantly through their committees and newspapers. The Wellington colonists set up their own administration.

None of these people could easily appreciate the priority given to Maori needs. Hobson had to exercise his authority backed only by £2000 squeezed unwillingly from the New South Wales exchequer, a handful of police and Justices of the Peace, no troops whatever, and a staff drawn from the small pool of educated men whom Sir George Gipps could spare. James George, a plain-spoken baker who settled in Auckland, called them 'a strange lot of cast-off old Sydney officials'.[10] With a few exceptions Hobson came to rely on those he promoted himself, like Captain W. C. Symonds and the brothers Willoughby and Edward Shortland, who belonged to Plymouth families whose worth he knew.

10. 'Remembrances', APL.

Inevitably the Lieutenant-Governor found his public life a thicket of thorns; but behind him, happy and secure, stood his home and his family. Whatever his critics might say about him, nobody had a harsh word for his wife. 'There is an excellent trait in Hobson', wrote his chief surveyor Felton Mathew, 'he is so fond of his wife and family and so desirous of having them with him.'[11] At a vice-regal dinner for fifty gentlemen in Auckland's Royal Hotel, the toast 'to Mrs Hobson and the ladies' included these words: 'Her kindness, urbanity and hospitality have elicited the highest encomiums and emotions of respect and esteem from all who have the honour of knowing her.'[12] After the Governor's death the *Auckland Times,* a bitter opponent of his administration, had kind words for his widow: 'The unobtrusive, silent course of habitual benevolence which has marked her path among us has not been unobserved because it has been retiring and noiseless.'[13]

11. *The Founding of New Zealand,* p.22.

12. *New Zealand Herald and Auckland Gazette,* 24 July 1841.

13. 12 September 1842.

The Treaty that Captain William Hobson was bound by honour and duty to secure was signed at Waitangi on 6 February 1840 by some forty-five Northland chiefs, and by many others later. In this way the Maori gave their consent to British rule in exchange for certain undertakings which they were not to know would be disputed from that day onwards. They were to receive all the rights and privileges of British subjects, and to have the full, exclusive and undisturbed possession of their lands, forests, fisheries, and taonga (things of value) as long as they wished to retain them. As a shield against exploitation, further land sales were pre-empted by the Crown. Certainly the Treaty of Waitangi was hasty, and what it conveyed to the Maori in their own language was not the same as what it conveyed to Hobson. Nevertheless, the new Lieutenant-Governor was perfectly sincere in his intention to honour its pledges.

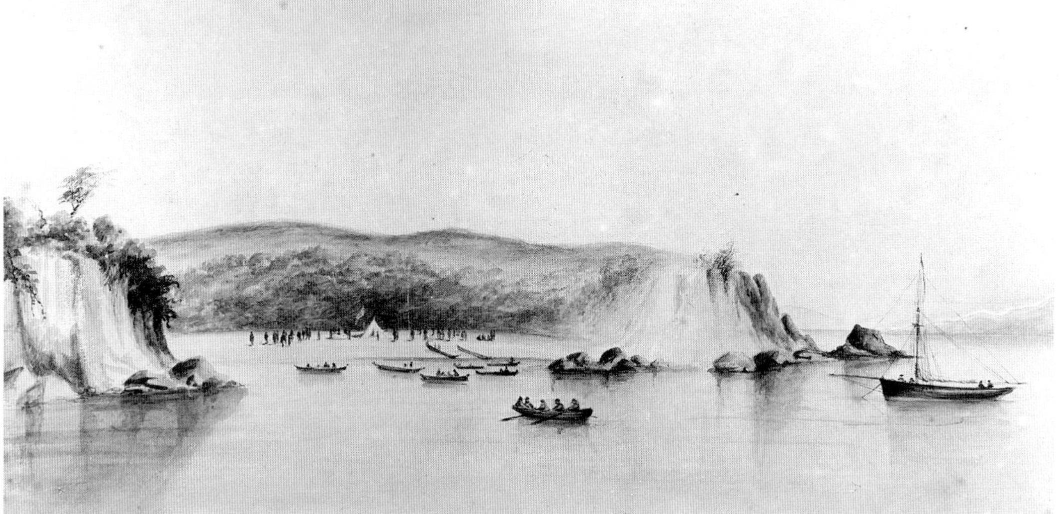

W. Jordan, *Signing of Treaty of Waitangi by Maori chiefs at the Entrance to the Tamaki River, June 1840*, 255 x 360 mm
Auckland Institute and Museum

Unhappily, on 1 March, while on a voyage which was meant to include Wellington, Hobson suffered a stroke at the Waitemata Harbour, and had to be sent back to the Bay of Islands with his right arm and leg paralysed. Alarming messages arrived in Sydney to throw doubt on his recovery and the peaceableness of the Maori. In great haste, Major Thomas Bunbury was despatched with eight officers and eighty soldiers, and with orders to take over the Government if necessary. With him on HMS *Buffalo* sailed Eliza Hobson and her children. They landed on 16 April and to their great relief found William recovering in the house of a missionary at Paihia.

This was a temporary refuge, for the purchase had already been approved of the first Government House, an existing building in the Bay of Islands at a place to be named Russell (see Plate **56**). The family were soon in residence. In her 'wooden palace', Eliza wrote to her friend Emma Smith in Plymouth, she was as happy as ever in her life. The farm adjoining the house gave great pleasure; and the children made pets of the poultry and cows, and received pocket money for their care of the chickens.[14]

14. Letter 29 June 1840, Hobson MS Papers 46, folder 4.

But Russell was only a temporary capital; for Hobson had been instructed to select a site suitable for communication with the Maori tribes who were then, as now, most numerous in the North Island. A much-travelled missionary, Henry Williams, was consulted and without hesitation he recommended the Waitemata Harbour. A short portage across the Tamaki isthmus led to the Manukau, whence a second portage led to the Waikato River; and this was a well-established route to the interior. The land was almost vacant, for it had been depopulated when the Ngapuhi of the north had armed themselves with muskets and swept southwards, killing thousands and driving the survivors far inland. The defensive pa on the volcanic cones which studded the landscape were all deserted.

After peace was restored in the 1830s, the Ngapuhi were still watched with caution. In 1835 the ariki of the Waikato tribes, the famous warrior Te Wherowhero, moved northwards. At Awhitu on the Manukau Peninsula he announced his readiness to protect the entire area, and he sealed that promise by settling first at Mangere and then at Onehunga. The Ngati Whatua under Apihai Te Kawau built a pa at Karangahape (Cornwallis) on the northern shore of the Manukau, while the associate Te Taou went to Okahu on the Waitemata. Somewhat earlier the remnants of Ngati Paoa returned to their land at Waiheke Island and the Tamaki estuary. However, their total numbers were not large and a Pakeha presence could be an additional guarantee of security.

At a combined runanga (assembly) at Okahu it was decided to go and ask the Queen's representative to come and live beside them. With their delegation went Captain William Cornwallis Symonds, who was already living among Maori at Kaipara as agent for a modest colonising venture, the Waitemata and Manukau Land Company. An army officer on long leave from his regiment, Symonds came from a Plymouth family well known to the Hobsons; his father was Surveyor-General to the Navy and his brother had served on HMS *Rattlesnake*.[15] The seven rangatira (chiefs), including Te Reweti Tamaki, Te Kawau's influential nephew, easily persuaded Hobson to come and see for himself; but this first Waitemata visit was cut short by his illness.

15. Letters 20 December 1836 and 31 January 1837, Hobson MS Papers 46, folder 1.

In July 1840 the cutter *Ranger* brought the Lieutenant-Governor back. Among his companions was the Colonial Surgeon, Dr John Johnson, who had a great eye for land. Captain David Rough, the future harbourmaster, later recalled how they anchored for the night off the Sentinel (Watchman Island).

> Dr Johnson, an accomplished artist, was the first to call attention to the inviting appearance of the country. . . . I offered to leave the cutter and remain behind to take soundings and examine the shore at low water before daylight next morning.
>
> Just as the sun rose I climbed the cliffs to where Ponsonby now is, and beheld a vast expanse of undulating country, mostly covered with fern and manuka scrub; several volcanic hills in sight, and, near the shore, valleys and ravines in which many species of native trees were growing, whilst the projecting cliffs and headlands were crowned with pohutukawa trees. . . . But there was not a sign of cultivation or human habitation, the nearest native village being out of sight. . . . not even a canoe was to be seen on the spacious surface of the Waitemata. . . .

> When the cutter returned His Excellency, accompanied by Dr Johnson, Mr Clarke and myself, landed and walked along the shore to what is now called Freeman's Bay. All we saw appeared favourable for the site of a settlement. Captain Hobson was much pleased, and without fixing on a particular spot for a site, we returned to the Bay of Islands. Soon after our return orders were given to make preparations for sending officers, workmen, and stores to the Waitemata.[16]

16. 'The Early Days of Auckland', APL.

John Johnson had the pleasure of painting the scene when the Union Jack was raised on Point Britomart immediately after the deed was signed for the first purchase of land from the Ngati Whatua tribe (see p.148). It was as lively a celebration as could be produced by perhaps three hundred people: six officials and one of their wives (Sarah Mathew); seventy-five members of the worker families, brought to begin work on the town; the crew of the *Anna Watson* which brought them from the Bay of Islands; the crew also of the *Platina* from England via Wellington, with the makings of Government House on board; and a large assembly of Maori with the four rangatira who had signed the land deed. They all cheered the flag, and the ships fired their guns in salute; and then, in Sarah Mathew's words, 'her Majesty's health was rapturously drunk with cheers loud and long repeated from the ships, to the very evident delight of the natives'. There followed a luncheon and a regatta with two boat races and one canoe race, while in the evening Captain Rough entertained with songs and his guitar, despite having shouted himself hoarse in honour of the Queen.[17]

17. *The Founding of New Zealand* pp.192-3.

The name of the town, *Auckland,* was cut into the flagstaff. It was chosen in honour of Lord Auckland who, as First Lord of the Admiralty, had secured Hobson's appointment to HMS *Rattlesnake,* and soon afterwards, as Governor-General of India, had continued his interest in Hobson's career. The master of ceremonies was Captain Symonds who was now Police Magistrate, standing next in rank to the Lieutenant-Governor. Confident of his abilities, Hobson had successfully applied to Sir George Gipps to have his army leave extended.

Point Britomart has long ago vanished through harbour reclamations, and so has Official Bay where the gentlemen had the finest building sites. The merchants were allotted Commercial Bay to the west of Point Britomart, where the Horotiu stream wandered down the gully which soon contained Queen Street, and where deep water came close to the shore. Round to the east where Grafton Gully ended in swampy land was Mechanics Bay (see Ashworth sketches, pp.34, 148). Here the workmen pitched their tents, replaced them with tiny cottages, and finally abandoned them for more convenient locations around Chancery Street, leaving their Bay to its sawpits, ropewalks and brickyards. St George's Bay soon gained a few better-class homes; and when the Chief Justice and the Attorney-General arrived they established themselves at Judges Bay — the only one of those charming coves which has survived the reclamations.

Thus the three distinct classes of officials, business people, and workers were separated by geography as well as by differences in education, occupation, and income, until some of the merchants became prosperous enough to merge with the administrators into one upper class and to share the more select neighbourhoods. In Hobson's time they were struggling and complaining loudly. There was no production as a basis for trade: it was Maori produce that supplied the new town. Land purchases prior to the Treaty of Waitangi had still to be validated by Commissioners; land purchases after the Treaty had to wait on surveys and on Government deals with the Maori.

Although he was soon to be blamed for the stagnation and frustration, the Lieutenant-Governor was greeted with éclat when he made his official entry into Auckland with his wife and family on 14 March 1841. They were received by a guard of honour, cheered by the settlers and many Maori, and led in procession to the newly erected Government House.[18]

18. David Rough, 'The Early Days of Auckland'.

Even then, this impressive and spacious residence (see Plates **3** and **8**, and p. 112) was not quite ready for occupation. Eliza and William were using a nearby cottage and the children were sleeping in the raupo schoolroom when, the very next month, a distinguished guest arrived. She was Lady Jane Franklin, wife of Sir John Franklin, then Governor of Van Diemen's Land (Tasmania). This intrepid woman was later to gain prominence through her strenuous efforts to trace the Franklin expedition, which disappeared in the search for a north-west passage across the Canadian Arctic.

Lady Franklin had come up from Wellington where she had stayed with the New Zealand Company leader, Colonel William Wakefield. Hostility between the two centres was obvious and she took care to be tactful. Despite an injury to her foot, which necessitated her being carried about, she accepted with alacrity the opportunity to attend a missionary hui (gathering) at Port Waikato. Captain Hobson was to address it, but became unwell and had to turn back at Onehunga.

Government House was in better shape when Lady Franklin returned, and soon she was so much at ease with the Hobsons and their 'four very nice children' that she offered to house William junior if he could be sent to an appropriate school in Hobart. She was there when the news came through that New Zealand was declared a colony independent of New South Wales, with Hobson elevated to the status of Governor. This gave 'great satisfaction, not to the Governor only but to everybody, and congratulations and addresses are pouring in upon him', Lady Franklin wrote to her husband. 'Now that I know Capt. Hobson I feel a great interest in and regard for him also, an interest not the less lively because I cannot help thinking that though he may yet be spared a few years longer, that his years are not many.'[19]

19. Letter 24 April 1841, in George Mackaness (ed.), *Some Private Correspondence of Sir John and Lady Franklin,* Part II, pp.14-19.

She judged correctly. Governor Hobson never regained sufficient health and vigour to follow his decided inclinations and travel around the Maori districts. Only one such journey proved possible, in April and May 1842, and even then he could get no further than Otawhao (Te Awamutu). If he had been able to establish further afield the close accords he achieved with the Maori of Auckland, the outcome of these important founding years could have been very different.

As it was, he was bound to rely on reports from his officials; reports to which his wife would surely have listened, for his correspondence shows that he shared his experiences with her.

Captain Symonds represented the Governor at the Port Waikato hui attended by a thousand Maori, and continued a remarkable expedition with the German scientist Dr Ernst Dieffenbach, and Lieutenant Abel Dottin Best. Although Symonds had duties to perform, including an attempt (which proved unsuccessful) to catch two European fugitives from justice, these three men set out to learn rather than instruct, and all three have left illuminating accounts.[20] Dieffenbach was unusual for his time in that he did not assume any innate superiority of European over 'primitive' cultures. Lieutenant Best had insatiable curiosity. None of them was restricted by evangelistic attitudes which tended to dismiss Maori culture as 'heathen'. Their own religious beliefs were indeed less rigid than those of their newly converted Christian guides, who could not be persuaded to travel on the Lord's Day.

20. Ernst Dieffenbach, *Travels in New Zealand; The Journal of Ensign Best,* ed. Nancy Taylor; W. C. Symonds, copy of extracts from his Journal, MS, Hocken.

At Otawhao, where the mission station was a vigorous centre of education and agriculture, Best recorded: 'A Mr Merrett whom we met at Mr Morgan's has expressed a wish to join our party which will certainly be granted as he has some little knowledge of the language and is moreover a good draughtsman.'[21] The very next day, five miles further on at a kainga called Ngahuruhuru, Joseph Jenner Merrett sketched a dramatic incident which became widely known through the lithograph which appeared as a frontispiece to Volume II of Dieffenbach's *Travels.* The rangatira Te Waru, having declared his determination to abide by British laws, brought forward his sixteen-year-old daughter to be judged by the Magistrate. Her brother had committed suicide after his adultery with a slave, whereupon the girl had killed the slave. Symonds listened attentively and then, realising that the daughter had not done wrong in the light of Maori tikanga (custom), was content to have her dismissed with a lecture by the missionary John Morgan.[22]

21. Best, *Journal,* p.297, 26 April 1841.

22. Dieffenbach, v.2, pp.38-39; Best, *Journal,* pp.298-9; Symonds's Journal, 27 April 1841. See also poem 'Te Waru' in the *New Zealand Journal* 1843, p.113, unsigned but in Merrett's ballad style, and Plates **24, 25** of this Album and corresponding note.

Lieutenant Best must soon have overcome the doubts he recorded as to whether Joseph Merrett could do justice to the scene, and to other scenes as they travelled. By the time Merrett left the expedition on the eastern shores of Lake Taupo, his interest and skill in depicting Maori life would have been established. Possibly this led to his close association with Edward Shortland; for these two men between them provided most of the Maori content of Mrs Hobson's Album.

Edward Shortland, a family friend of the Hobsons from their Plymouth days, arrived in New Zealand early that year (1841) and soon commenced that eager study of Maori life, language, traditions, customs, and culture which has made him such a valued authority. He was very likely to have been present when Dieffenbach and Symonds described their travels to Eliza and William Hobson at Government House. Almost immediately afterwards he travelled as Private Secretary to the Governor on the much-postponed visit to Wellington on board the Government brig *Victoria.*

'I cannot bear to think of his going', wrote Eliza to her friend Emma Smith, 'for they have treated him so ill, they deserve nothing at his hands.'[23] But she declined to go with him as he wished, and with good reason; for in the same letter she confided that she might be in need of more baby-linen; and she was afraid of sea-sickness. Under the circumstances, perhaps the three views of that New Zealand Company settlement contained in the Album were quite sufficient (Plates **30, 38, 39**).

23. Letter 4 August 1841, Hobson MS Papers 46, folder 4.

Hobson himself was prepared to be conciliatory, but had nothing in his hands to give, so slender were his resources. The Wellington leaders had a string of complaints to deliver when he arrived on 20 August 1841.

First — it had taken the Governor a very long time to come at all.

Second — he had planted his capital on the empty ground of the Waitemata when they already had a substantial and increasing immigrant population centrally placed for the two islands. (They neither understood nor approved the policy towards the Maori for which Auckland was more central, or the simple fact that Hobson had been directed to the northern tribes in the first place.)

Third — when they had set up their own self-governing Council, he had reacted sharply to this apparent challenge to his authority and declared it illegal. His emissary Willoughby Shortland, who was sent with the backing of thirty soldiers to straighten things out, did not improve matters.

Fourth — he had advertised in Wellington for tradesmen and sawyers to build his new town, offering attractive wages and free passages; thus enticing away some eighty workmen brought out by the Company. (They nicknamed him 'Captain Crimp' for that.)

Therefore the Governor was coolly received; and he was powerless to assist with the most pressing problem of all: how to gain title and access to the land they were hoping to farm. The land commissioners had yet to come.

Hobson then sailed to Akaroa where he concurred with the leaders of the French community that Port Cooper (Lyttelton Harbour) could not be settled by the New Zealand Company so long as the French claim to have purchased the whole of Banks Peninsula was yet to be investigated.[24] This was bad enough — and then the Wellington people were further outraged to discover who else was aboard the *Victoria*. Hobson's companions actually included the Protector of Aborigines George Clarke, 'in the position of interfering between the native and the settler'; and the 'northern barbarian Te Wherowhero'. News came that the ship had anchored off the Kapiti Coast to allow communication with 'the dreadful murderer Raupero [Te Rauparaha], who possessed no land and lived on a small island. . . .'[25]

24. *GBPP* 1842 [H.C. 569], pp.164-7.

25. *New Zealand Journal*, 20 July 1844, p.521.

Very little is known of this surprising meeting between the Governor's party and, if not Te Rauparaha himself, his front-ranking rangatira Te Hiko. Edward Shortland preserved a record of a letter written subsequently by Te Rauparaha to Te Wherowhero, begging him to continue working for peace between Maori and Pakeha, a plea that he repeated in Governor FitzRoy's time.[26] These two

26. Shortland MS 86B, Hocken; Patricia Burns, *Te Rauparaha*, pp.221-2; *GBPP* 1844 [H.C. 33], pp.128-9.

powerful and sagacious chiefs saw clearly the advantages to be gained from co-operation, and acted accordingly. In later years, for both of them the relationship with the government of the day deteriorated; but it was real and valuable so long as the perceived interests of the two sides coincided. Hobson could be clumsy and tactless when dealing with colonists, but he did not underestimate the Maori leaders.

After Wellington, it must have been a tonic to be received back in Auckland 'by Government officers and other gentlemen and a large concourse of assembled inhabitants . . . with loud cheers, and greeted with hearty demonstrations of welcome'.[27] But the following month came a tragedy: the loss of the Hobsons' close friend and trusted Magistrate, Captain William Cornwallis Symonds.

27. *New Zealand Herald and Auckland Gazette,* 13 October 1841.

The Waitemata and Manukau Land Company, whose agent he was, had at last brought out an emigrant ship with twenty-six men, women, and children from Scotland. The *Brilliant* was anchored behind Puponga Head on the north shore of the Manukau on 23 November 1841, when a messenger came over from Orua Bay to ask if there was a doctor on board to attend the missionary's wife, Elizabeth Hamlin, a brave woman with a large family whose husband was absent at the time.

The *Brilliant* had no doctor and so Captain Symonds himself, with two other Pakeha and the Maori who had brought the message, set out in the ship's longboat with medicine. On that notorious stretch of water the longboat capsized and only the Maori survived, to report that Symonds swam a long time in his heavy clothing before he drowned, or perhaps was taken by a shark. His body was never found. (Mrs Hamlin however recovered.)

This was more than a personal tragedy. If he had lived, Symonds would have been administrator after the Governor's death, instead of Willoughby Shortland in whom Hobson's confidence was misplaced. Symonds was well liked for his personality and respected for his capabilities, and all Auckland mourned for him. Dr John Johnson later sketched for Mrs Hobson the place where the tragedy occurred (Plate **31**).

With the Magistrate gone, it was fortunate that the Chief Justice (William Martin) and the Attorney-General (William Swainson) had recently arrived from England. They were soon to have a testing time with the first trial of a Maori for murder. The case was a sensation at the time, controversial for both peoples, and a very sad human story.

Motuarohia in the Bay of Islands was farmed by John Roberton, a sea captain who had survived many stormy seas to settle down with a wife and family, only to be drowned before their eyes in the autumn of 1840. His widow Elizabeth remained on their island farm, using hired help. On 30 November 1841 her employee Thomas Bull, aged 35, was abusive (not for the first time) to his fellow-worker Maketu, who retaliated by killing him. According to his own account, when Maketu told Mrs Roberton, she also abused him, whereupon he killed her too, with her small daughter and a half-Maori child, Isabella Brind, who was in her care. He then pursued the Robertons' seven-year-old boy to the top of a cliff and threw him over, returned to the house and set fire to it. George Clarke junior, who knew Maketu's family well and was interpreter at the trial, afterwards wrote that insane rages were hereditary in Maketu's family.[28] He was only sixteen or eighteen years old.

28. *Notes on Early Life in New Zealand*, p.41.

The smoke from the burning house alerted two merchants of Kororareka to go to the island and investigate. Soon the horrified town was demanding that the murderer be dealt with. But the Bay of Islands had one magistrate, two constables and no soldiers at all, and not even enough residents to take action if the arrest of Maketu was resisted. The Maori quickly gathered in great numbers on Motuarohia.

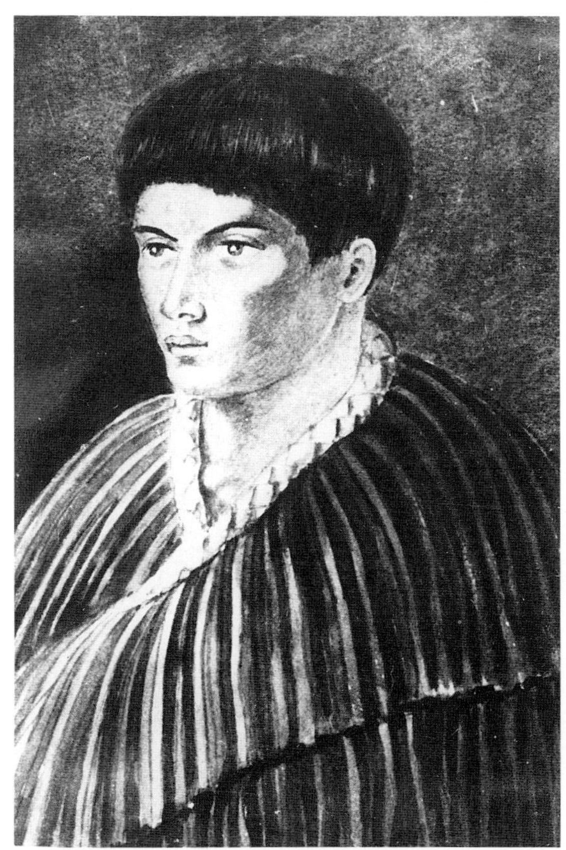

Artist unknown. *Maketu hanged at Auckland 1842*, watercolour, 266 x 199 mm
British Library

Maketu was well-born, the son of the rangatira Ruhe, connected with Pomare and others of mana. From the standpoint of Maori tikanga his action, at least in the case of Thomas Bull, could be considered as utu (repayment). But what of the foster-child Isabella, granddaughter of the rangatira Rewa? Her relatives in turn could claim utu for her death; and where would be the end of the conflict?

The agitation among the Maori led to rumours among the Pakeha that the Maori were about to rise against them. However, the issues were resolved at a hui brought together by Rev. Henry Williams at the Paihia mission on 16 September. Resolutions signed by an impressive list of rangatira, including Maketu's father, were sent to the Governor. These Ngapuhi leaders regretted the actions of Maketu, which were his alone, and gave assurances that they had no intentions of rising against the Europeans in their midst. Maketu was given up.[29]

Ngapuhi were not of one mind, however. Hone Heke was among those who thought Maketu should be dealt with by tribal custom, and that to hand him over to Pakeha justice was to diminish Maori independence. His resentment over this issue was a factor in his rebellious felling of the flagstaff at Kororareka three years later.

At the inquest Maketu frankly related what he had done, and he was taken to Auckland for trial. The officials and the settlers saw this as a triumph for the acceptance of British law. Henry Williams expressed a different view in a letter to James Busby: 'The disturbance arising from the capture of Maketu was happily suppressed, but I do not hesitate to say that had not the grandchild of Rewa been one of the victims, thereby bringing all the Ngapuhi tribes as auxiliaries to the Europeans in the event of war, the result of the affair would have been far otherwise.'[30]

29. Hugh Carleton, *The Life of Henry Williams*, v.2, pp.42-43.
30. ibid. p.46.

The trial before Chief Justice Martin was expected to make a suitable impression on the Maori, and according to George Clarke junior it did; but it was still a strange procedure in their eyes. At the last minute Maketu was provided with a defence lawyer, who had to improvise. But why go to such lengths in arguing whether a man was guilty when he repeatedly said that he was? And once he was condemned, why not kill him at once, instead of keeping him in a cell within sound of the hammering as they built the gallows, his 'house of death'?

His kinsmen begged the Governor to allow them to take Maketu out and deliver a blow with the mere from behind, in their own honourable manner. But English custom prevailed. A church service was held in the Courthouse, where everybody who was anybody (including the Hobsons) prayed God to send His grace into the heart of the poor prisoner; and during Maketu's seven days of agonised waiting, the Rev. Churton saw to his baptism and penitence (see Plates **6, 52, 53** and corresponding catalogue notes).

The hanging was a public spectacle to which the populace rolled up a thousand strong. It might appear to the colonists as retribution and a deterrent; but by Maori standards the whole business was stupid and cruel. A man had to die: let it be over and done with.[31]

31. Maurice Lennard, *Motuarohia*, gives a detailed account of the whole affair.

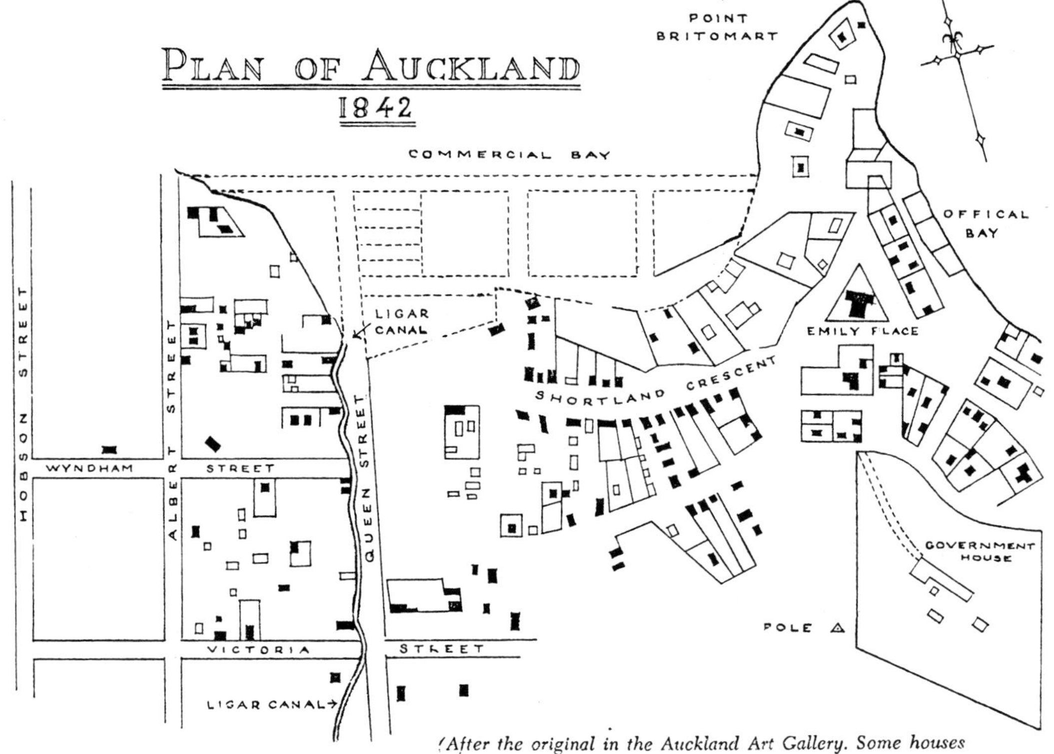

(After the original in the Auckland Art Gallery. Some houses were not filled in on the original.)

Plan of Auckland 1842, reproduced in 'Historic Auckland' by John Alexander [?1961]

There was only one benefit to the people of Auckland in the Maketu trial. The mucky state of Queen Street, where the Horotiu stream flowed sluggishly through accumulated debris, was a continuing cause of complaint. Was a Chief Justice in full regalia expected to leap across it, or tramp through it and soil his gown? A bridge was quickly built at Victoria Street so that the Courthouse could be reached with a modicum of dignity.

The artist and architect Edward Ashworth found conditions much the same when he arrived in October 1842, splashed ashore on slippery rocks and saw that 'two great dead pigs were lying on the beach & the dogs ever & anon giving a tug at their entrails'. He continued:

In the cottages of this hopeful town were to be seen here & there Scotch mechanics some in work & some not. They had just arrived from Glasgow in a Govt emigrant ship that was wrecked a few months after, as if in judgment for her halfheartedness in bearing in her bosom these poor deluded wretches to semistarvation on a desolate shore. The men looked too neat & civilised for colonial life, their wives & children walking about barefoot or treading clothes in tubs as washerwomen seemed more in harmony with & suited to the savage aspect of the spot — a group of children might be seen dipping pieces of bread into a frying pan of pork fat seasoned with young onions. . . .

Commercial Bay was fringed by some storehouses all weatherboard & 2 or 3 inns & behind these was the chief thoroughfare Shortland Crescent, here a number of emigrants were at work reducing the hill, levelling & filling to produce a gradual inclination; an utter disregard being paid to the sites of houses hastily reared on allotments which had cost the owners large sums. Many of these houses or rather their occupants had to make themselves an access down a loose earth slope by a stepladder. Others removed themselves upstairs & threw out a sort of platform or drawbridge from their first floor to the level of the road; some screwed up their weatherboard dwellings with lifting jacks to the new level; others were left at an immeasurable distance above the street & quite invisible behind the steep banks of earth thro which the cutting was made. . . .

I found New Zealand as might well have been expected, a colony commenced at the wrong end; Town civilization wretched as were its untraceable streets of board cottages had taken the precedence of the rude agricultural labour that is necessary to prepare every country to afford subsistence to its inhabitants. . . .[32]

32. Edward Ashworth MS Journals [brown notebook], ATL.

Even in the desirable quarter of Official Bay the roads were a hazard. The Justice's wife, Mary Ann Martin, has described how a ball was held at Government House when the weather was bad. Nobody gave up. Some of the ladies borrowed jackboots, tucked up their skirts and waded through the quagmire; and one who

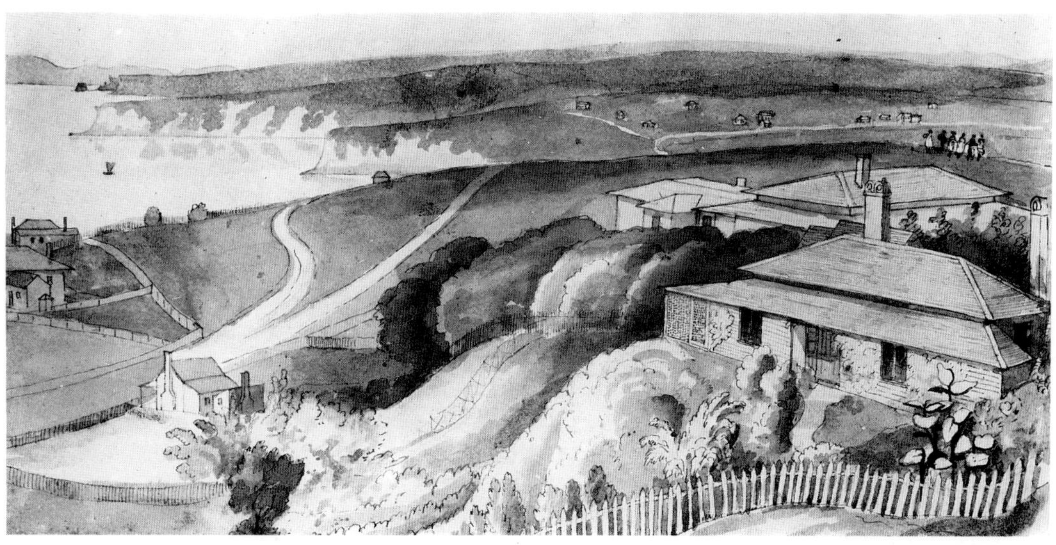

Edward Ashworth (1814–1896), *Residences, Official Bay, Auckland* [1843], ink and sepia wash, 140 x 210 mm
Alexander Turnbull Library

fell in simply stopped at the house of a friend to clean herself up. One chivalrous husband wheeled his wife to the ball in a wheelbarrow.[33]

The Hobsons were amiable hosts. Before the church was built their drawing room was the venue for weddings. When the fiancée of one of the officials arrived from Sydney she stayed at the house until the wedding day and had Lila Hobson for her bridesmaid. The governess brought out from London, Ellery Short, was married there to the harbourmaster David Rough. These weddings were always followed by a ball, and the Governor danced the first quadrille with the bride. Afterwards the happy couple simply walked together to their new home.

Hospitality seems never to have faltered, although four days before her second Christmas in New Zealand Eliza Hobson bore her fifth child, Margaret — an event given only brief notice in the newspaper.[34] Emma was then only two years old; but a young baby and a toddler in the house would create no social impediment where there were servants. To the Hobsons, all their babies were a blessing.

The townspeople seized every opportunity to enjoy themselves. On 29 January 1842, the second anniversary of Hobson's arrival in New Zealand, there was a regatta involving five whaleboats, three gigs, and an unlimited number of Maori canoes. Loyal toasts were drunk on board the *Portenia,* and in the evening the Governor Hobson Hotel in Shortland Crescent was brilliantly illuminated. So began the tradition of celebrating Auckland's Anniversary Day with a regatta.

It was the last such celebration for William Hobson. In mid-year, when he was facing bitter attacks from merchants seeking remedies, which he was powerless to provide, for the current economic stagnation, he was frequently too unwell to attend to public business; and on 10 September a second stroke ended his life.

The Governor was buried at Grafton with full military honours, and public animosities were laid aside. 'The interment took place accompanied by the most striking demonstrations of respect and affection', reported the *Auckland Times.* 'We can bear testimony, from experience, of the kind and urbane course of conduct adopted in his private life, towards every individual who had the honour of his acquaintance.'[35] 'He was the poor man's friend,' wrote James George in his 'Remembrances'.

The Maori crowded into the town early in the morning, mourning in their own style, sitting on the ground and keening in unison. They were directed to the rear of the procession, where 'almost every male carried a musket, but with intuitive politeness they abstained until the military salute had been fired, after which their demonstrations were rather noisy. Most of the females had their hair fantastically ornamented with wreaths of supplejack, in full blossom at the time.'[36]

The message sent to Queen Victoria by Te Wherowhero asking for a new Governor as good as the one who had recently died (Plate **7**) should be read in the context of this genuine mourning. Hobson's approach to the Maori was friendly. He respected their customs, and recognised that his authority could go only as far as the Maori would allow it. In those areas beyond the fringe of Pakeha

33. Lady Martin, *Our Maoris,* p.13.

34. *New Zealand Herald and Auckland Gazette,* 22 December 1841.
35. *Auckland Times,* 15 September 1842.
36. *New Zealand Journal,* 18 March 1843, quoting the *NZ Gazette.*

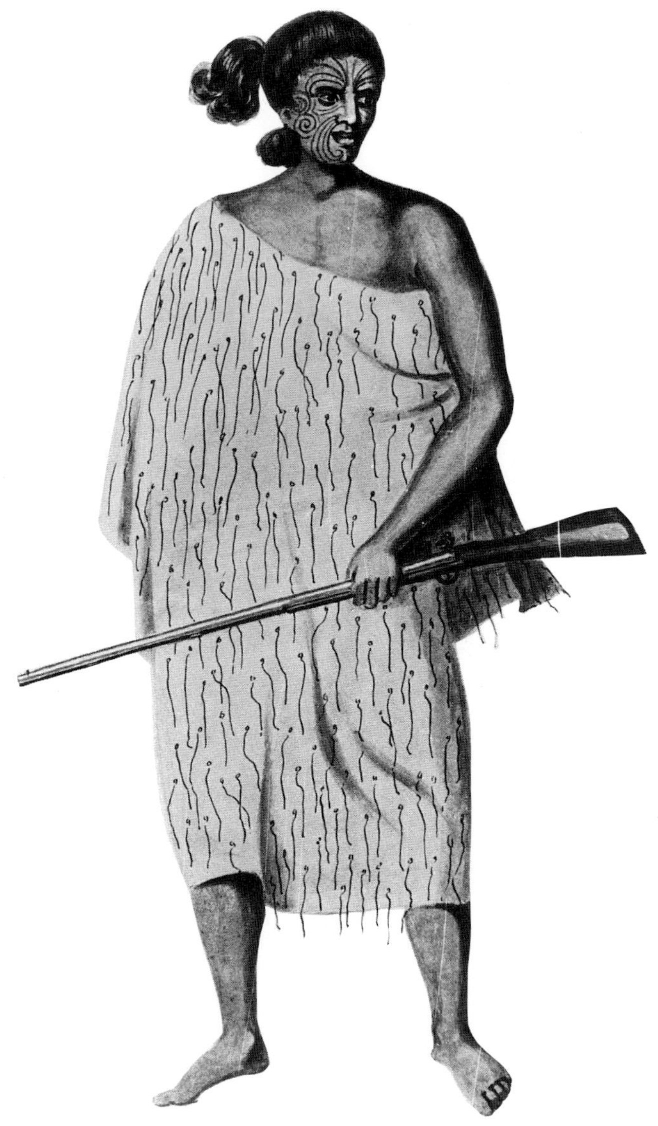

Joseph Jenner Merrett (1816-1854), [*Rangitira with musket* 1842], ink and watercolour, 337 x 237 mm
British Library

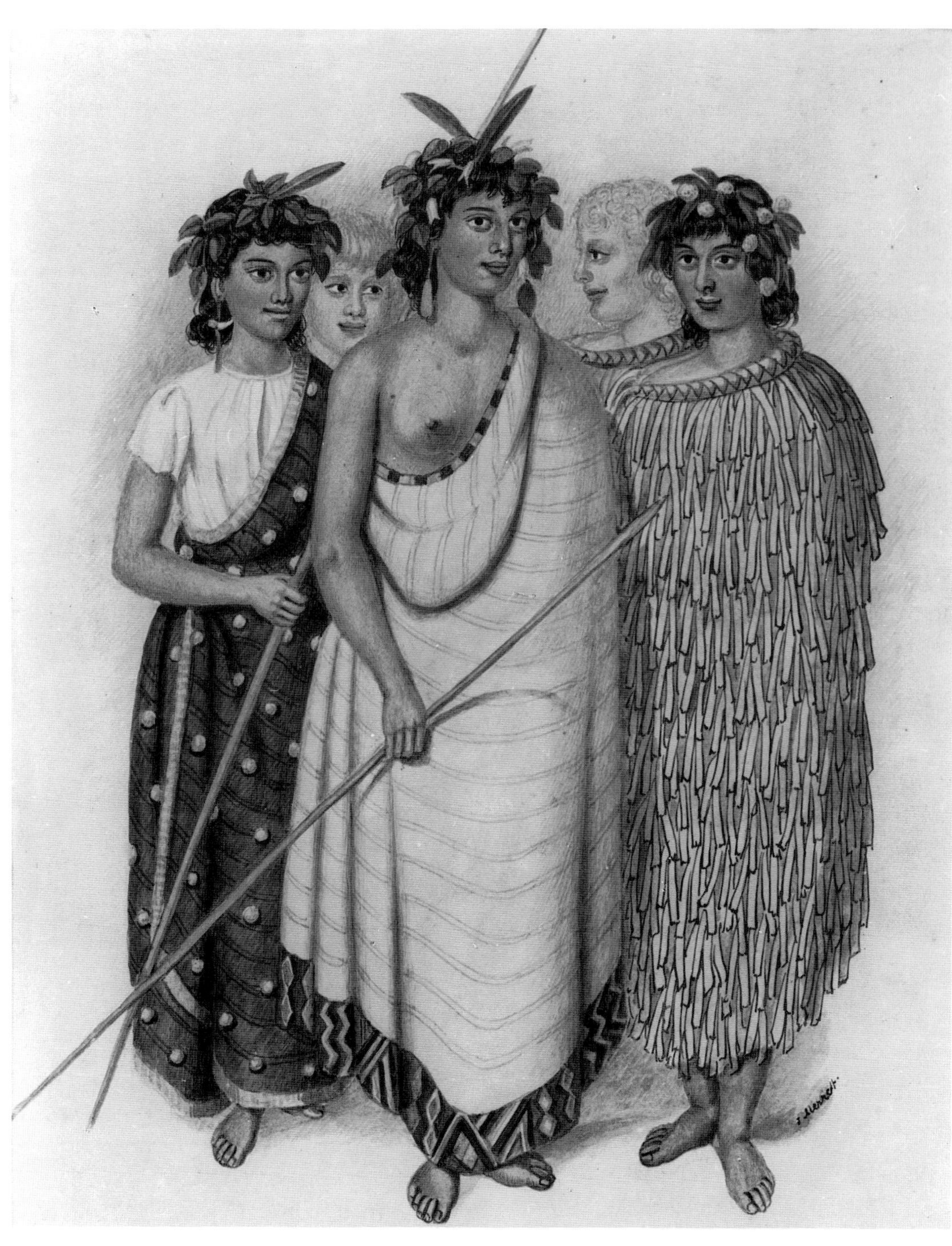

Joseph Jenner Merrett (1816–1854), [*Maori women wearing wreaths, 1842*], ink and watercolour, 241 x 183 mm
Hocken Library

settlement the Maori lifestyle continued much as before, with only such innovations from European contact as the Maori chose to introduce. A kind of dual control was to persist in the colony for the first twenty years, until the supremacy of the settlers was enforced by the wars in the key districts of Taranaki, Waikato and the east coast of the North Island.

Edward Shortland described in his diary on 4 November 1842 a visit to the pa at Kaitotehe, on the Waikato River near Taupiri. 'In a short time old Te Wherowhero came towards me, when I rose to meet him. This was the first time we had met since Hobson's death, on which account he saluted me with his native lament, and cried most bitterly for about 10 minutes, when he nosed me. His old wife (Wai-matau) followed his example, being carried on her "amo" [litter].'[37]

37. Journal of a journey to Matamata, Tauranga and Waikato, Hocken MS 22.

Although Te Wherowhero did not sign the Treaty of Waitangi he was at one with Hobson in trying to get the best from the new relationship of the two races. Hobson for his part must also have recognised that the security of Auckland depended heavily on the mana of Te Wherowhero. It was only when the pressure of settlers and speculators to obtain the land became relentless, that the ariki of the Waikato tribes turned from co-operation to resistance and became, as Potatau I, the first Maori King.

In Hobson's time the Maori from far afield enjoyed a lively trade with Auckland in pork, fish, potatoes, kumara, wheat, maize and melons. The Governor was well received on his journey southwards as far as Kawhia and the Waipa Valley in April 1842.[38] Serious problems there were, and a deep uneasiness as to what British rule might have in store — but the grievances which oppressed Captain Hobson in the last months of his life came more from the settlers than from the Maori.

38. Described in *The Journal of Ensign Best* and in Shortland's Journal, Hocken MS 21.

Historians have passed widely varying judgments on the career of New Zealand's pioneer Governor. This is how he appeared in the eyes of his widow:

> The Office to which Captain Hobson was thus promoted was arduous as well as honourable. Few Governments but have trials and difficulties, but in the new Colony of New Zealand these were accumulated and peculiar, arising from the Native population, the character of many of the Europeans who had settled on its shores, the disappointed Agents of a powerful company, the extravagant claims set up by individuals to the territory, and the limited means at the Governor's disposal.
>
> Zealously, courageously & disinterestedly did Governor Hobson endeavour to carry into effect the instructions of her Majesty's Government, and to promote the welfare of the Colony over which he was placed. Many were eager to possess themselves of land there, or make money by trafficking in it. Governor Hobson desired not only to be free from reproach but afford no possible ground of suspicion. When he sank to his grave under his anxieties and labour, so far had he been from using his office or station for his own enrichment, that *he did not possess, nor had he ever possessed so much as an inch* of the coveted colony . . . on the contrary, through the expenses of his outfit, his honourable spirit, and his inability to attend to his personal concerns, the small property which he possessed when he received his first appointment to New Zealand, had been diminished.[39]

39. Copy of a memorial asking for a pension, Eliza Hobson to Lord Stanley, Secretary of State for the Colonies, 4 December 1843. Hobson MS Papers 46, folder 6. Italics in the original.

Eliza Hobson herself was bound by no such constraints, for she was facing long years of widowhood with no expectation of assistance from the British authorities.

She bought land at five successive auctions, costing £726 altogether: town lots in Parnell near the Domain, suburban land around the beginning of New North Road, and 220 acres of farm land somewhere in the 'County of Eden'. Edward Shortland acted as her trustee. The investments were ultimately profitable and some of this land remained in family ownership for up to three-quarters of a century.[40]

40. *NZ Gazette*, 1842-43, pp.4, 29, 50, 144. Also records of sales by Sir Alexander Meadows Rendel and family, Auckland Lands and Deeds Office.

Eliza began her new life in England in straitened circumstances. Long after her return she was writing to Lord Auckland seeking his good offices to recover £750 realised by the sale of her husband's effects in New Zealand, and put to interim use by Acting-Governor Willoughby Shortland. Her great concern was the children's education: 'The thought of having neglected anything I might have done for the benefit of our children would be a continual grief to me.'[41]

41. Letter 29 July 1846, Hobson MS Papers 46, folder 5.

We do not know whether she ever received this £750. It does not seem that she received any pension, but she did succeed in having her son William launched on a lifetime career in the Navy, after writing to Sir G. Cockburn pleading 'the character and services of his father'.[42]

42. Letter 24 September 1844, ibid.

During the nine months of her widowhood spent in New Zealand however, Eliza Hobson remained at Government House in her accustomed lifestyle. The artist and architect Edward Ashworth, whose hand in compiling this beautiful album is very evident, has left us a vivid account of his first meeting with Eliza and her children. Unable to find other employment he announced himself as a 'Teacher of Architectural, Perspective and Landscape Drawing' and soon received an invitation to call at Government House.

> I expected to find the widow of the late Governor an elderly, prim, pompous & ceremonious lady; to my surprise I was introduced to the presence of one comparatively young, beautiful, most amiable & unaffected; it would have been difficult to have heard her speak 5 words without admiring & feeling interested in her. The drawing room she sat in was so grand compared to the generality of the Auckland apartments, redolent with perfumes artificial as well as the natural ones of a splendid bouquet of English flowers in Nov: — a gilt chandelier, a few paintings, a handsome piano & some cases of highly ornamental books, and last but not least a beautiful child of about 3 years [Emma], with blue eyes & a profusion of jet ringlets that was playing in one of the fauteuils, that I almost fancied myself in the regions of romance. The very landscape out of doors had its wildness curtailed by being seen thro a broad verandah screened with white trellis work.
>
> Mrs H., referring to my card, arranged that I should attend 3 times a week to teach her eldest daughter & son, & so prepossessing was her manner that I could not but anticipate a very pleasant employment. . . .
>
> A second visit to Government House introduced me to my two pupils; The boy [William], an only son, a stout intelligent looking lad of 11, with a quickness and readiness beyond his years, which won the heart very soon, though his idleness bid fair to estrange it again; however it was smooth water for the first few days, 'new brooms sweep clean.' But the young lady [Lila]: she it was that I had the greatest curiosity to see; & in she came with the sweetest &

> most modest smile & with a manner far above all vulgar bashfulness or childish awkwardness presented her drawing book for my inspection.
>
> She might have been 12 or 13, rather slender & tall for her age. . . . If this young girl shone in personal beauty, — the lustre of her mental acquirements & her sweetness of temper lost nothing by comparison. The concern she evinced, when her brother in any of his stubborn fits, was insolent to me; her mild gentle & persuasive rebukes addressed to him, the tact & cleverness with which she would manage the younger children, who, poor things, for company's sake must come and play beside us, the elegance & politeness of her manners & conversation (evidently Mamma's associate), made me feel a regard for her and admiration as of one far more mature in years. . . .[43]

43. Edward Ashworth MS Journals [green notebook].

Perhaps these young pupils were looking on as Ashworth applied himself to the preparation of the Album.

Shortly before the family sailed for England aboard HMS *Tortoise*, Eliza Hobson was honoured at a public assembly with the delivery of this public address:

> We cannot but deem it a matter of just consideration, that the chief place in Society in this infant Capital should, from the earliest period of its formation, have been filled by a Lady, who, both in public life, and in private station, has so admirably fulfilled the various duties of social life, as to call forth a spontaneous expression of respect from a whole community. . . . If, after performing the duties which now call her to England, Mrs Hobson should again be drawn hither by the ties that must always connect her to New Zealand, her return would be welcomed with sincere and heartfelt joy.
>
> We would conclude this expression of our feelings by assuring Mrs Hobson that, in leaving Auckland, she carries with her the sincere sympathy, the unfeigned respect, and the kindest wishes of the whole of its inhabitants.[44]

44. *Southern Cross*, 10 June 1843.

We have found no report of a Maori farewell, although there must have been one. Perhaps, when Eliza Hobson and the children stood ready to board the pinnace which ferried them out to HMS *Tortoise*, Wiremu Hoete Ririkakara was there with his people to deliver in flowing oratory the sentiments of his written poroporoaki (Plates **22, 23**).

The Governor's widow never remarried, and she never returned to New Zealand; but her links with the country were never severed. Occasionally her Auckland friends were able to visit her at Penlee House in Plymouth. And with her, at all times, were the words and images to keep in mind those vivid years when a colony was founded: the gift of Mrs Hobson's Album.

Contributors to the Album

Janet Paul

We are presented, as was Mrs Hobson, with an album. It contains fifty delightful drawings and watercolours, two manuscript poems, letters from two distinguished Maori chiefs, Potatau Te Wherowhero and Wiremu Hoete, a translation of Maketu's last words and seven pages giving written examples and comment on Maori customs, songs and proverbs.

For Mrs Hobson they were gifts from friends, reminders of shared experience. She would have recognised the Maori scholarship of Edward Shortland, her husband's private secretary, who became Sub-Protector of Aborigines. She had seen St Paul's Church grow from William Mason's original drawings and would have appreciated the accurate detail of the chief surveyor, Felton Mathew, in his reminder of her first home in New Zealand. She had probably watched her children's tutor, Edward Ashworth, draw the facade of Government House and had herself been drawn, in ink, by the Colonial Surgeon, John Johnson.

She would have been familiar with the expert watercolours of John Guise Mitford, a young son of Anglo-Irish gentry, who worked as a minor official. Although Mrs Hobson did not travel south of Auckland, she would have often listened to her husband and their friends tell travellers' tales of Maori customs, ceremonies and modes of living recorded by the one man in early Auckland who described himself as 'artist': Joseph Jenner Merrett.

For Mrs Hobson, these works were reminders of known people and places seen, or spoken of, during the three and a half years she spent in Russell and Auckland; but for us, who study this Album 150 years later, the guides are less certain. Eleven different people contributed to the Album, but of the fifty drawings and paintings only five works are signed or initialled; a sixth drawing bears an implied signature, since part of a manuscript on its verso is signed 'J. Merrett'. For the remaining forty-five works we can only suggest likely artists: attributions which may, in time, give way to different certainties.

Some attributions can be made with assurance. When we have smaller studies of the same subject in a known sketchbook or journal or in a well-documented collection, legitimate parallels can be drawn, given that a number of art curators have judged certain drawings to be 'by the same hand'. If we can establish the artist of one of these versions, on historical and biographical grounds as well as graphic style, then we can be safe in ascribing the whole group.

Some earlier attributions have already been changed as more knowledge is made available. For instance, when Dr Hocken and his wife went to England in 1903 they called on Mrs Hobson's descendants in Plymouth to see this family album. Mrs Hocken copied from it two pictures of the founding of Auckland which were attributed to Dr Johnson, as were also two paintings of Government House (Plates **3** and **8**). In 1966, when the Alexander Turnbull Library bought 'Journal of a Voyage from London to New Zealand & to Australia & China 1842-4', by an architect, Edward Ashworth, that second attribution was seen to be mistaken. An Ashworth sketchbook[1] contains a small detailed drawing, 'Government House, New Zealand', which corresponds exactly in style and treatment of architectural

1. Ashworth, Sketchbook, pp.30-31, ATL.

detail to the watercolours of that subject in the Hobson Album. To avoid confusion, we have made clear in the Catalogue when a previous attribution is superseded.

In the same way, a painting which has for years been catalogued 'artist unknown' may be found to belong to a body of work by a hitherto undiscovered artist. This happened in 1974, when the Alexander Turnbull Library bid at Sothebys, London, for thirteen early watercolours, mainly of the thermal region, Auckland, and Russell. Six were bought by the Turnbull Library; the remainder, re-auctioned in Wellington, are now in private hands. 'Puwai Island and Mt Tarawera' is a good

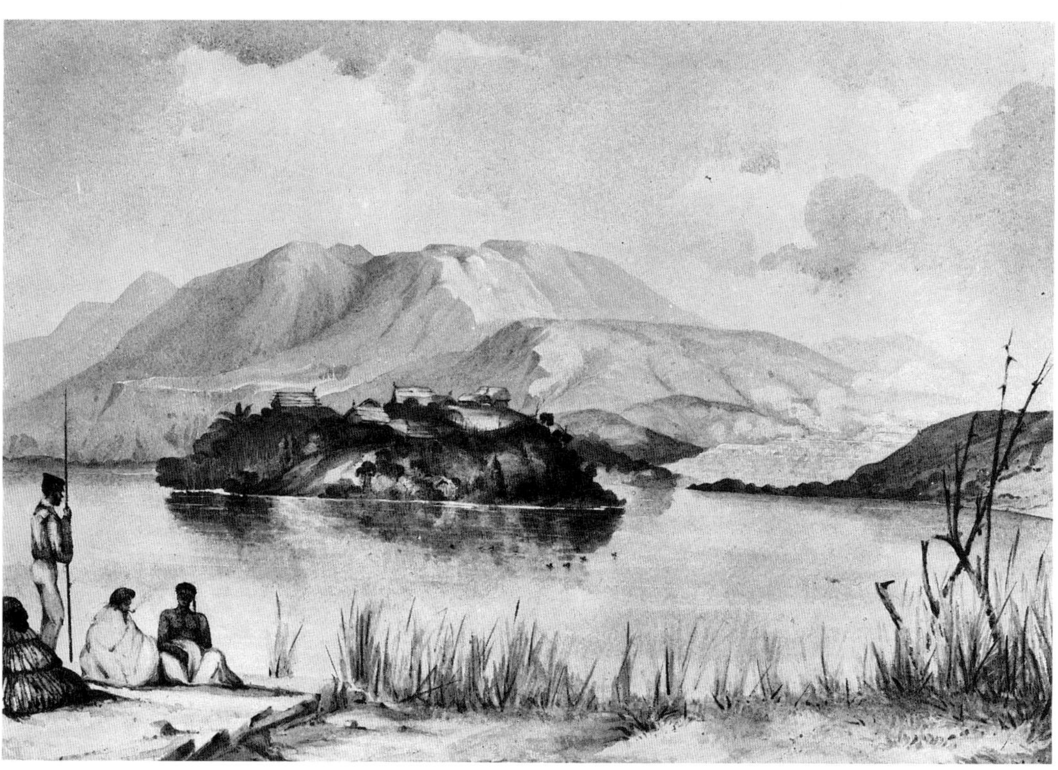

John Guise Mitford (1822–1854), *Puwai Island and Mt Tarawera* [*c.* 1845], watercolour, 226 x 324 mm
Private collection.

example of this artist's style. On one of the Turnbull watercolours was the name 'Guise Mitford'. At first it was thought that this could be the name of an early traveller in the tradition of Augustus Earle or George French Angas, or even of a previous owner; but a search for the name Mitford in National Archives disclosed letters dated 8 July and 3 August 1844 to the Acting Collector of Customs in Auckland from the Sub-Collector in Russell.[2] The Sub-Collector's handwriting resembled pencil inscriptions on mounts of the Turnbull Library acquisitions and provided evidence to identify the painter as John Guise Mitford.

2. Nat. Archives, I.A. Col. Sec., 44/1563 and 44/1786.

John Guise Mitford (1822-1854) has consequently been recognised as the artist responsible for other early watercolour landscapes hitherto catalogued as 'artist unknown' in the Turnbull and other public collections. Amongst these are two watercolours and two sepia wash drawings in the Hobson Album (Plates **14, 18, 19** and **20**). In an essay on John Guise Mitford, Roger Blackley includes another

(Plate **15** of the Album) and also attributes to the same artist 'The Grafton Gully' *c.* 1842/43, in the collection of the Auckland City Art Gallery.[3] Blackley also states: 'Geographically, the available work ranges over the Bay of Islands, Auckland and its environs, the Waikato, and the central lakes: Rotorua, Tarawera, Rotomahana and Taupo'.[4] Blackley also questions the title 'Near Wellington' of a watercolour now in private hands. However, J. G. Mitford was in Wellington before he moved north. He was appointed 'Clerk' in the Customs Department, Wellington, on 14 December 1851, with a salary of £130 p.a.[5] On 5 April 1842 he was appointed 'Collector's Clerk' in the Customs Department, Auckland; a promotion which increased his salary to £150.[6] He would have joined his brother, George Manners Mitford, who worked in the office of the Colonial Secretary, and other young men who lived around Official Bay and worked for the government. Most of Mitford's paintings of the Auckland area would have been done between March 1842 and March 1843. We can confirm their dating from sketchbook copies by K. Staples Alexander, who inscribed each page with the title and date of the original as well as with the date of his copy.[7] These copies include three Auckland images and one 'River Waikato at Pukatia Dec '44', of which the originals are not yet traced.

Mitford painted Auckland's volcanic cones with a rare accuracy of observation and technical skill. In April 1843, one year after his Auckland appointment, John Guise Mitford was appointed Sub-Collector of Customs at the Port of Russell, at a salary of £200 p.a.[8] Mitford may then have had little time for painting. In letters written to the Acting Collector in Auckland, he complained of combined customs, post office and treasury duties which forced him to work on the Sabbath. He worried also at having to keep government funds in his lodging house.[9]

We get a different picture of the artist from *The New Zealand Journal of John Brown Williams of Salem,* who was appointed, 10 March 1842, to be United States Consul at the Bay of Islands. Williams wrote, 'Her Majesties Officers at the Bay have their hours for business, 10AM to 2PM, in this small place of about 205 inhabitants'. He singled out for disapproval 'the Sub-Collector J. Guise Mitford, . . . toiling hard for this world's pleasure . . . living licentiously' in 'such splendid sin' that Williams looked forward to the time when the Eternal Judge would call to account this 'half educated upstart of a boy'.[10]

Edward Ashworth's lively glimpse of Mitford as a customs officer is more sympathetic. When his ship called at Kororareka, 31 January 1844, Ashworth commented ironically on the variety of duties imposed by 'the now economizing New Zealand Government'.[11] Stringent economies had added police duties, and extended Mitford's responsibility to make him 'Sub-treasurer of the Northern District', until the Customs office in Russell was eventually closed.

In October 1844 Mitford returned to Auckland to negotiate for the last quarter of his salary[12] before leaving on a southern journey to the thermal area, from December until early March 1845, during which time a great part of his known work was done.

3. Blackley 1983, p.51 footnote 2.

4. Blackley 1983, p.47.

5. Nat. Archives, I.A. 12/3 Blue Book 1842.

6. Nat. Archives, I.A. 12/5 Blue Book 1843.

7. Alexander, Sketchbook, APL, NZP 134.

8. *NZ Government Gazette,* 12 April 1843, by notice dated 10 April 1843, p.105.

9. Nat. Archives, I.A. 44/1563, 44/1786. In Letters to Col. Sec. 8 July, 3 August 1843.

10. *The NZ Journal 1842–1844 of John B. Williams of Salem, Massachusetts,* pp.65 & 87.

11. Ashworth, Journal, Brown notebook typescript pp.11-12, 2 February 1844.

12. Nat. Archives, I.A. 12/6 Blue Book 1844 shows that Mitford still held his appointment as Sub-Collector of Customs at Russell at the end of 1844.

It is likely that on his return Mitford sent these carefully inscribed watercolours to his family near Dublin; they would, perhaps, have illustrated a journal or descriptive letters. However, no written account by him is known, nor are there any New Zealand watercolours dated later than 1845. His name appears with those of his two brothers, George Manners Mitford and Charles Venables Mitford, on an application for 900 acres on Great Barrier Island, but there is no evidence of land being taken up.[13] Una Platts's dictionary of nineteenth-century New Zealand artists cites John Guise Mitford as Port Boarding Officer in Auckland in 1852. Mitford family records give the date of his death as 1854 but do not tell where this occurred. He may have returned to Ireland.[14]

13. Nat. Archives, Old Land Claims file.

14. Micro MS 689, ATL.

For other contributions to Mrs Hobson's Album we can begin with the few works which are signed or initialled. Plate **56** is the only drawing signed 'Felton Mathew', titled 'Government House — Russell — Bay of Islands — New Zealand. 6 Apl. 1840'.

Felton Mathew (1808–1847) was an English surveyor working in New South Wales from 1829 and listed in the Surveyor-General's Department as assistant surveyor, and after 1837 as 'Town Surveyor'. He was appointed Surveyor-General under Captain Hobson and travelled with his party in HMS *Herald.* His career is well documented in printed sources: Ruth Ross, in *New Zealand's First Capital,* gives in full detail his part in choosing and planning a proposed town at Okiato, renamed Russell. Like many early settlers, Felton Mathew and his wife, Sarah, both kept journals. These were published in 1940. In the central panel of a four-part watercolour panorama of the Auckland Harbour we are given a glimpse of the Surveyor-General and his assistant at work.

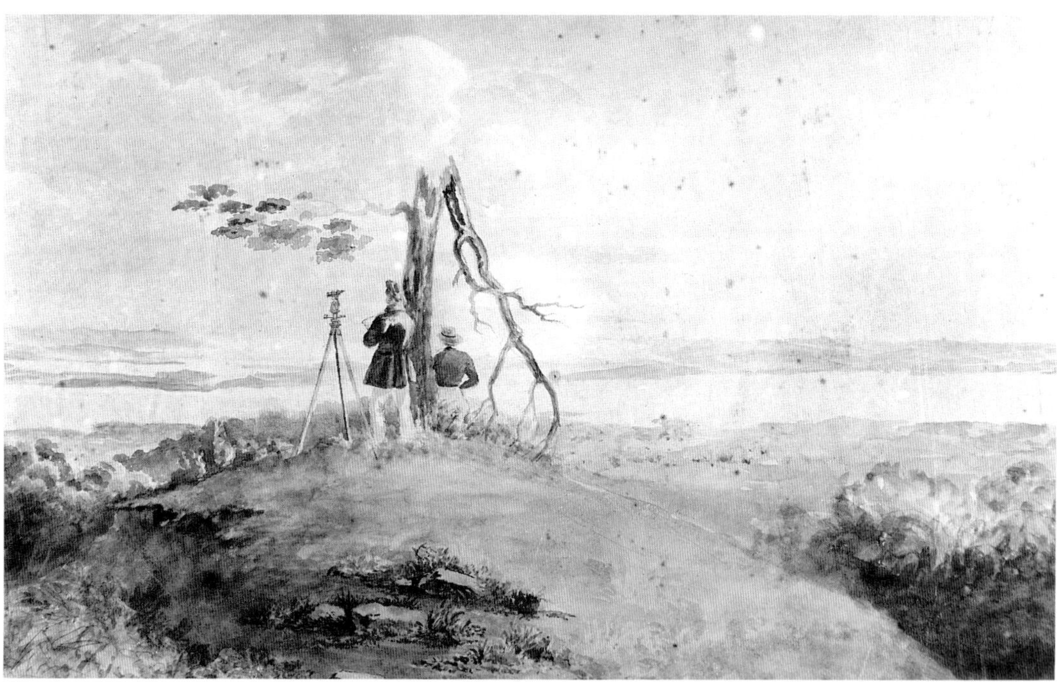

Thomas Bunbury (1791–1861), [*Panoramic view of Auckland Harbour, looking westward from the summit of Rangitoto,* 1841], 400 x 550 mm. Shows Felton Mathew taking a round of angles for a trigonometrical survey.
Auckland Institute and Museum

On Plates **28** and **60** are three ink and wash drawings which are initialled 'J. J.'. Una Platts identified these as the work of John Johnson (1794–1848) when she prepared the catalogue *Early Colonial Artists* for the Auckland City Art Gallery. The Auckland Institute and Museum also holds drawings by Dr John Johnson.

The vigorous linear style of these works, with their consistent use of a sloping, widely spaced ink hatching and a monotone wash, permits additional attribution to John Johnson of 'And the solitary places shall be made glad' (Plate **29**), 'Entrance to the Harbour Manukao from Puponga Head' (Plate **31**), as well as 'The First Government Settlement in the Waitemata River' (Plate **43**).

Dr Johnson was also one of half a dozen officials appointed in Sydney to assist William Hobson. He travelled on HMS *Buffalo* with Eliza Hobson to the Bay of Islands and set out for Waimate to attend the sick Governor on 19 March, two days after his arrival. Here he kept a brief diary and made the only New Zealand sketch we have of Eliza Hobson.[15] Dr Johnson became very active in early Auckland society, an enthusiastic gardener and dutiful citizen easily persuaded on to committees to found a public library and museum or to build a new Presbyterian Church or to raise money for a monument to Captain W. C. Symonds. Johnson made drawings to record outstanding events or houses in which particular people lived.

15. Johnson, Diary, unnumbered page at end, APL.

As a general rule it has not been possible to use the neatly handwritten Album titles as evidence of authorship, but Johnson does appear to have provided idiosyncratic titles in his own handwriting; the same hand inscribed the poem 'To Mrs Hobson' (Plates **54, 55**) and the title and names on the map 'View of the entrance to the Harbour Manukao from Puponga Head' (see p. 137), which was found on the back of the drawing 'Entrance to the Harbour Manukao [Manukau] from Puponga Head' (Plate **31**). Similarity of style confirms that this black ink and grey watercolour is also the work of John Johnson.

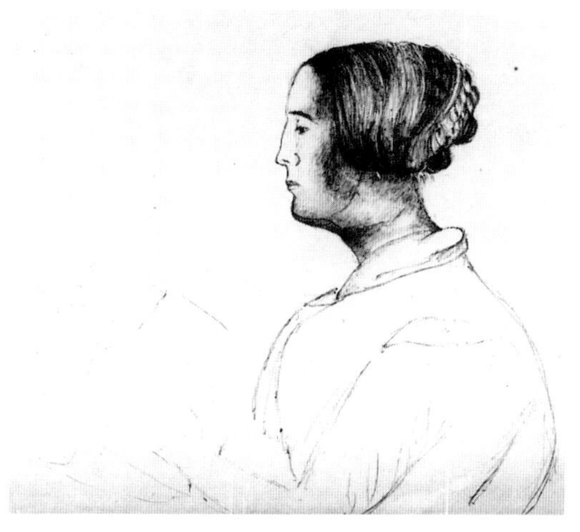

John Johnson (1794–1848), [Untitled sketch of Eliza Hobson, 1840]
Auckland Public Library

Difficulties of attribution are not confined to unsigned work. In the Hobson Album a group of three pencil drawings are signed 'B. Connell' in two different ways: 'Wellington from the London' (Plate **30**) and 'Kaiwarra Warra from the Petoni Road Wellington' (Plate **38**) are both signed, in pencil, in a flowing script. Plate **39**, 'In "Te Aro" Flat Wellington', has a more upright signature and a printed rather than cursive capital 'B'. The shipping indexes do not show any 'B. Connell'. They do list a William Connell with a wife (unnamed) and three children who arrived on the ship *London* in Wellington, December 1840. Records of the Grafton Cemetery name William Connell's wife: Isabella Connell, who died on 1 March 1895. Plate **30** is 'Wellington from the London'. It is tempting to believe that we have identified the artist; but would the William Connell, the first Postmaster, who served in the Department of the Colonial Secretary and then became an auctioneer, and later a member of the first Auckland Provincial Council, have sported two different signatures, signing himself unofficially 'B' (as short for Bill?) and officially 'William'? Or was his wife called 'Bella' and was she the artist? We have no evidence of other work signed by 'B. Connell' held in New Zealand.

There are, however, three drawings in the Rex Nan Kivell collection in Canberra which are attributed to B. Connell. The titles inscribed on the works are 'Mungaroa Bridge, Upper Hutt N.Z.', 'Pakuratihi River in Wairarapa NZ' and 'Auckland Harbour from the Bastion Rock'. None is dated. The Alexander Turnbull Library holds an unsigned watercolour (see p.144) which is so close a version of the Hobson Album drawing 'Te Aro Flat' that it is logically attributed to B. Connell. We can only say that this artist is at present named but not identified. The Auckland City Art Gallery has an ink drawing by an unknown artist of the west side of Queen Street, 1852, in which Connell & Ridings Auction Mart is prominent on the right.

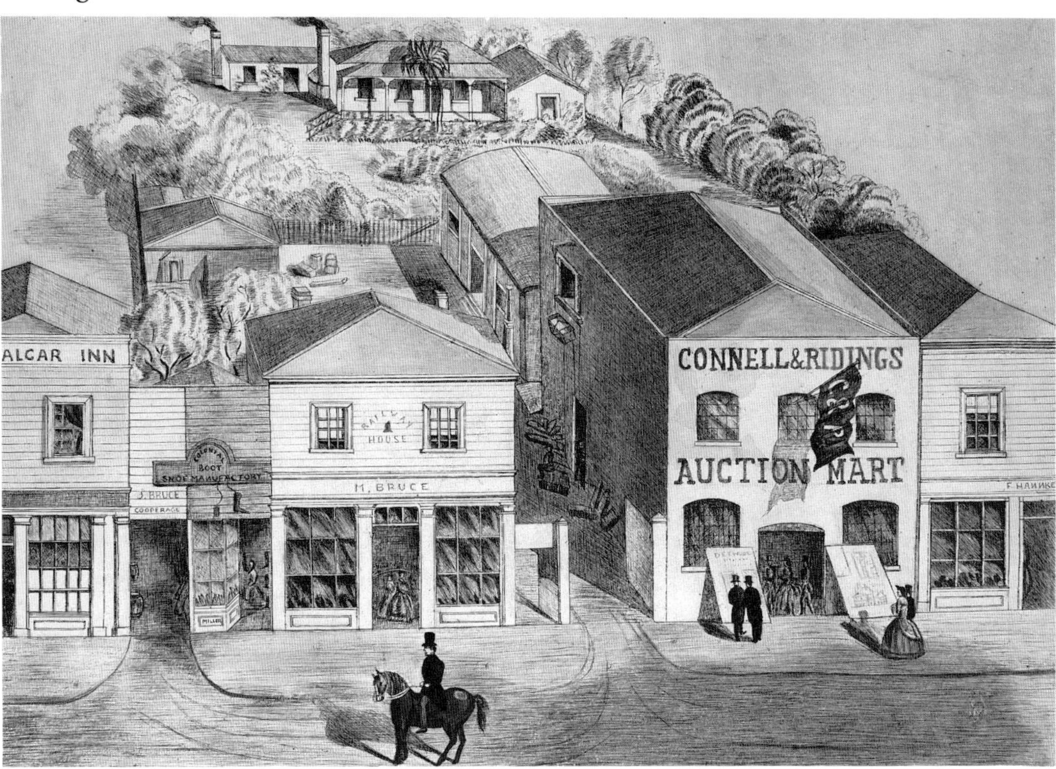

Artist unknown, *Connell & Ridings Auction Mart, c.* 1852, pen and ink with watercolour, 315 x 428 mm
Auckland City Art Gallery

The assessment of Maori texts required special scholarship. The Maori Studies Department of the University of Canterbury has assisted, with Christine Tremewan contributing the modern translations and catalogue notes for all Maori texts. She has found textual authority to attribute the collection of unsigned Maori texts to Edward Shortland (1812–1893). We are then left with possibly five unnamed contributors who provide the bulk of the paintings and drawings. Their parts have had to be assigned from the evidence of other work and this has been the most teasingly difficult task and the one most open to error.

We have already given reasons for attributing three works to John Guise Mitford. One further contributor of architectural elevations was relatively easy to trace. He is William Mason (1810–1897), the first government architect, whose three drawings of the west and east fronts and side elevation of the Metropolitan Church of St Paul are reproduced on Plates **46** and **47**. A biography by John Stacpoole (1971) establishes Mason's work and deals with the design and building of this first Anglican church.

We have already mentioned another young architect who, as tutor to the Hobson children, was closely associated with Mrs Hobson. His work became known in New Zealand only after the Alexander Turnbull Library acquired, in 1966, the journals and sketchbook kept during his fifteen months' residence here, as well as paintings of Mauritius, Cape Verde Island, Melbourne, Sydney, Batavia, Hong Kong and Gibraltar. Edward Ashworth (1814–1896) had arrived at Auckland in October 1842, six weeks after Governor Hobson's death, expecting to find in a young colony plenty of work for an eager architect. He was sadly disappointed. Ashworth spent his first few months learning the art of housekeeping and coping with the 'oviparous propensities of blowflies'. Fortunately he continued to keep and illustrate lively journals. While he made a meagre living by teaching, he asked himself what to do. 'I determined to build a little house of my own . . . live rent free, for the veriest holes containing 2 board rooms were letting at from 10s to 15s per week. I went to work to purchase a spot of ground in the town.'[16] He bought a corner allotment on High Street with an east boundary only 5m wide. 'My edifice was about 12 feet square and when with the assistance of a fellow passenger I had got 3 sides up, I engaged a bricklayer to build a chimney on the 4th side. . . .'[17]

16. Ashworth, Journal to be sent to England [Green Notebook] typescript p.30.

17. ibid., p.31.

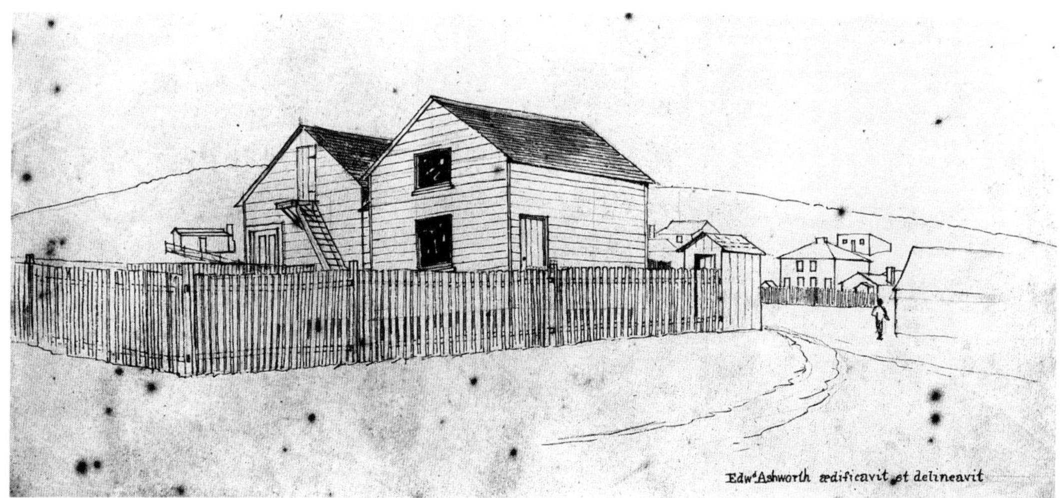

Edward Ashworth (1814–1896), *Edwd Ashworth aedificavit et delineavit,* 1843, ink and wash, 110 x 230 mm
Alexander Turnbull Library

He had other sad lessons to learn, apart from finding 'stout sturdy maggots of 2 days growth'[18] on his corned beef. In misguided attempts to profit by lending at current high interest rates, but without adequate securities, he lost more principal than he gained interest. His journey to the Waikato in December 1843 was an unsuccessful attempt to get repayment of a loan. He returned to Auckland, sold his house and set sail for Hong Kong. Ashworth does not mention Mrs Hobson's Album in his journals, although his name is among those on the farewell address

18. ibid., p.39.

presented to Eliza Hobson.[19] We have to posit Ashworth's involvement from his position in her household and from his vigorous and individual style of figure drawing. Sepia wash and black ink studies in his sketchbooks make links in content and style sufficient to establish Ashworth's hand on Plates **3** and **8**. Specific references in his journal and one particular sketch of a tree (reproduced on p. 111) also allow us to be certain that Ashworth drew the frontispiece to the Album, and to deduce that the neat lettering of the title page and italic titling in the first half of the Album are most probably his work.

19. *Southern Cross,* 10 June 1843, p.1 col.3.

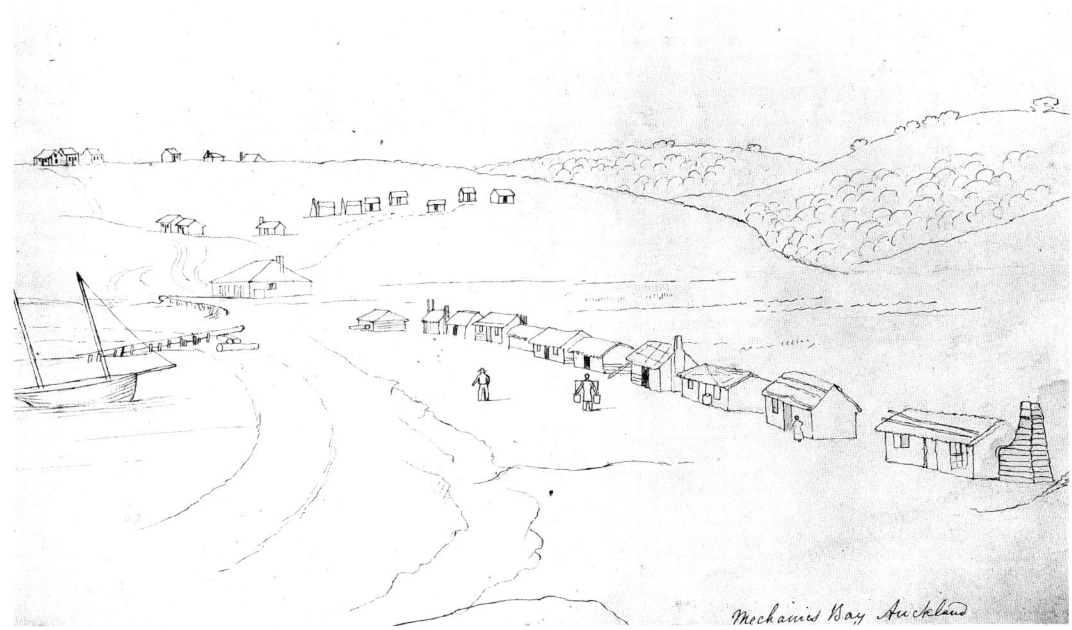

Edward Ashworth (1814–1896), *Mechanics Bay Auckland,* 1843, pencil, 200 x 310 mm
Alexander Turnbull Library

All Ashworth's sketches in and around Auckland were done between November 1842 and the end of January 1844. He drew the progressively changing settlements of Auckland. His style melds architectural accuracy with a free bold simplification of natural forms. 'Residences, Official Bay, Auckland' and 'Mechanics Bay, Auckland' are works in the Alexander Turnbull Library which closely resemble pen and wash drawings held in the Auckland City Art Gallery — 'Fort Street, Auckland', 'Princes St' and 'Commercial Bay, Auckland 1843'.

The crisp clarity of Ashworth's style can be seen in a watercolour, 'Queen Street *c.* 1843', held in the Auckland Institute and Museum Library; but in a landscape, when groups of buildings are no longer the main focus, determinants of style are less individual. However, an identified watercolour, 'Auckland from the Government Domain 1843', reproduced in Una Platts's *Lively Capital,* Plate 1, establishes evidence of Ashworth's use of colour, his way of drawing flax, and his handwritten ink inscription on the image. These similarities lead to the attribution to Ashworth of a watercolour of Auckland Harbour (Plate **44**). Its forms are flatter and more angular than the watercolours of the same landscape by John Guise Mitford (Plates **18, 19** and **20**). Where Mitford uses cobalt and ultramarine blues, this painter uses a colder prussian blue and balances the colour composition with a strong brownish orange. The drawing of foreground flax also recalls Ashworth's view in the Auckland City Art Gallery. Moreover, strong supposition is confirmed when we compare a known Ashworth drawing 'Auckland looking NW' (ATL A208/18) with this watercolour. Its content is identical. Some aspects of style and technique, including surface abrasions with some sharp instrument to indicate light on water or to highlight the edges of rounded forms of foliage, suggest that Ashworth may also be the artist of 'View from above Grafton Gully showing graveyard and Government House', [1843] (Plate **45**). This is one of a near-identical pair of watercolours. The other, 'Entrance to the Auckland Harbour' (Plate **19**), has been attributed to John Guise Mitford. Both appear to have been painted from the same viewpoint; both look over the bush-filled Grafton Gully to the slope on which a cemetery is fenced and beyond to the distant Government House, the Waitemata Harbour, and part of the North Shore and Rangitoto. The painter of Plate **19** tilts his forms nearer to the picture plane, the painter of Plate **45** diminishes the distance and sharpens the edges of far cliffs, and uses tone rather than colour to build substance. It is possible that the two painters sat side by side as they worked; but the two compositions are so similar that one artist may have made his own version of the other's and both put them in the Album for Mrs Hobson to puzzle over the authorship — which by Mitford, which by Ashworth?

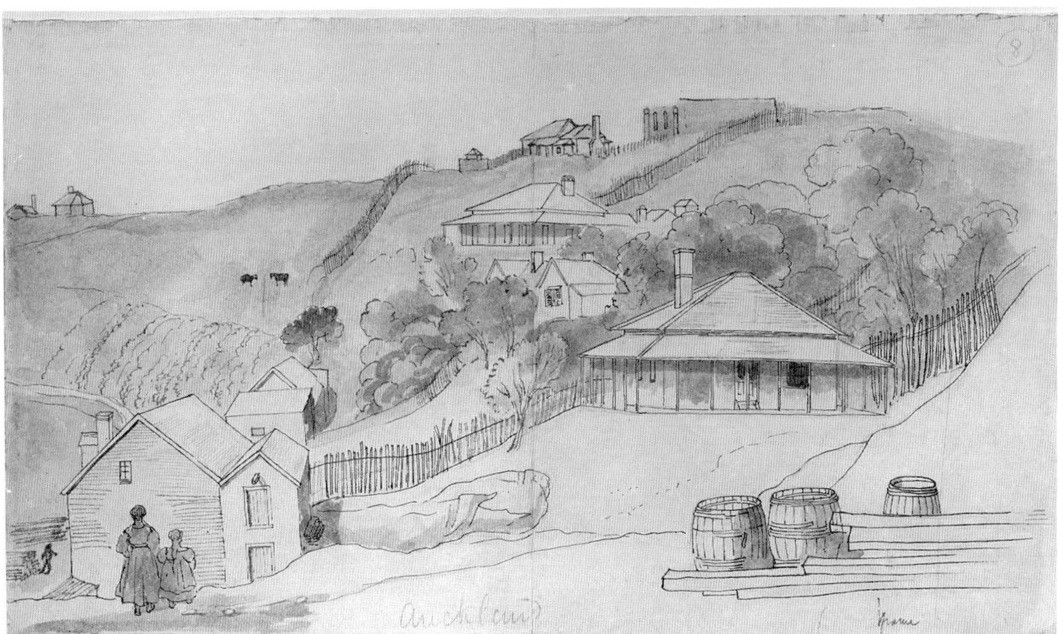

Edward Ashworth (1814-1896), *Auckland,* 1843, pen and ink with wash, 177 x 302 mm
Auckland City Art Gallery, presented by Sir Cecil Leys, 1935

There is in the Album a second puzzle pair: two versions of a portrait of Maketu (Plates **6** and **53**). Maketu's trial and hanging — the first for multiple murder —

were unhappy and significant events in Hobson's brief time as Governor, but important as they were, would the one artist include two different records of the protagonist? Yet both versions have close links with the style of one particular artist. And here we are at the nub of the problem: how to ascribe these and the remaining twenty-five pages in the Album, which include eleven figure paintings, fourteen landscapes and one poem. The fourteen landscapes are so consistent in style and medium that they can safely be ascribed to one hand. But whose? They could only have been done by a painter who was conversant with Maori character and custom and familiar with the great pa on the Waikato and Waipa, at Otawhao, Maungatautari, Matamata, in the thermal areas around Ohinemutu and Rotomahana, and with the people and landscape of the East Coast near Tauranga and Whakatane.

It is tempting to accept the guidance of Dr T. M. Hocken, who put Edward Shortland's name to four Album-associated works which the Hocken Library acquired from Shortland's widow.[20] Shortland's friendship with the Hobson family was a continuation of family and naval connections in Plymouth. Edward Shortland (1812–1893) studied medicine after graduating from Pembroke College, Cambridge, in 1835. He came to New Zealand in April 1841 and was appointed Private Secretary to Hobson on 25 June 1841, a post he held for one year. He began at once to study the Maori language and was soon, according to his friend Abel Dottin William Best, seeking opportunities to converse and gather waiata, chants, and stories from 'our friends the Maories'.[21]

In April 1842 Shortland accompanied Hobson, William Martin and Best, with Meurant as interpreter, on an expedition into the Waikato. They went up the Waipa to Otawhao and returned by the west coast. Shortland's account, which extends his Journal observations,[22] was published in the *Auckland Standard,* 9 May 1842, under the signature 'A Gentleman of the Governor's Party'. Many of the drawings in the Hobson Album seem chosen particularly to illustrate Hobson's journey, which was taken to acquaint himself with Maori life. If Edward Shortland were the artist he would have had ample opportunity to make drawings of New Zealanders or of these particular landscapes. His grasp of Maori language and etiquette showed his sympathy and friendship for the people, which was reciprocated.

On 4 August 1842 the *Government Gazette* confirmed Edward Shortland in his appointment as Police Magistrate and Sub-Protector of Aborigines in the district of Tauranga. From 2 July to 21 August he had travelled via Coromandel to Katikati. It was in his journal of this trip that Shortland made his only references to drawing, with the phrase 'Take a view of the country about Totara' (6 July).[23] The journal includes two drawings only: one, a tentative sketch in pencil (so light that it cannot be reproduced here), is titled 'Manga Kowai group scraping potatoes'; the other is a fine ink diagram, 'He moko',[24] with names given for the elements of facial tattoo patterns (reproduced on p. 114). In his 'Journal of journeys', Shortland, visiting Taipari's pa at Maunga Tapu, wrote: 'obtained an excellent view

20. Plates **4, 9, 13** and **53**; see also pp.112-4.

21. Best 1966, pp.333, 344.

22. Shortland, Journal of an expedition . . . April 1842, Hocken MS 21.

23. Shortland, Hocken MS 21, entry for 6 July 1842.

24. Shortland, Hocken MS 22, pp.44-45.

of the country below'[25] — words which might possibly imply that he made a drawing. But apart from these examples, the only other evidence of Shortland having any ability to draw are some ink sketch maps in his 'Notebooks: Middle Island (1843-1844)' of river courses near Oamaru (three pages), the river Waitaki (six pages) and 'Direction of coast from Taumutu' (two pages).

There are no other original drawings or paintings amongst the Shortland papers in the Hocken Library, nor are there works in any other New Zealand or Australian picture collection attributed to Edward Shortland.

On examination, all four works in the Hocken picture collection attributed to Edward Shortland proved to be careful copies of rougher and more vital drawings in the Hobson Album. Three of these are in sepia wash, ink and china white, and one in watercolour. It is possible, but unlikely, that Shortland made the copies himself. It is much more probable that he paid the professional artist, Joseph Jenner Merrett, to make the copies for him. In the days before photographic reproduction it was common practice for artists to make copies of their own and of others' works. Finding the drawings among Shortland's papers, Dr Hocken may have assumed that Shortland was the artist. If the attribution which Hocken gave to Shortland came originally through the Rendel family, then we must conclude that Edward Shortland obtained all these drawings from Merrett and presented them to Mrs Hobson. He may have employed this man, who was later described as 'a sort of travelling sketchmaker'[26] to record particular places and significant figures or customs.

We are now left with upholding our attribution to Joseph Jenner Merrett of nearly half the works in Mrs Hobson's Album. Joseph Jenner Merrett (1816-1854) was a writer and painter living in New Zealand from 1840 — if not earlier[27] — who tried to make his living from both activities. He was well read[28] and he had had experience of life 'in other colonies'.[29] From a watercolour in the Turnbull Library [Christ carrying the Cross], we can suppose that Merrett may have had some training in art. He had lived in England and claimed that he 'studied anatomy and physiology under a clever teacher, a brother in law of my own who is a physician of considerable talent Dr Howslip of Burlington Street'.[30] He also claimed to have been 'extensively engaged' there when he advertised for work as a surveyor in the *New Zealand Herald and Auckland Gazette* of 30 March 1842. He had sufficient fluency in the Maori language to advertise (*Times*, 9 July 1844) his ability to handle land purchases from the Maori, and to be employed as an interpreter by the government in 1845. Amongst letters to the Protector of Aborigines and Native Secretary, 1841-1853, is one directing payment to 'Mr Merrett who accompanyed the volunteers on the late expedition to the Bay of Islands as interpreter up to the 27 instant inclusive'.[31]

In 1841 Merrett lived with,[32] and in 1843 married, a young woman of Ngati Koura, a sub-tribe of Waikato located at Kihikihi and Whatawhata. Her name as shown on the death certificate of her daughter Ani Gage (died 7 February 1920) was Maria Rangitetaea Koa. The name in regular use was Rangitetaea. There were

25. Shortland, Hocken MS 20, entry for 9 December 1842.

26. By Dr T. M. Hocken.

27. Phelan to Marian Minson, Letters TL/3/1/1, 24 August 1983 and 14 September 1983 detail Merrett's friendship with her great-great-grandfather, John Edwards, 'a life-long friend of the artist J. J. Merrett . . . they met and formed a lasting friendship when both were employed in Sydney'. Edwards came as a trader to Kawhia in 1835 or 1836. 'Merrett followed at a later date and also resided at Kawhia.' Both men moved to Waipa valley and built a house 'in the native style'.

28. Best 1966, p.300: 'Our companion had a copy of *Don Juan*'.

29. This fact and Merrett's appreciation of literature are given in an article, in which he lists books in 'a library selected with no ordinary taste . . .' in the cabin of a coastal schooner. *Sydney Morning Herald*, 19 June 1846, p.2 col.1.

30. Letter from Joseph Merrett to H. E. Capt Grey. Nat. Archives G13/1 48/21, *c.*15 October 1848, in box letters 11 Jan 1841–27 March 1852.

31. Nat. Archives, C I.A. 4/271 p. 192, 31 May 1845.

32. Letter from Morgan to A. N. Brown, 1 May 1843, Parliamentary Library, Microfilm Papers Reel for 1842-45.

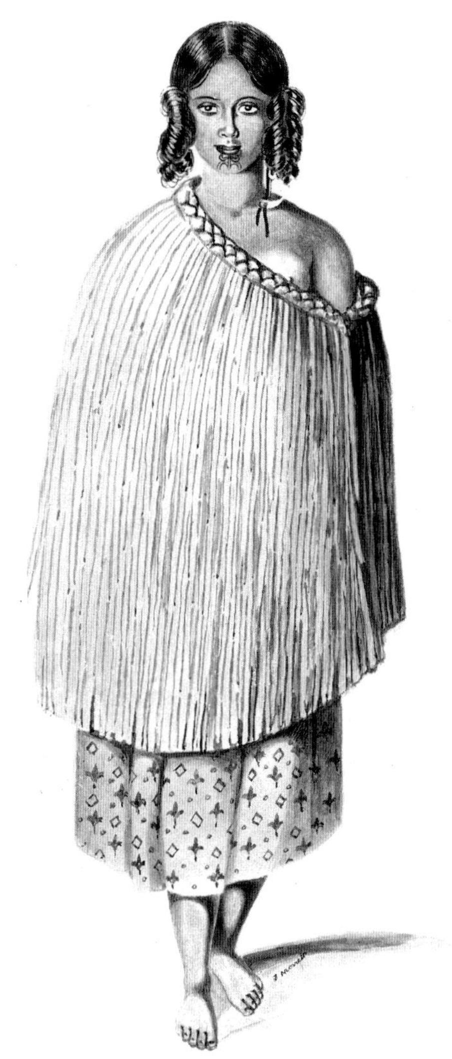

Joseph Jenner Merrett (1816–1854), *Rangitetahi [Rangitetaea], a young woman of the tribe Ngati Koura,* watercolour, 240 x 330 mm
British Library

at least two children, with many descendants, who now spell the name 'Merritt'. Since Merrett's spelling of Maori followed pronunciation in an idiosyncratic way we can be satisfied that the poem 'Rangi Kawau' (Plate **32**) was written in praise of his young wife, whose portrait he painted (Plate **33**). This unidentified watercolour in the British Library signed twice 'J Merrett' and dated 1845 may well be a later portrait of Rangitetaea with a completed chin moko and a more demure hairstyle.

Joseph Jenner Merrett's work has survived because of its historical and anthropological value. Original watercolours and lithographs made from his drawings are held in the Rex Nan Kivell Collection, Australian National Library, Canberra; Mitchell Library, Sydney; Auckland Institute and Museum, Auckland Public Library, Auckland City Art Gallery; National Museum and Alexander Turnbull Library, Wellington; the Hocken Library, Dunedin; and the British Library, London. There are many variants of the same composition, with different supplied titles. For instance, there are four watercolour compositions[33] of a Maori girl whose European dress shows above a fine korowai-ngore. She wears a shark's tooth as an ornament and a European ring on the third finger of her right hand. In each painting she is flanked by stylised flax bushes, on the far left a decoratively treated ponga fern and on the far right part of a triple-coned volcano and some sea. No version is signed or dated, nor title inscribed.

Most of the work in the public collections or in private hands has been given tentative dates ranging between 1844 and 1850, but from our evidence some could have been as early as the 1841 drawings for Charles Terry. Merrett's reputation has so far been mainly connected with the large documentary watercolour 'Native feast held at Remuera Auckland NZ 1844';[34] and 'The New Zealand Festival 11 May 1844', a keyed lithograph published from that, which is a slightly different record of the same occasion:[35] a reputation augmented when Merrett also published a series of portraits made at the Bay of Islands in February 1845. The most

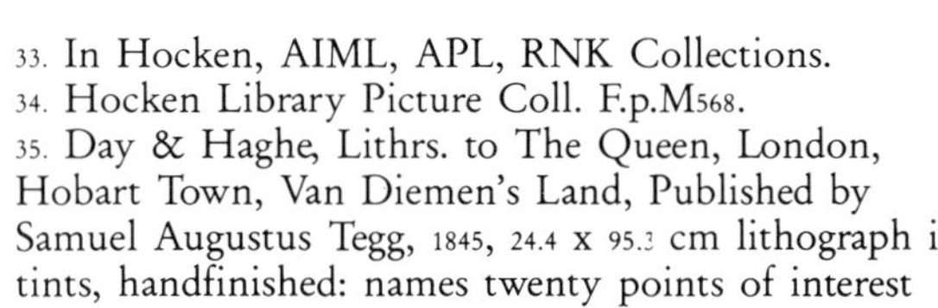

33. In Hocken, AIML, APL, RNK Collections.
34. Hocken Library Picture Coll. F.p.M568.
35. Day & Haghe, Lithrs. to The Queen, London, Hobart Town, Van Diemen's Land, Published by Samuel Augustus Tegg, 1845, 24.4 x 95.3 cm lithograph in tints, handfinished: names twenty points of interest with a key.

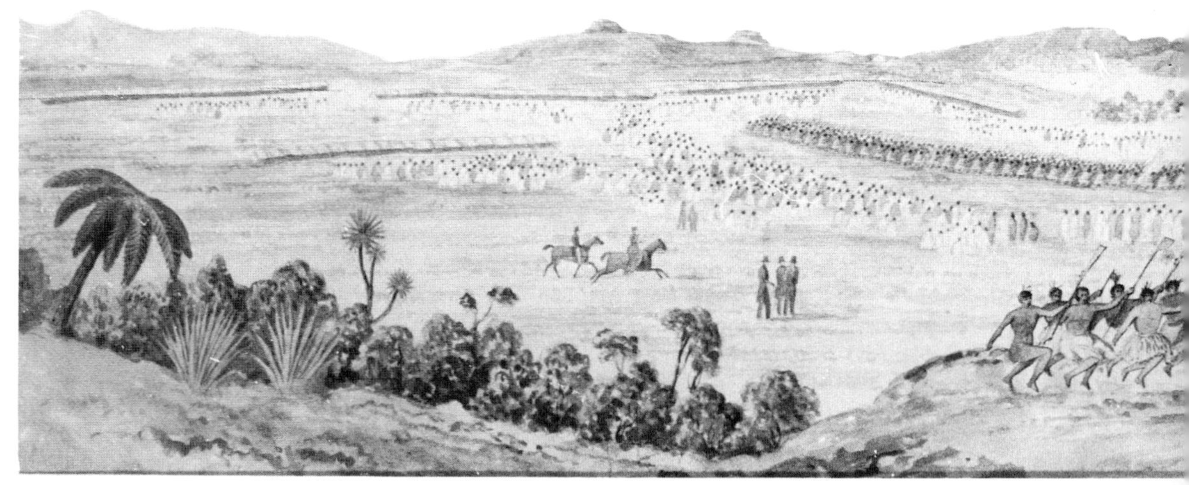

frequently reproduced is the lithograph of his combined portraits, entitled 'The warrior chieftains/of/New Zealand/Harriet Heki's wife. Heki, Kawiti/Drawn by Josh. Merrett. Drawn in stone by W. Nicholas.'[36]

For Merrett's connection with the Hobson Album we have to look back for work published in 1842 or 1843. One of the earliest books to be profusely illustrated is Charles Terry's *New Zealand, its Advantages and Prospects, as a British Colony,* published in London in 1842. Among its twelve lithographs, five are of Auckland, three are portraits of Ngati Whatua chief Te Kawau and his two sons, and the remaining four are landscapes further south. One of these, 'Fortified native village/ A pa on the Lake Okataina on the East Coast' is unmistakably by the artist who contributed Plate **62**, 'The Pah of Okatina on the Lake of [the same] Name'.

The Hobson Album drawing includes figures and clear details of the carved gateway, which were fudged by the English lithographer who interpreted the original drawing. That Merrett is the artist of both works is confirmed by a note on the title page of Sir George Grey's annotated copy of Charles Terry's book in the Auckland Public Library, which reads 'The Sketches and Likenesses by "Merritt"'. Once this connection has been made, the fact that two of the drawings attributed to Merrett have holograph poems on the back in Merrett's handwriting gives further confirmation. We can be satisfied with the correctness of all the landscape attributions to Merrett. The figure drawings, though, seem sometimes to be too proficient, to have more sense of body structure than the rather pretty simplifications one has come to associate with his figure groups.

With those Hobson Album and Charles Terry pictures known to be by Merrett, we can now find further supporting evidence of the range and sympathy of Joseph Jenner Merrett as a sensitive recorder of Maori life in the 1840s. Merrett is the

36. Published by Mr Wm Ford, George St Sydney, Lithog. to W. M. Brownrigg, surveyor, 45.6 x 31.5 cm lithograph in tints, handfinished: signed on plate W. Nicholas, 1846.

Detail from title page of *New Zealand, its Advantages and Prospects, as a British Colony* by Charles Terry, 1842, inscribed by Sir George Grey on his own copy 'The Sketches & Likenesses by "Merrett"'.
Auckland Public Library

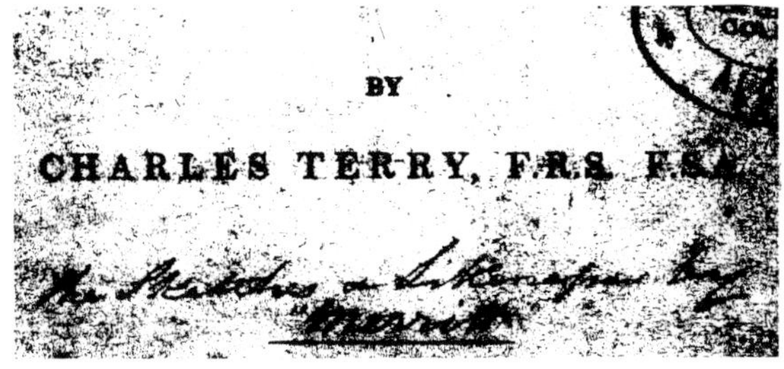

BY

CHARLES TERRY, F.R.S.

Joseph Jenner Merrett (1816–1854), *Native feast held at Remuera Auckland NZ 1844,* ink and watercolour, 284 x 912 mm
Hocken Library

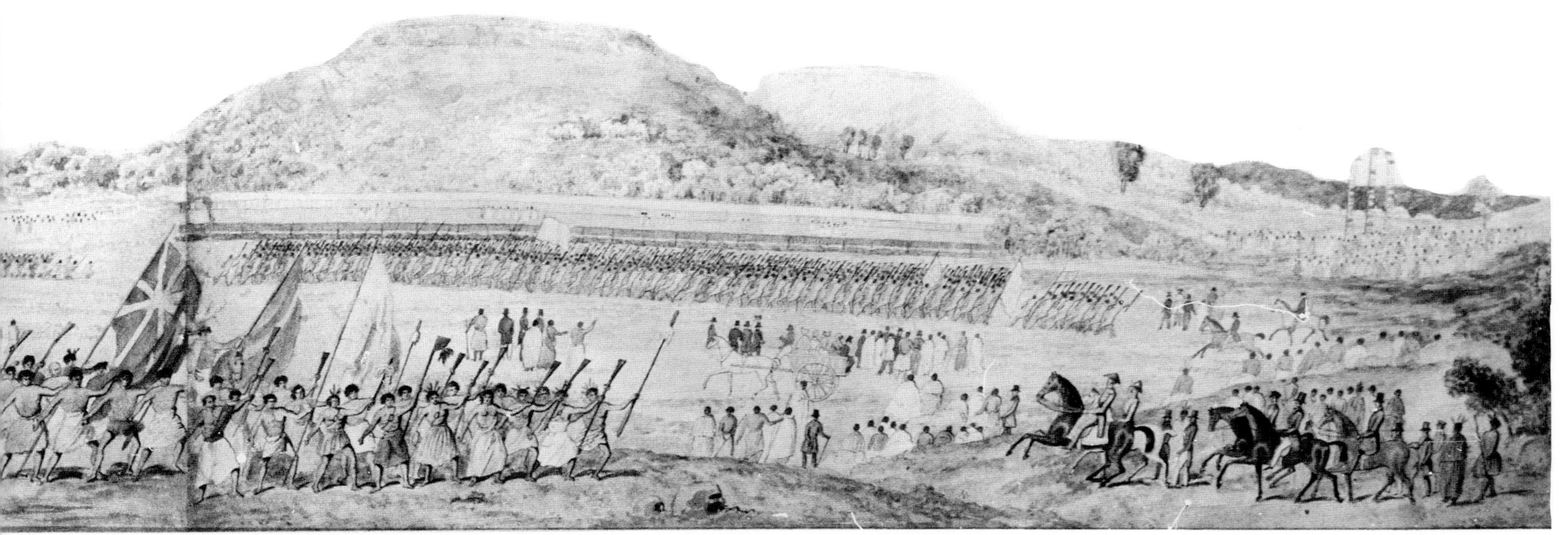

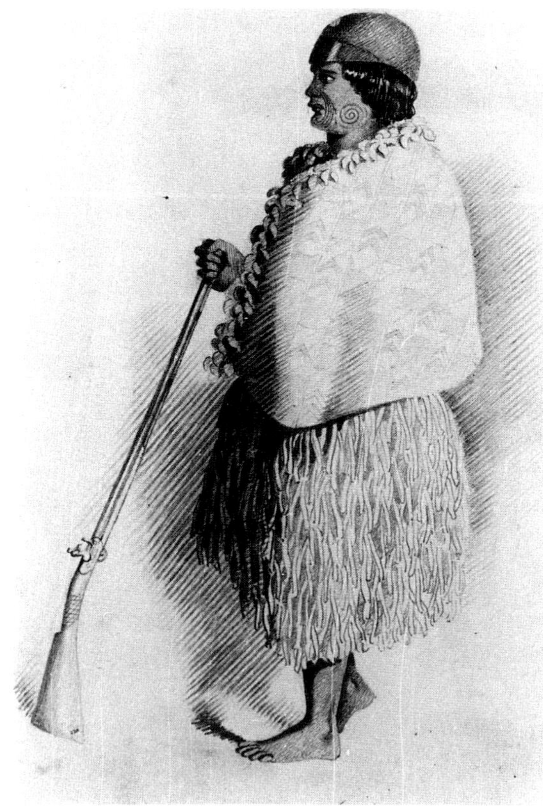

Joseph Jenner Merrett (1816-1854). A confirmed example of Merrett's style: the original drawing of Hone Heke from which the artist made one of his published lithographs of the Chiefs of New Zealand.
British Library

documentary artist of many hitherto unidentified drawings in London. It is Merrett's work which dominates the 'New Zealand Pictorial Scrapbook, Drawings and Sketches illustrative of New Zealand 1845-1854', an album presented to the British Museum by Sir George Grey, 13 September 1854, which is now held in the Manuscript Room, British Library (ADD. MS 19953). In the notes to the catalogue we have tried to trace connections with Merrett's field drawings and for convenience have referred to the Pictorial Scrapbook presented by Sir George Grey as the 'Grey Album'. We find that many of the Hobson Album plates attributed to Joseph Jenner Merrett have prototypes in the Grey Album which are there inscribed in his handwriting. Such close correspondence with finished pictures made for Eliza Hobson's Album between 1841 and 1843 makes one question the dates on the British Library album. The dates 1845-1854 may simply refer to the period in which George Grey purchased his collection.

Merrett is likely to have completed the work for Mrs Hobson's Album before he worked for George Grey between 1845 and 1847, an association he underlined when he advertised his talent as 'Portrait and Landscape painter to H.E. the Governor. Studio in Mr Coolahan's new house at the back of the Exchange Hotel'.[37] Poems in the *New Zealander*[38] identify Joseph Jenner Merrett with the pseudonym 'Crayon': one in particular, a ballad 'The Lizard Rock', was described as written and illustrated by Joseph Merrett, 'dedicated to Gov. Grey and to be published in England'.[39] Merrett's struggle to make a living as an artist ended in disaster — poverty, ill health, imprisonment, and an early death. There is not space here to follow his descent, except to quote a letter from Merrett to George Grey dated 14 October 1848. Here the artist renews a previously refused claim to 'a crown title being granted to me for a certain tract of land situated in Manakau which I purchased from the Nga te Watua of O Raki', and tells the Governor that, by his own diagnosis, he 'is suffering from a very peculiar disease of the brain'. He ends with the sad paragraph,

> Would Your Excellency be kind enough to give me an order for two pair of blankets and twenty sheets of bristol card board and I will go into the interior for a month or two: and see if I can derive any benefit from a trip of that kind. All the productions of my pencil I will submit to your approval.[40]

It would require a complete catalogue of New Zealand sketches held in the British Library, Australia, and New Zealand, to do full justice to the work of Joseph Jenner Merrett. Recognition of his contribution here does acknowledge the importance of this observant, concerned and unhappy man whose pencil gives us vital anthropological information in one half of the pictures presented to Eliza Hobson.

37. *New Zealander,* advertisement 13 Nov. 1847, p.4, col.3.
38. *New Zealander,* 9 January, 20 March, 9 June 1847.
39. *New Zealander,* advertisement, 3 July 1847, p.3.
40. Nat. Archives. Merrett to George Grey, CS1/1 1848/78.

List of Album Plates

1 Title page: Mrs Hobson Government House Auckland, New Zealand *March* 184 [3]
2 Frontispiece: Costumes, Scenery, Specimens of Literature etc. of the North Island of New Zealand 1841, 1842, 1843.
3 Government House Auckland NW view.
4 View from ORakau of Maunga tautari with natives in the foreground digging. They dig while sitting in preference to standing.
5 Wakatani.
[Young Maori man of high rank]
6 Maketu.
7 Letter from Te Whero Whero, Chief of the Waikato tribes to Queen Victoria
8 Government House, Auckland showing the North Head of Waitemata Harbr.
9 A Native Game.
10 [Commentary on the 'Poi']
11 A Group of New Zealanders.
12 [Maori woman reading]
13 The Pah of Oinamutu on the Rotorua Lake: the carvings in this pah are particularly fine
14 Russell from Paihia, Wai Keri River
15 View of the town of Auckland from the opposite shore of the Waitemata
16 A Hot Spring in the Warm Lake of Rotomahana
17 [Part of poem 'Rangi Kawauw' and marginal notes in Shortland's hand]
18 Rangitoto, Mount Victoria and the North Head, from the Government Domain, Auckland
19 Entrance to the Harbour, Auckland
20 [Auckland Harbour]
21 A Native Chief dressed in a Dog's Skin mat, with a weapon called wahanoghi
22 Wiremu Hoete e Mata Kawana
23 Letter from a New Zealand Chief to Mrs Hobson on leaving for England
24 Ko te Waha o te Papa. Wakano
25 Kino Kino. Ohuia
26 [Two Maori Girls]
27 View on the lake of Rotorua. The island of Mo Koia in the Centre of the Lake
28 "And the Wilderness shall become the fruitful Field"
29 "And the solitary places shall be made glad"
30 Wellington from the 'London'
31 Entrance to the Harbour Manukao from Puponga Head
32 Rangi Kawauw
33 [Rangi Kawauw]
34 "Maori Songs."
35 "Maori Songs."
36 "Maori Songs."
37 "Maori Songs."
Major Richmond's Cottage Auckland
38 Kaiwarra Warra from the Petoni Road, Wellington
39 'Te Aro' Flat, Wellington

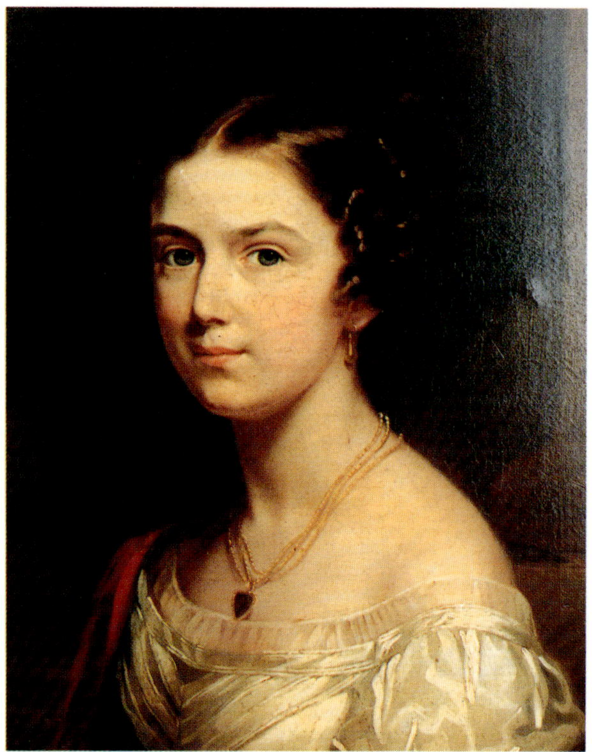

Mary M. Pearson, *Eliza Hobson* [*c.* 1827]
Rendel family portrait

1 [*Album page 1*

Title page

Mrs Hobson
Government House
Auckland, New Zealand
March 184 [3]

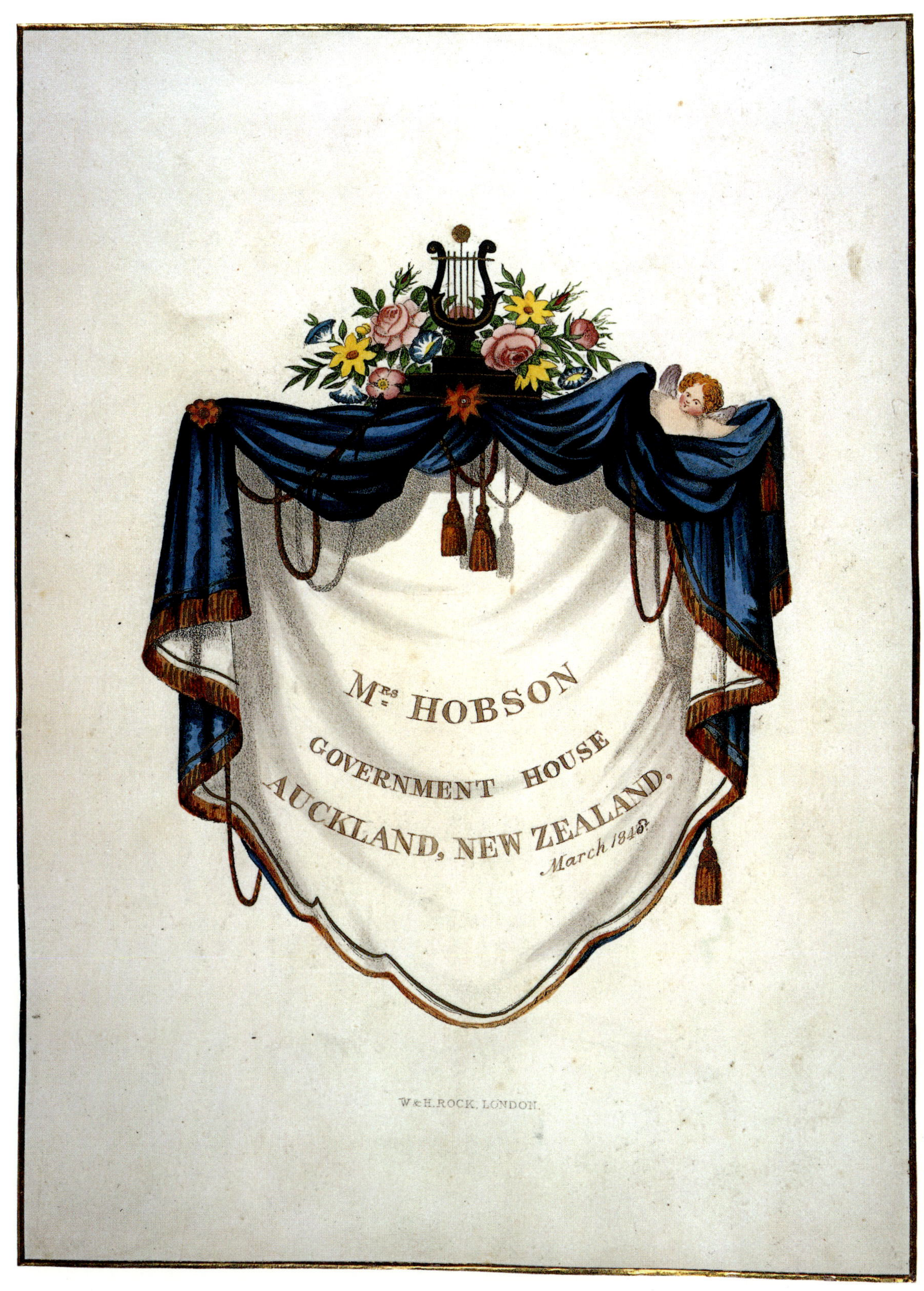

2 [*Album page* 3

Frontispiece

Costumes, Scenery,
Specimens of Literature etc.
of the North Island of
New Zealand
1841, 1842, 1843.

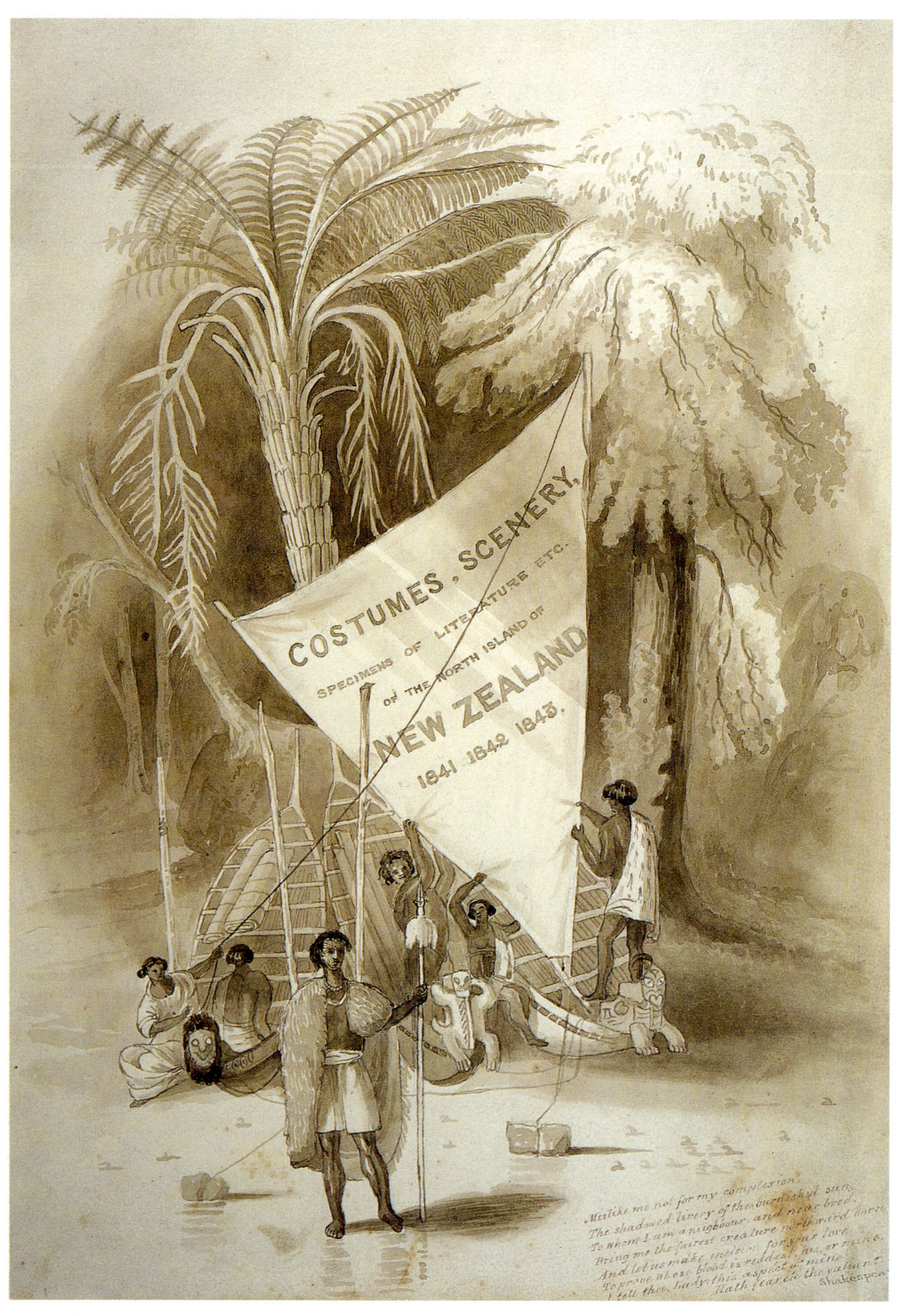

3 [*Album page 5*

Government House Auckland NW view.

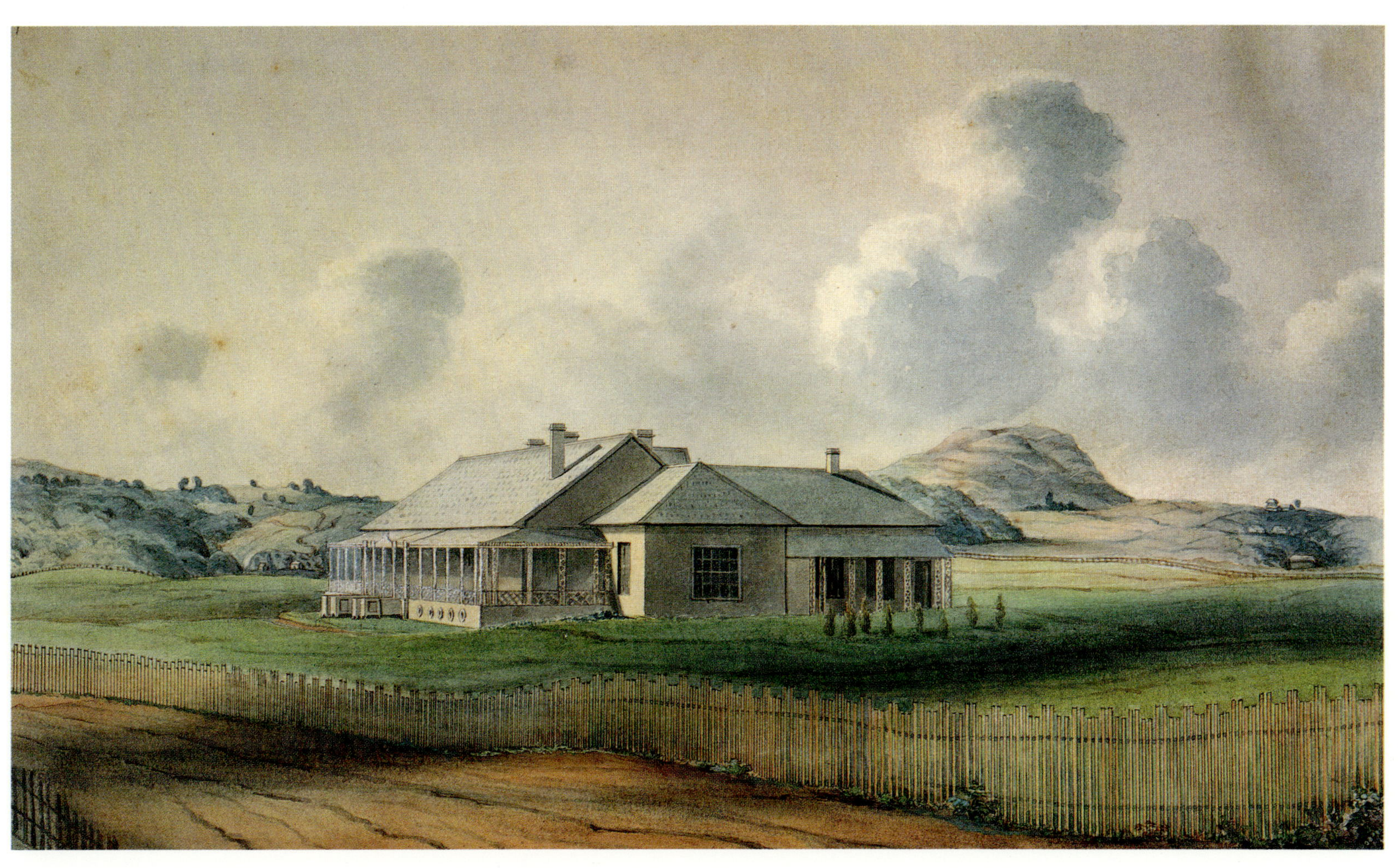

4 [*Album page 7*

View from ORakau of Maunga tautari with natives in the foreground digging. They dig while sitting in preference to standing.

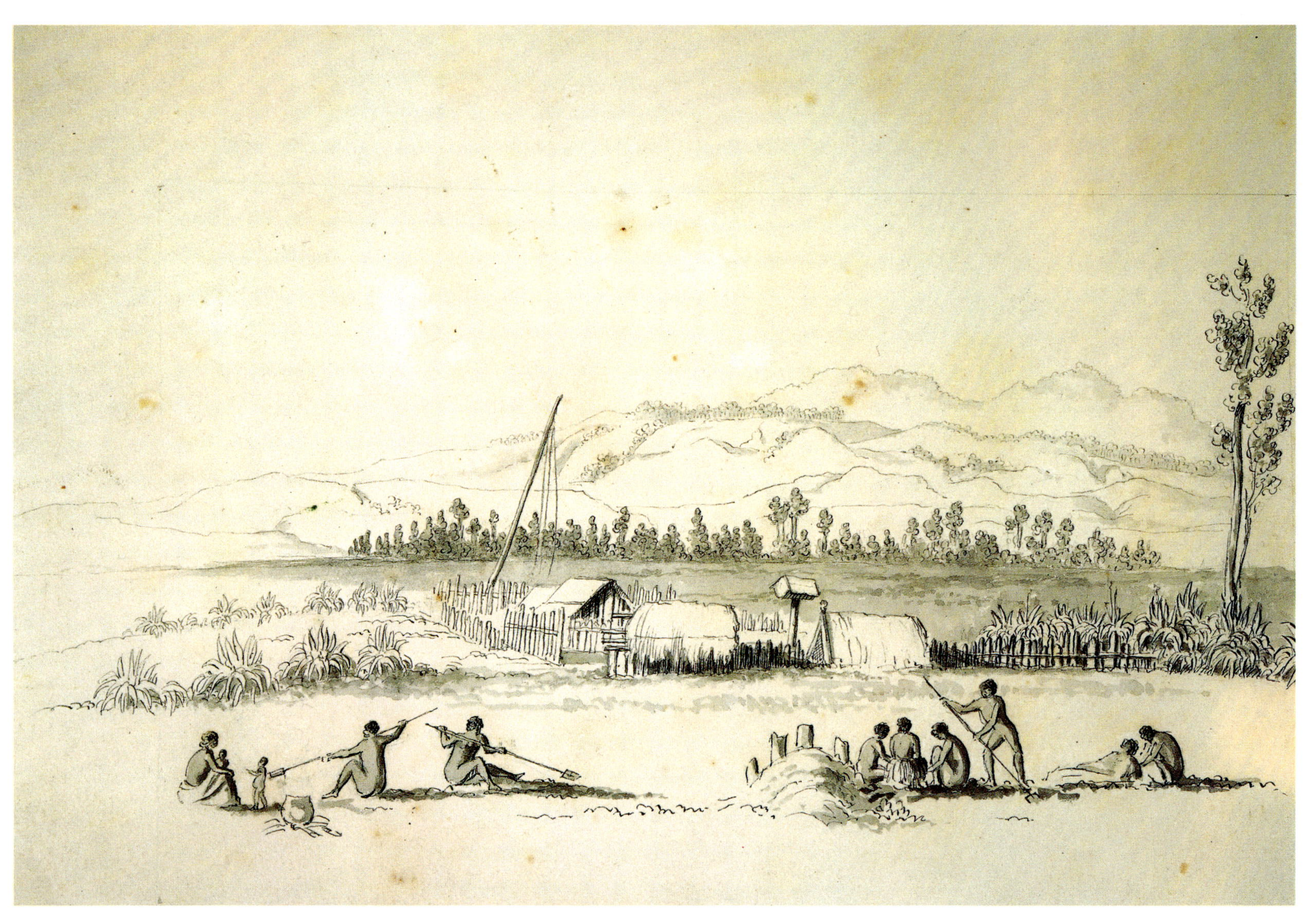

5 [*Album page 9*

Wakatani.
[Young Maori man of high rank]

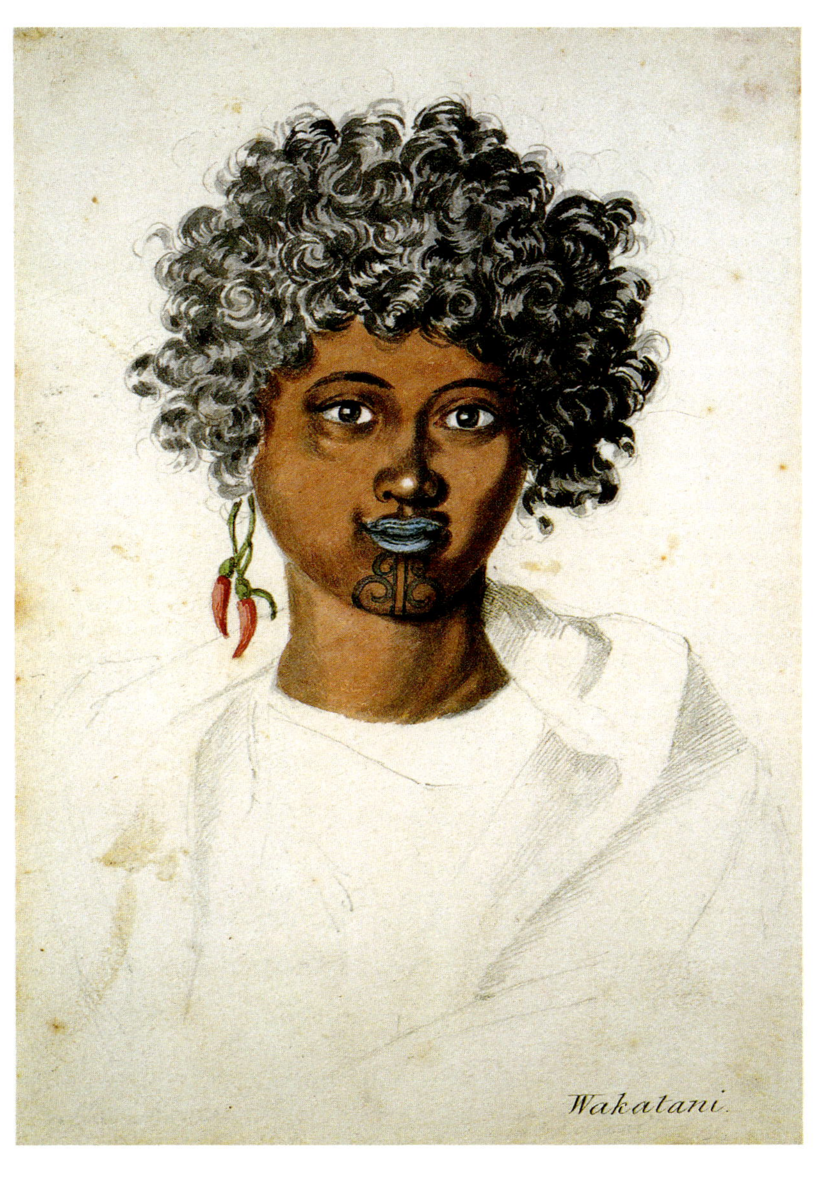

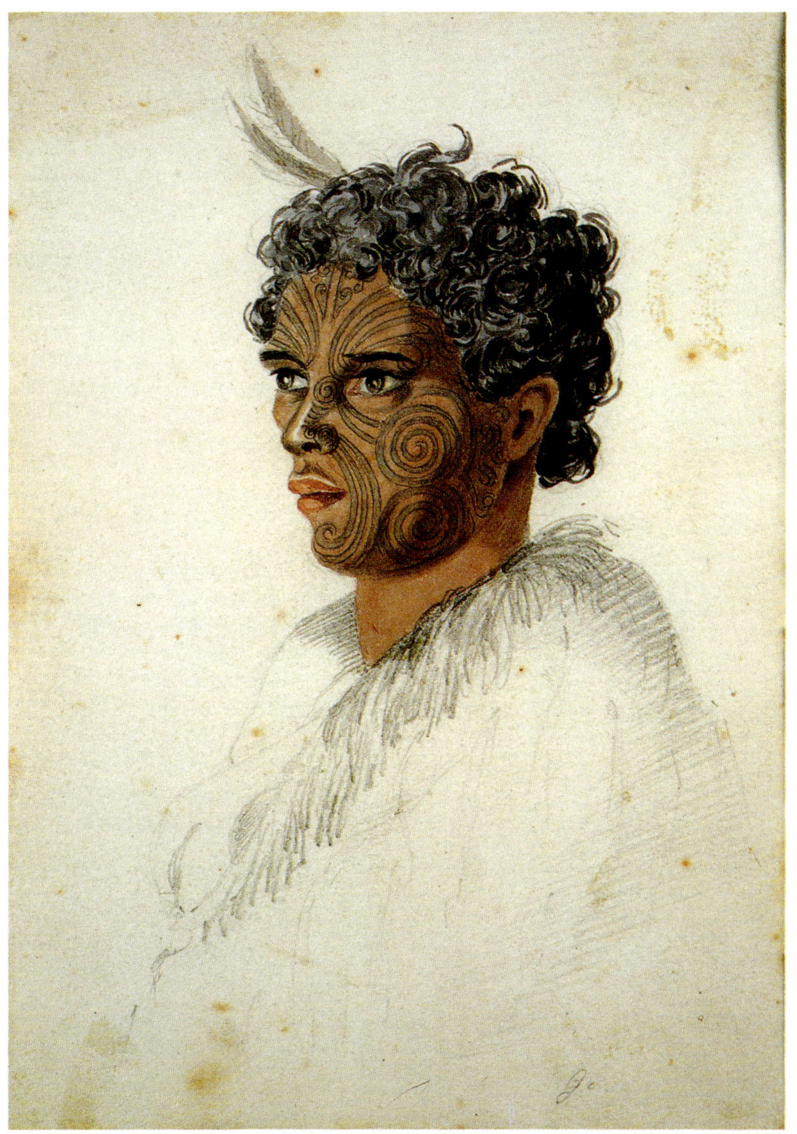

6 [*Album page* 11

Maketu.

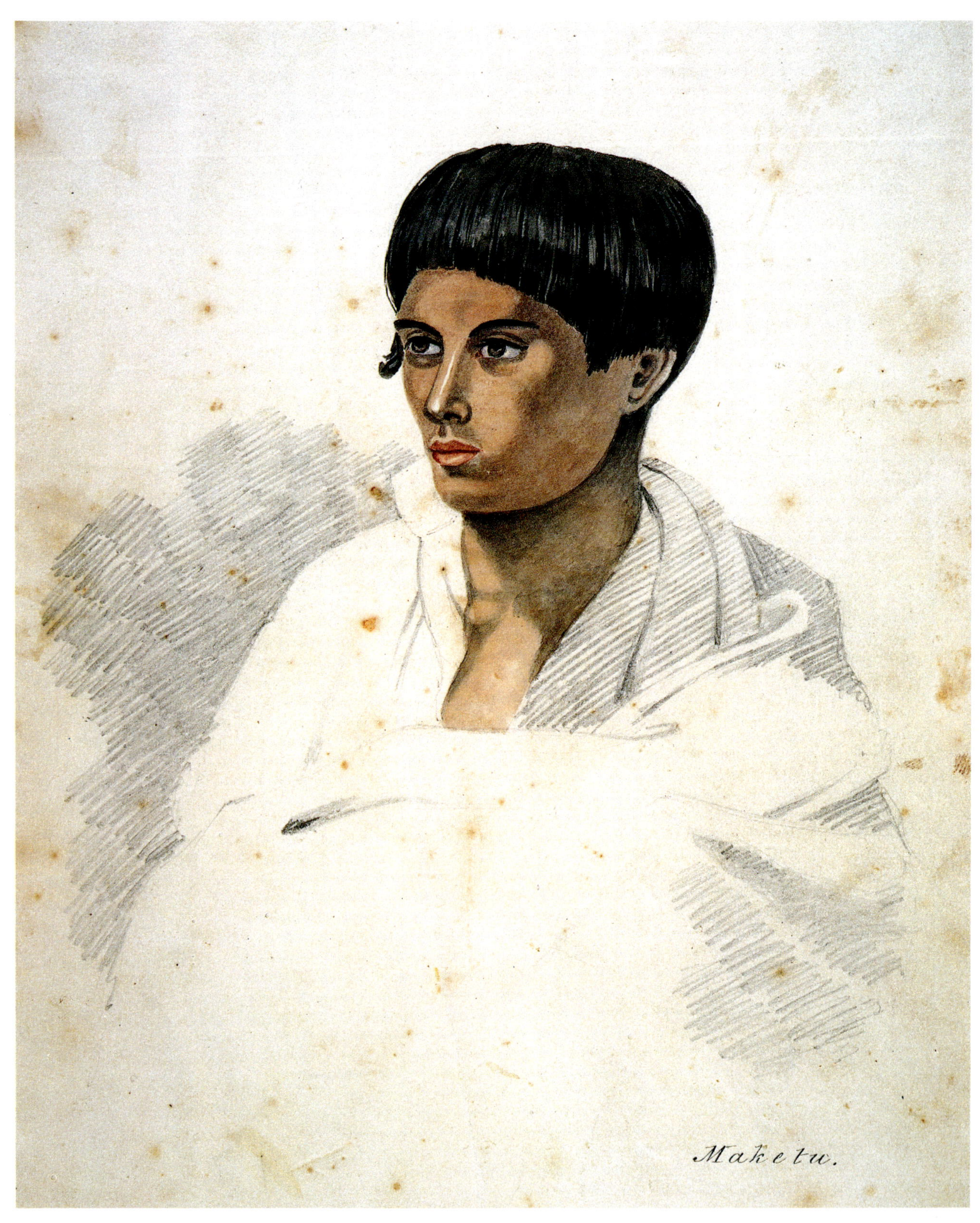

7 [*Album page* 13

Letter from Te Whero Whero,
Chief of the Waikato tribes
to Queen Victoria

Letter from Te Whero Whero, Chief of the Waikato tribes to Queen Victoria

E tai, e Wikitoria

Tena ra ko koe, He rahi taku aroha ki a koe, e noho mai na i tou kainga. He mea atu naku ki tetahi kawana mo matou, ko nga Pakeha o tenei motu. Kia pai, Mau e titiro iho te tahi tangata pai whakaaro, kei haere mai kikonei te mea kino; kei haere mai te mea tutamarika, te mea hikaka, ka wehi matou nga Tangata Maori, kia penei ano te pai me te kawana ka mate nei.

E kui, e Wikitoria, kia pai ra to korero ki te Pakeha; kia atawhai kei haere mai ki konei patu ai ia matou — e pai ana koki e ata noho ana matou. He iwi kino matou i mua, he iwi kohuru, he iwi patu, Inaianei ka noho marire; ka mahue i a matou te kino. Mau tenei ritenga koia; pai ai. E kui kia Atawhai

na to hoa na te Wherowhero

<u>Translation</u>

Good Lady Victoria

How fairest thou: Great is my love to you, who are residing in your country, My subject is, a governor for us and the foreigners of this Island. Let him be a good man, Look out for a good man, a man of Judgement. Let not a troubler come here. Let not a boy come here, or one puffed with pride we, the New Zealanders, shall be afraid. Let him be as good as this governor who has just died, Mother Victoria, Let your instructions to the foreigner be good. Let him be kind. Let him not come here to kill us. — seeing that we are peaceable. Formerly we were a bad people, a murdering people, a killing people. — Now we are sitting peaceable, we have left off the evil, It was you who appointed this line of conduct and therefore it is pleasing to us, Mother be kind.

From your friend Wherowhero.

8 [*Album page 15*

Government House, Auckland
showing the North Head of Waitemata Harbr.

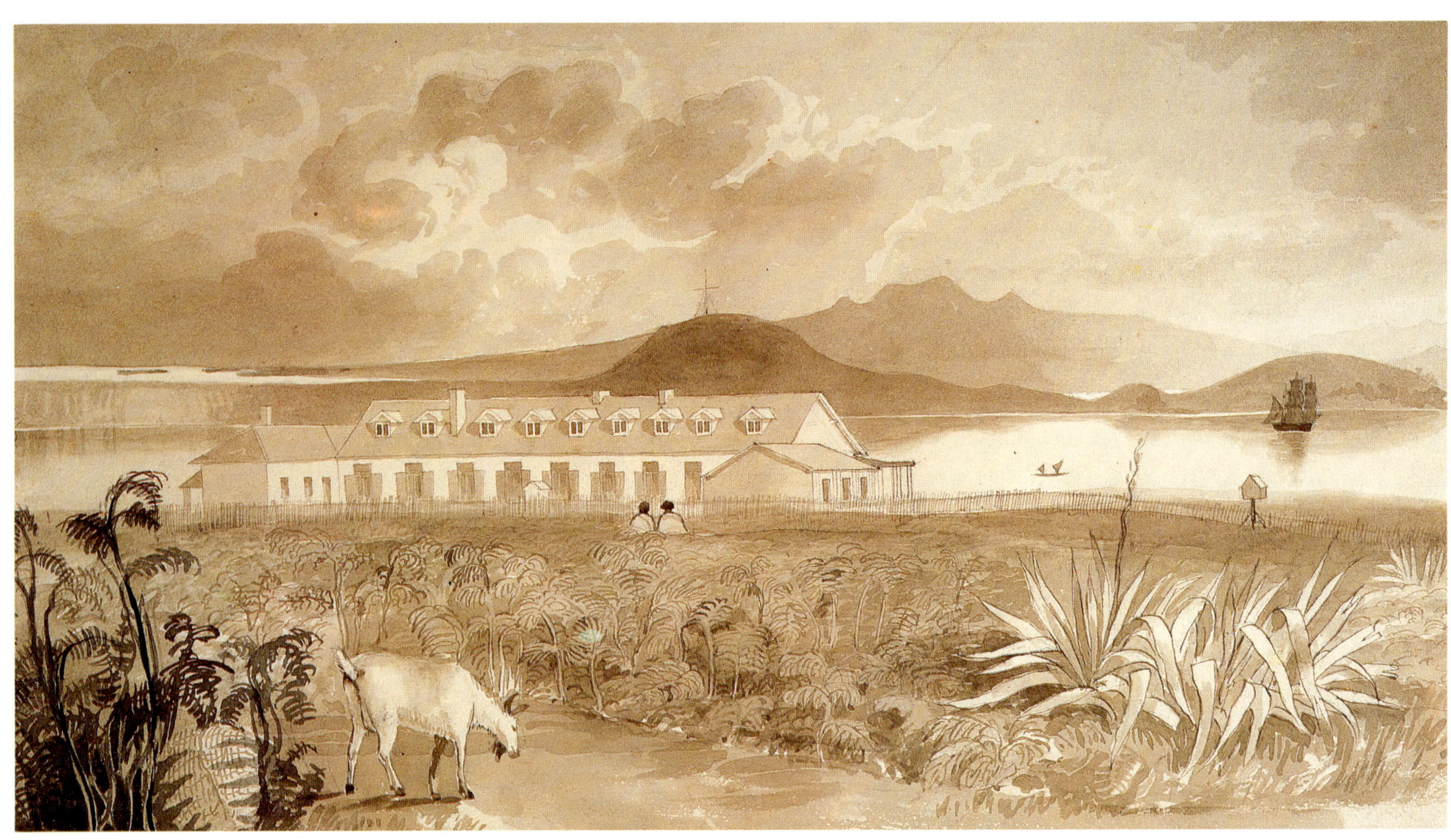

9 [*Album page* 17

A Native Game.

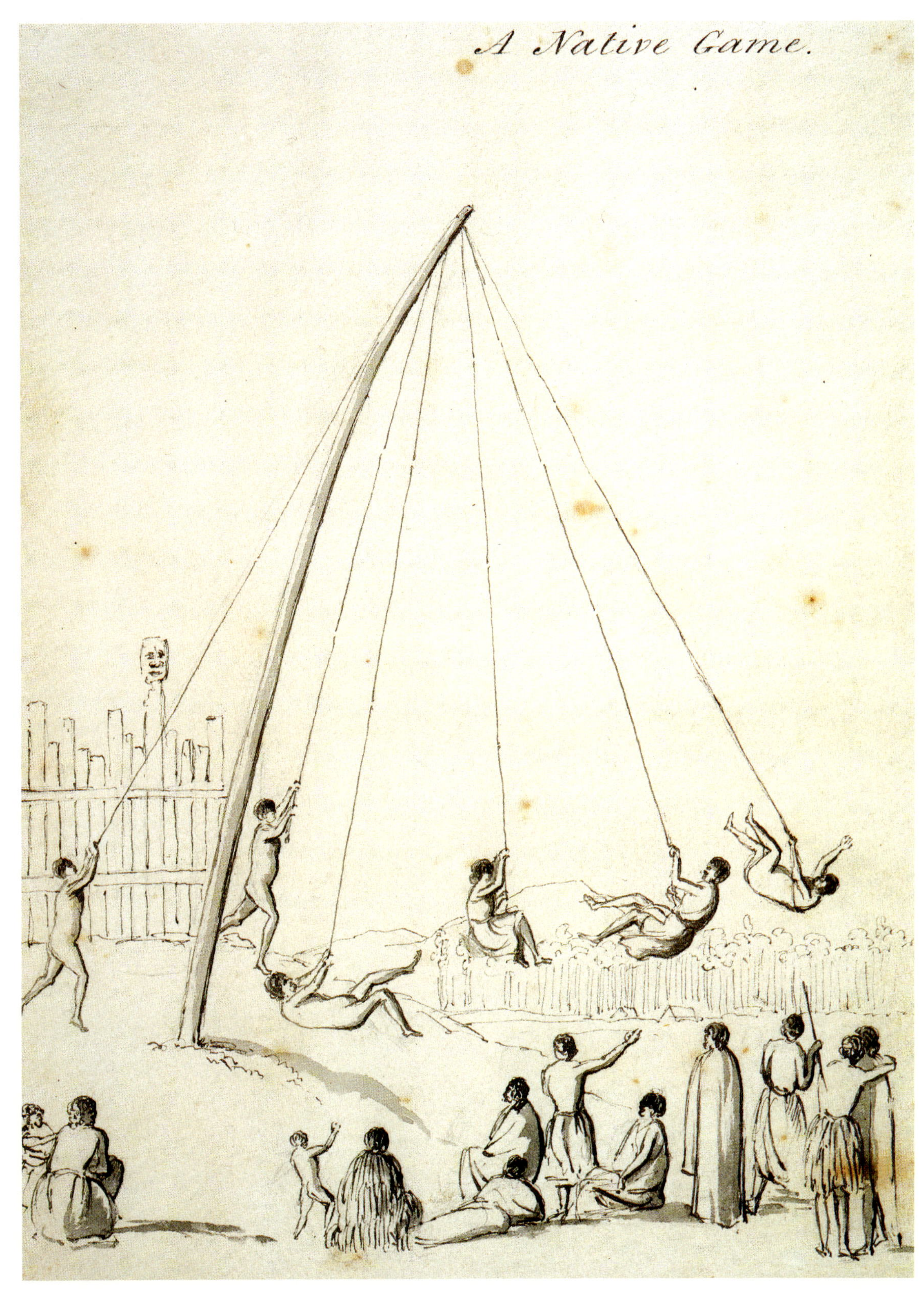

10 [*Album page* 20

[Commentary on the 'Poi']

The Poi a favourite plaything of the New Zealandes bears a conspicuous place in the history of these people. As seen in the accompanying drawing, it is simply an ornamented ball with a long string and is struck alternately with either hand the string being so managed as to cause the ball to describe a variety of figures. Simple as this may appear, to use it properly requires much manual dexterity only to be acquired by long practice.

The Poi is the love letter of the Maori. A young chief becomes enamoured of some beautiful Maiden doubtful if he has found favours in her eyes he secretly makes a Poi, which he ornaments after the most approved fashion. some trusty slave conveys this to the young lady taking care to name from whom it comes and that none witness its presentation; If favourable to the suit of her lover she plays with it on all favourable occasions. he sees it in her hands and overjoyed takes the first opportunity of assembling his friends and carrying her off, should he be disagreeable to the fair object of his affections she throws away the Poi.

In War the Poi is sent from Chief to Chief as a symbol of gathering, when Tuiva proposed to attack Maketu he sent Tai Pari (his friend) chief of Maunga Nui an ornamented Poi as an earnest of his intention and as a signal to Tai Pari to gather his people for war. This is only one instance of a general custom. I have seen the Poi sent on this occasion and so strictly tapued (or rendered sacred) was it, that none but Tai Pari would touch it.

In playing with the Poi a kind of chaunt accompanies the motion of the hands of which the following is a specimen.

E noho ana koki nga Petoni kei wakaneke kapai noa taku ringa i taku Poi, Ka te pukapuka te kai o taku poi, Ko Maketu ko te Reanuku ki te awaho. Ko Ikairo tona Atua Ko te Wakawae tou mea nia watu haere ki toto ki a ai toku mate e toku totonu he mea ka kaha kore tenei Iwi, kaumai koki ra te Poi. Haere ta ki — Tokirau he werore kau ana te rewa o te Kaipuke kite wakapu o — Kororarepa i a Tareha e karau panatu ai nau i homai tou Pouda ki Maketu. E Poi — E —

A small New Zealand word being the name of a Boundary on one of the Land Claims.

Tetutu ki tangaongaluwondakamarangi

Translation

The falling on the knees of Kamarangi.

11 [*Album page 21*

A Group of New Zealanders.

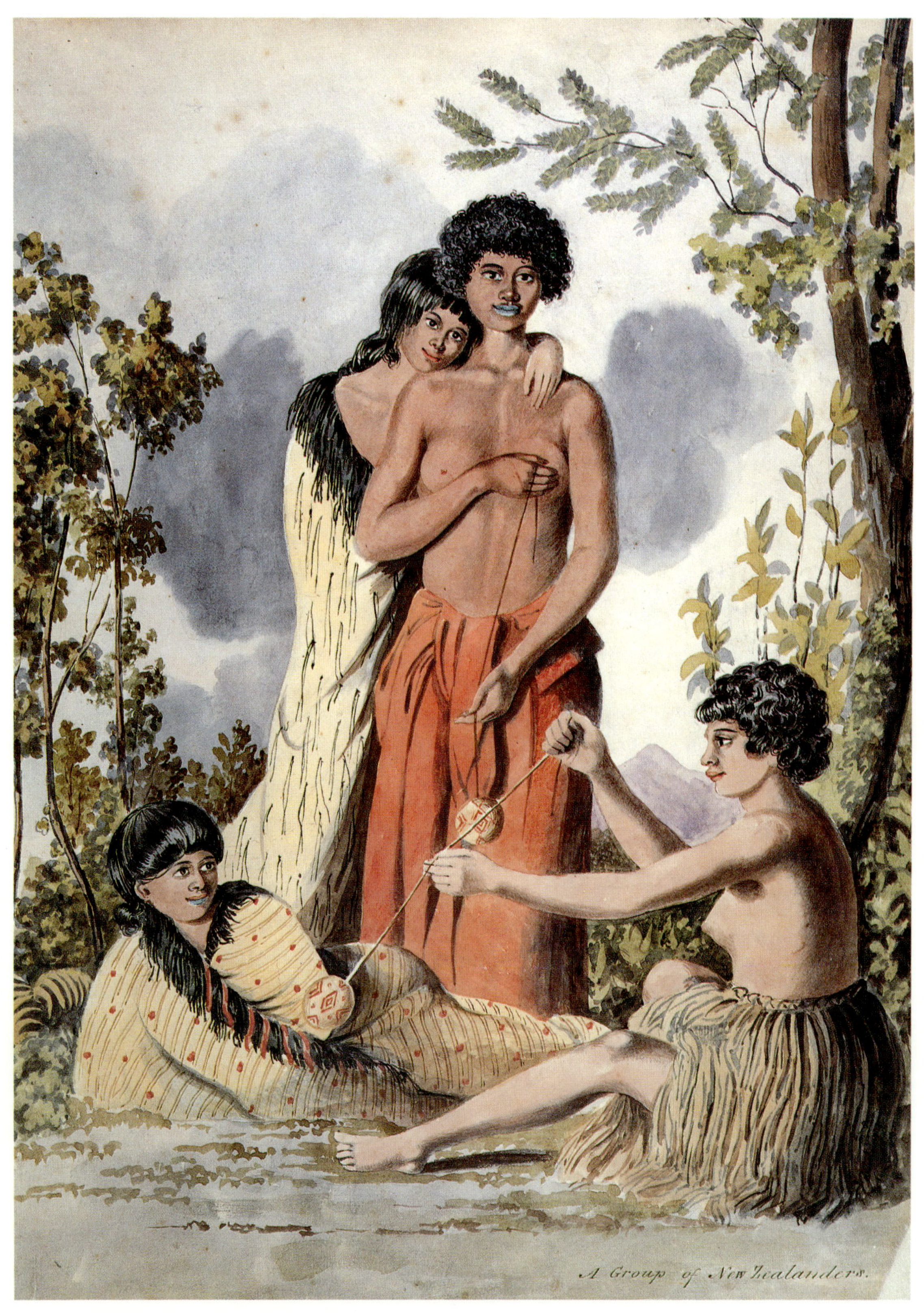

12 [*Album page* 19

[Maori woman reading]

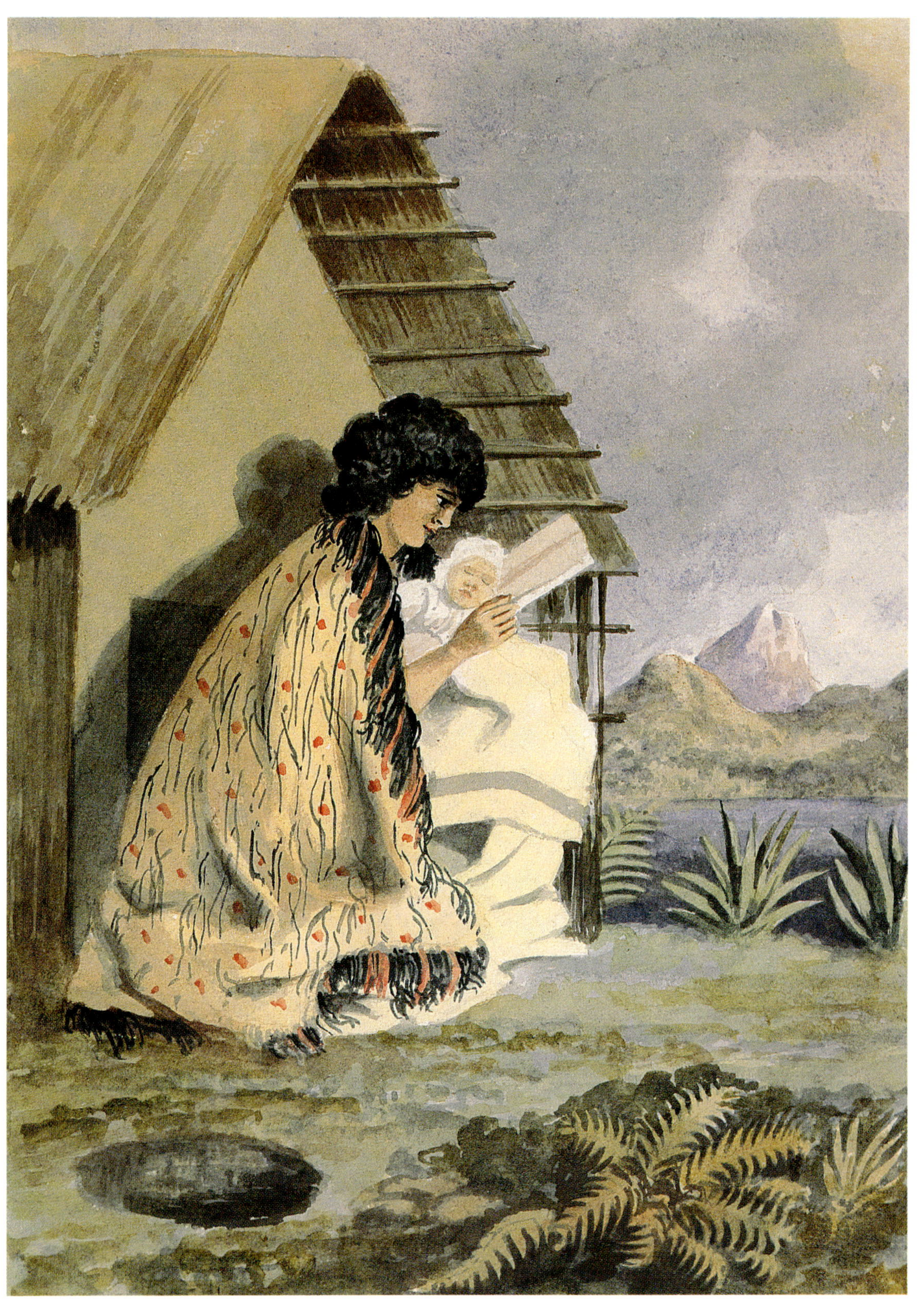

13 [*Album page* 23

The Pah of Oinamutu on the Rotorua Lake: the carvings in this pah are particularly fine

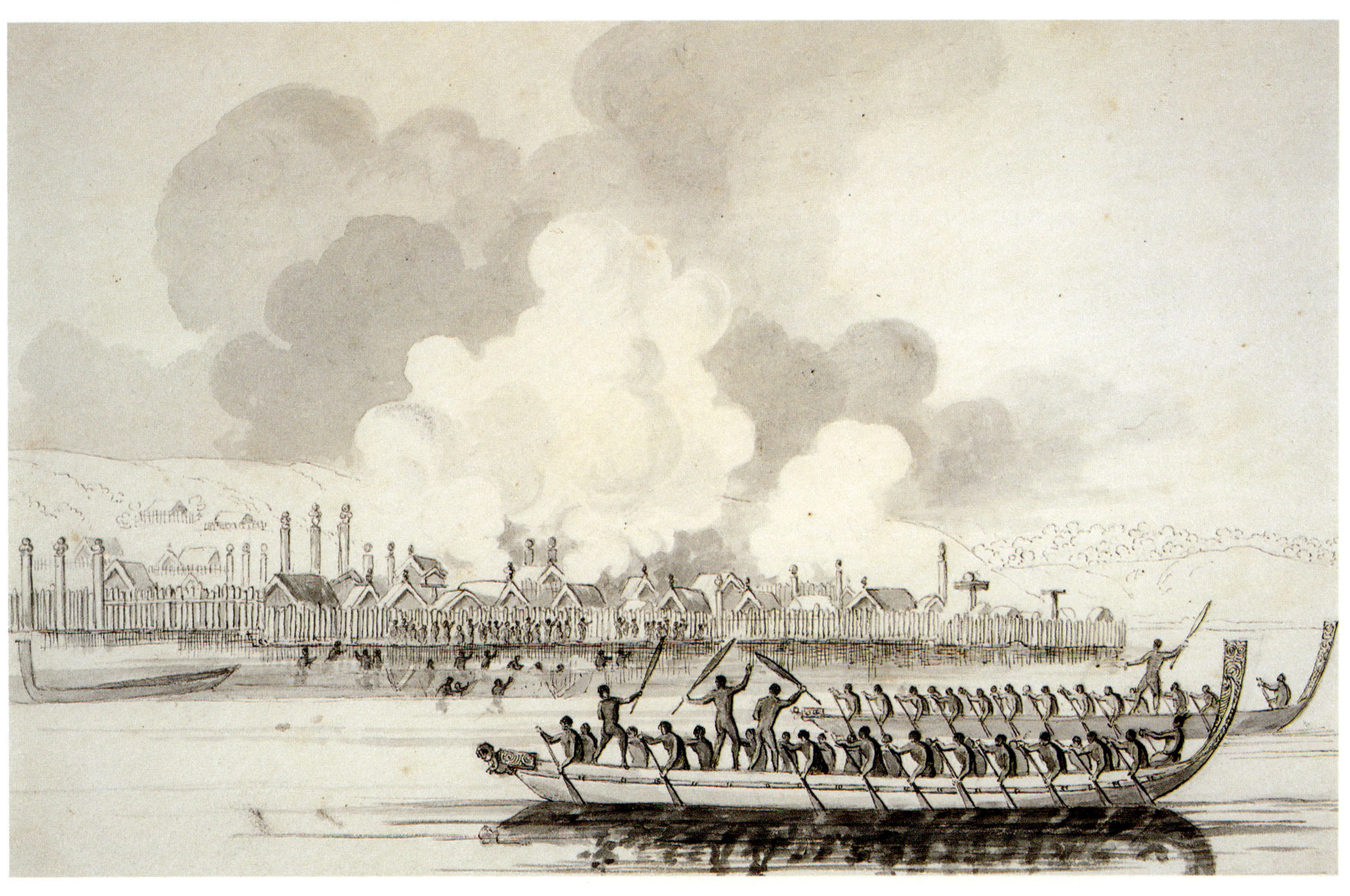

14 [*Album page 31*

Russell from Paihia, Wai Keri River

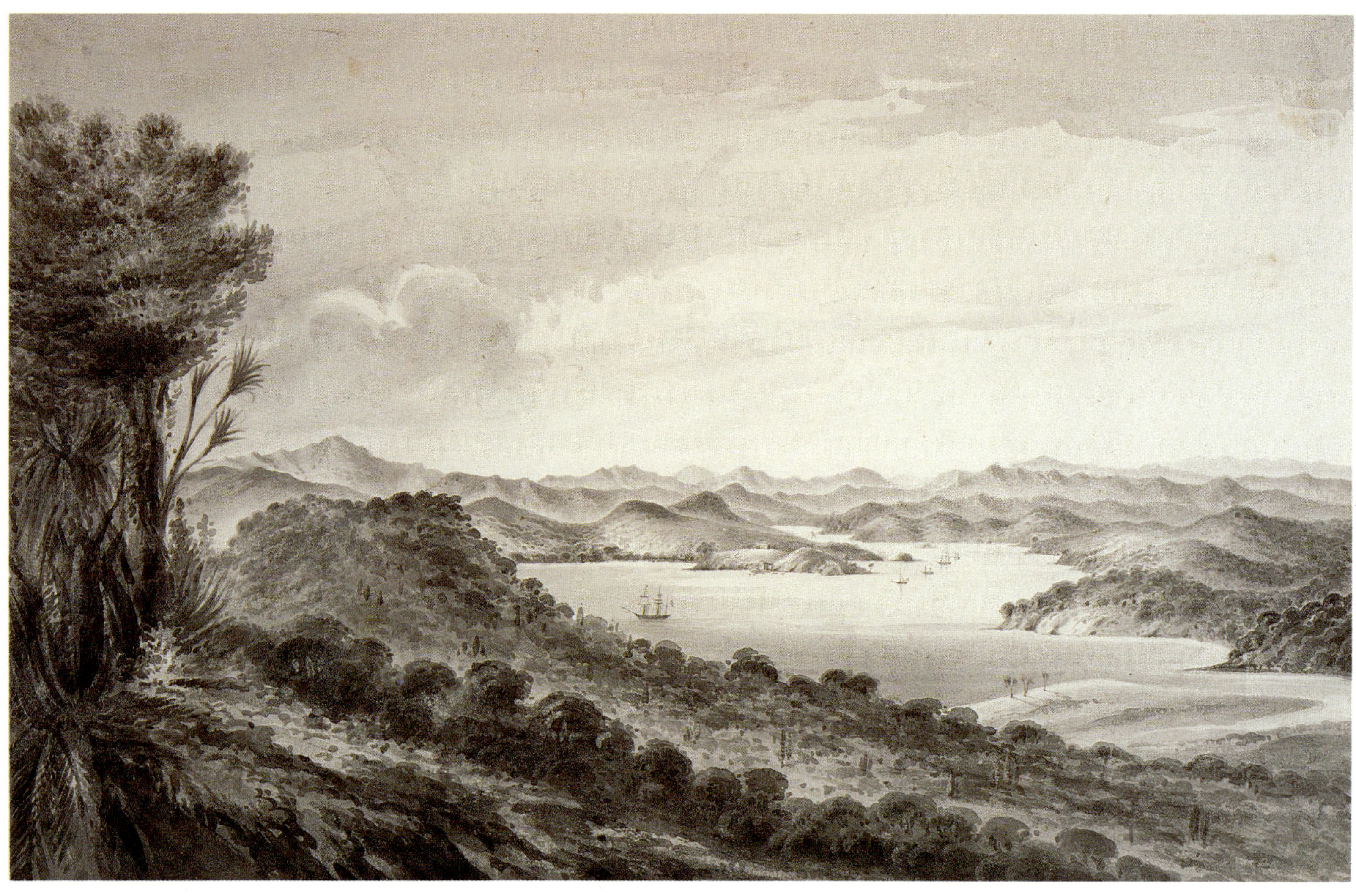

15 [*Album page* 33

View of the town of Auckland from the opposite shore of the Waitemata

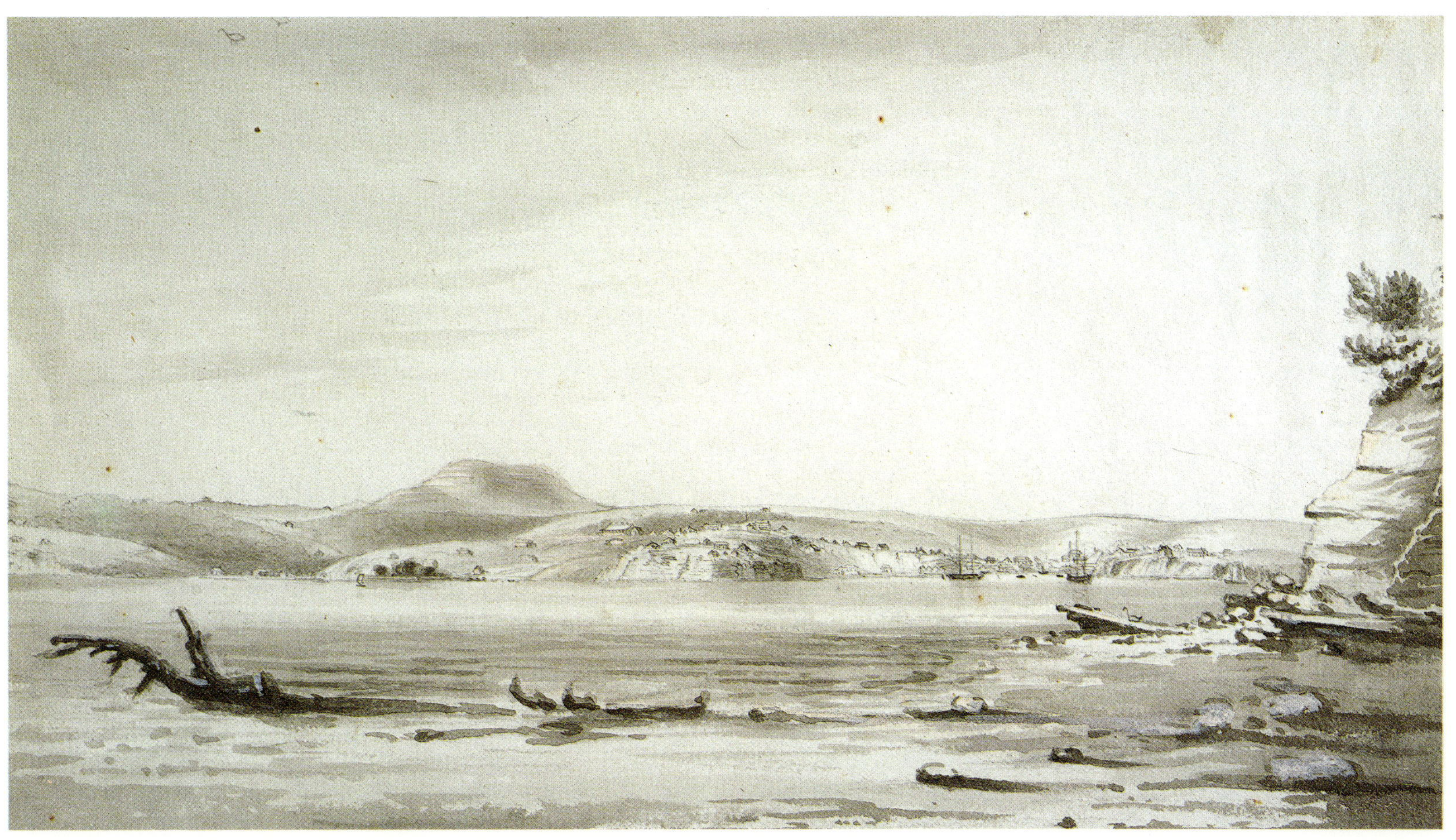

16 [*Album page* 37

A Hot Spring in the Warm Lake of Rotomahana

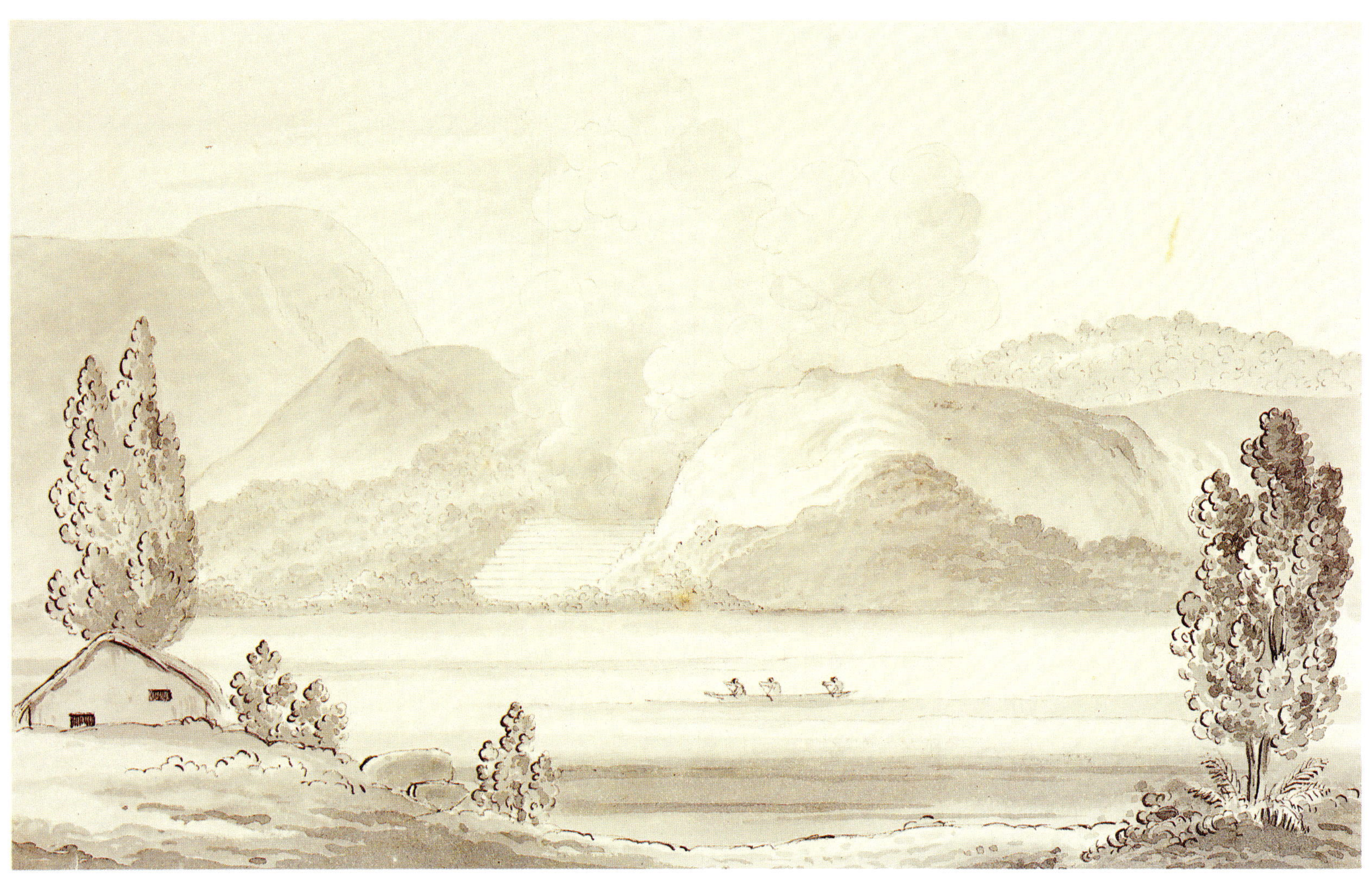

17 [*Verso of Album page* 37

[Part of poem 'Rangi Kawauw'
and marginal notes in Shortland's hand]

The lashes of her eyes were long
Such as we love to praise in song
Her lips were stain'd with blue.

To hunga's skill, her Kouwai show'd;
In graceful lines the carving flow'd;
Tis said, the artist lost his heart,
When first, the maiden's lips did part,
They held such brilliant pearls;
The richest copper could not win,
The slightest praise, when near her skin.
Above her breasts, a tiki hung,
Below the flax tatara strung,
Its leaves in waving curls.

With graceful ease she wound her way,
And sang her native roundelay;
It spoke of battles, love, and food.
With threats of drinking some one's blood
Twas quite a Maori song;
She climb'd the lofty forest trees
And pluck'd their fruits, with greatest ease;
Her mats were work'd with nicest skill
The richest fringe the edges fill
Its strings so black and long.

A shark's tooth dangled from her ear
A costly gem, the Maori's wear,
Its root was tipt with brilliant red
Bound to the ribbon by a thread,
A single waka kai.
She was indeed a rich brunette
Her eyes in sparkling lustre set;
Yet all her charms were soon forgot
When she put on that basilisk spot
The Dirty Kokowai

Tohunga a priest
in any craft.

Kauwai – The chin
between lower lip

carve
Tiki – an image of
or pounamu as the
stone, wh. is worn a

Tatara – name of th

kokowai – red earth
the body ~~and~~ ~~[illegible]~~
their garments are

Korowai – name of
with white & black

18 [*Album page 35*

Rangitoto, Mount Victoria and the North Head,
from the Government Domain, Auckland.

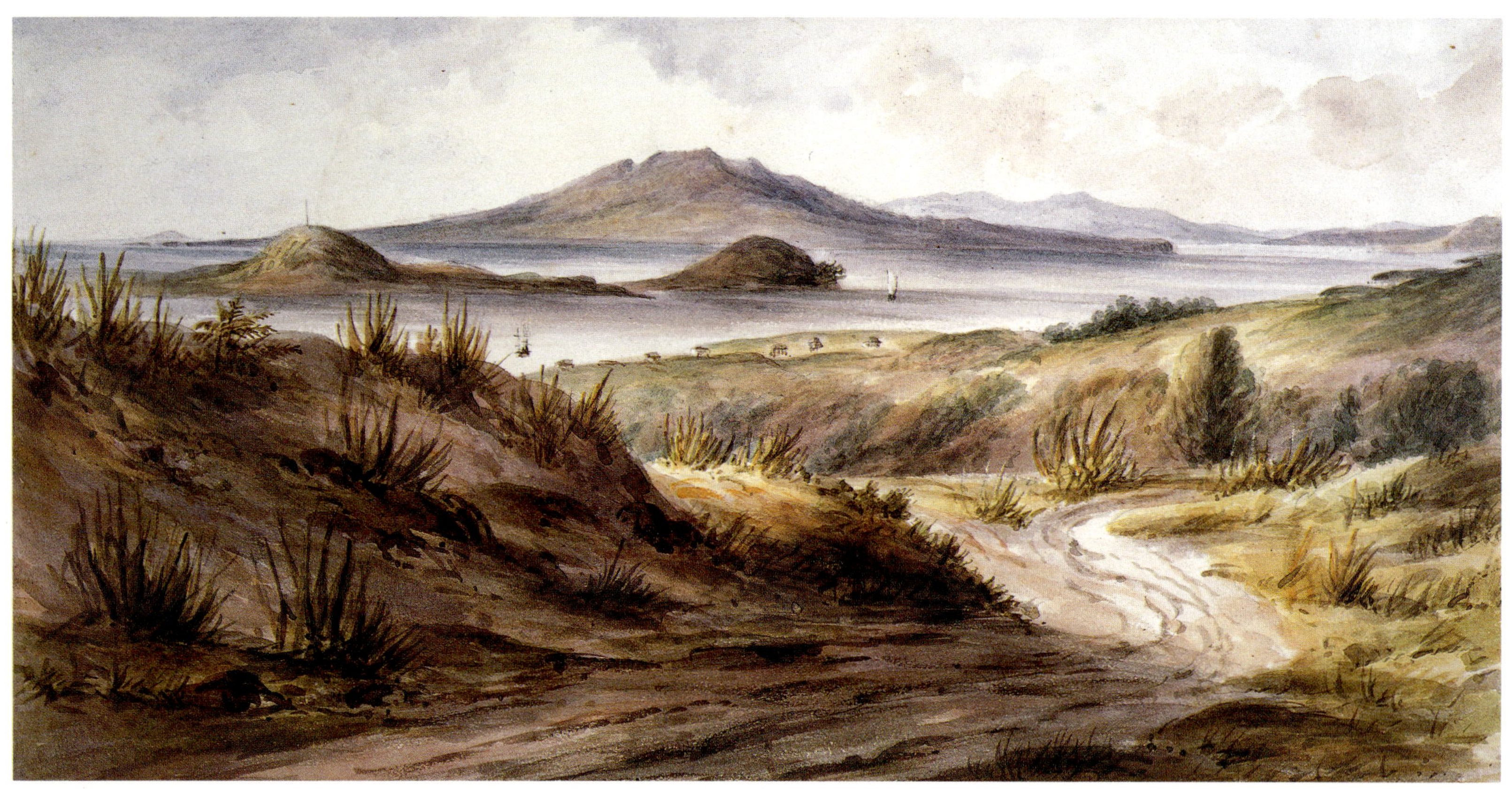

19 [*Album page 41*

Entrance to the Harbour, Auckland

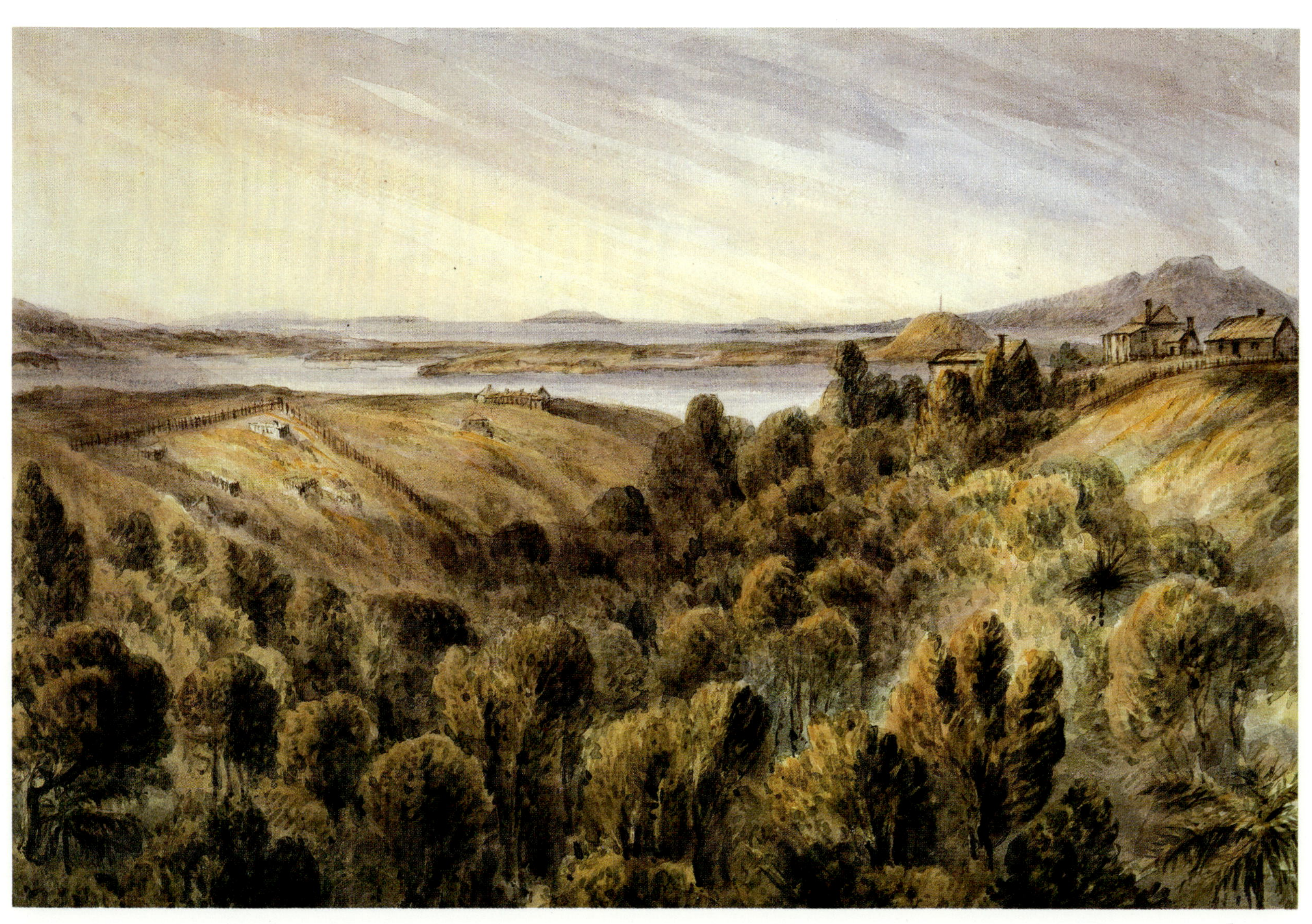

20 [*Album page* 43

[Auckland Harbour]

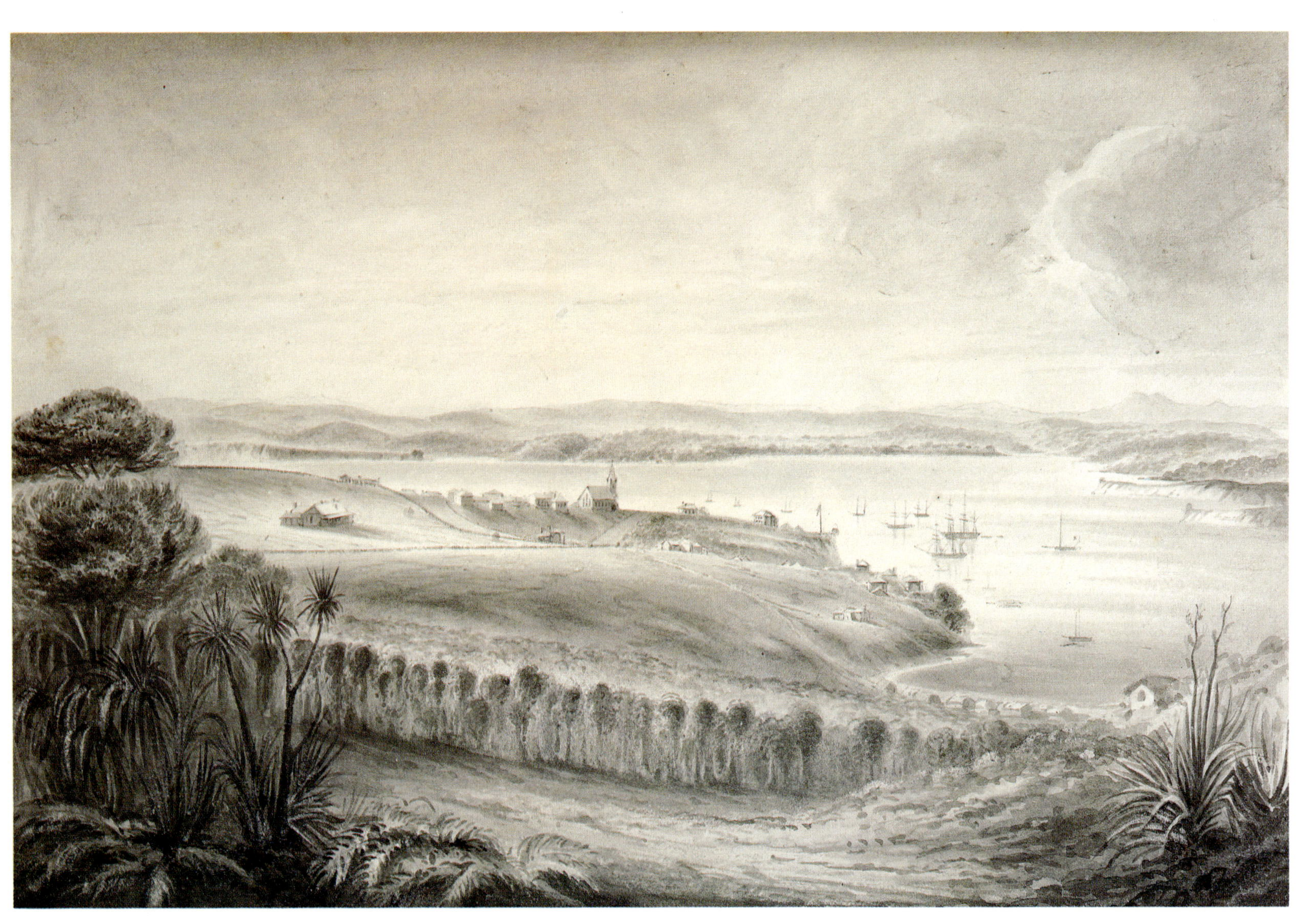

21 [*Album page* 45

A Native Chief dressed in a Dog's Skin mat, with a weapon called wahanoghi

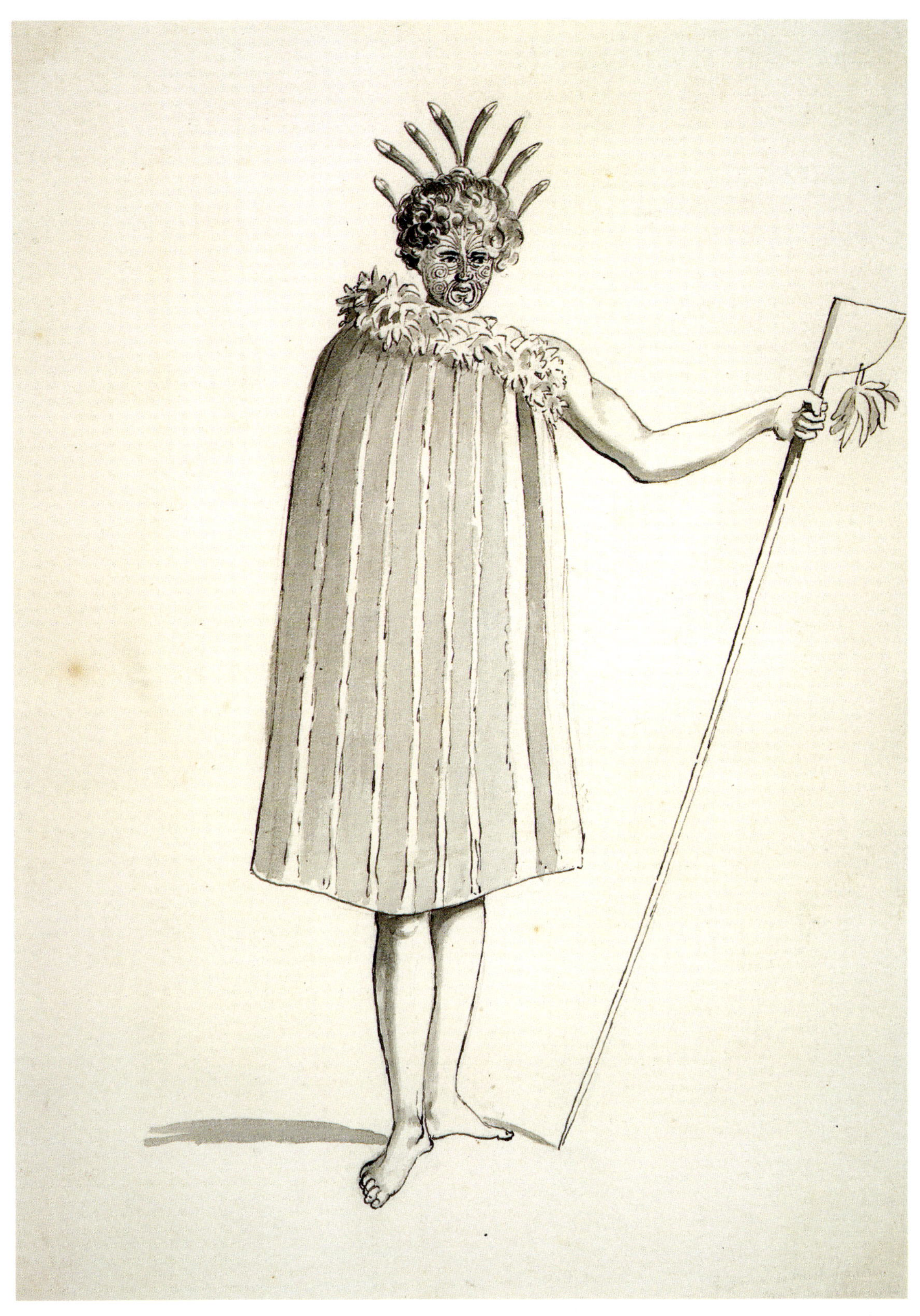

22 [*Album page 49*

Wiremu Hoete e Mata Kawana

Putiki Maehi 27 1843

E Kui e Mata Kawana.

Tena koe koutou ko tamarika.

E Kui e Mata tena koe te kanohi o to matou hoa ahakoa kua mate ai ko tona ahua kei akoe, koia taku rita aroha i tuhituhi atu ai kia koe, no te mea kua rongo au kia te Karaka, e hoki ana koe ki tou kainga koia taku reta poroporoaki ki a koe ki te ritenga o to matou Kawana tino pai ahakoa mate noa i a kahore ana whakaro he ki a matou, koia ka nui ai to matou aroha ki a ia ki a koe ki a au tamariki koki.

E Kui e Mata Kawana tena koe haere ra e kui ki tou kainga ka wha kina atu ra to korua nei ahua pai ko tou rangatira waiho ra matou i konei mihi kau ai ki o korua nei haerenga.

Tenei ano taku waita aroha kei akoe kei to matou nei hoa atawhia

Otahui tanga he mihi kau iho, E Kui te tikanga o tena kupu waiata aroha, mo korua, ko tou hoa. nga ro ana koe. nga ro ana a te Kawana, ko korua nei haerenga waiho kau i ko hei mihi ma matou.

E Kui haere ra e te hoa aroha, o nga rangatira o Nui Tireni ka whakina atu ra te kuru pounamou. He ai ano taku poro poro aki aroha ki a koe haere ra e kui ki tou kainga kahore he kupu ki a koe, haere ra e taku reta aroha ki a Mata Kawana.

Na tou hoa aroha

Na Wiremu Hoete.

23 [*Album page* 48

Letter from a New Zealand Chief to Mrs Hobson on leaving for England

Letter from a New Zealand Chief to Mrs Hobson on leaving for England —

Putiki March 27th 1843.

Lady – Lady Governor health to you and your children. Lady, Mother health to you, the eye of our friend, who though dead, has left his image in you, — therefore I write this letter of affection to you, because I heard from Mr Clarke that you were returning to your Native Land, therefore this is my valedictory letter to you. the semblance of our most Excellent Governor, who is dead, but who never had an evil thought towards us, on this account our love is great to him, to you, and to your children.

Lady – Lady Governor, health to you, Go Lady to your Native Land, the good qualities of yourself and himself will be acknowledged – Go and leave us here to regret and sympathise over your departure. This is my love song to you, to our kind friend – "Ceahuri tanga ke i mihi kau iho"

Lady the meaning of this love song is this, it is for you and your husand – you are about to be lost, and he is gone, and the departure of you both, will leave us only a theme of regret.

Lady go – kind friend of the Native Chiefs you will not be forgotten.

This is my loving valediction and farewell to you, go Lady to your Native Land, I have not a word to say

Go my affectionate letter to the Lady Governor

From your affectionate friend

William Jowett

24 [*Album page 55, top*

Ko te Waha o te Papa
Wakano

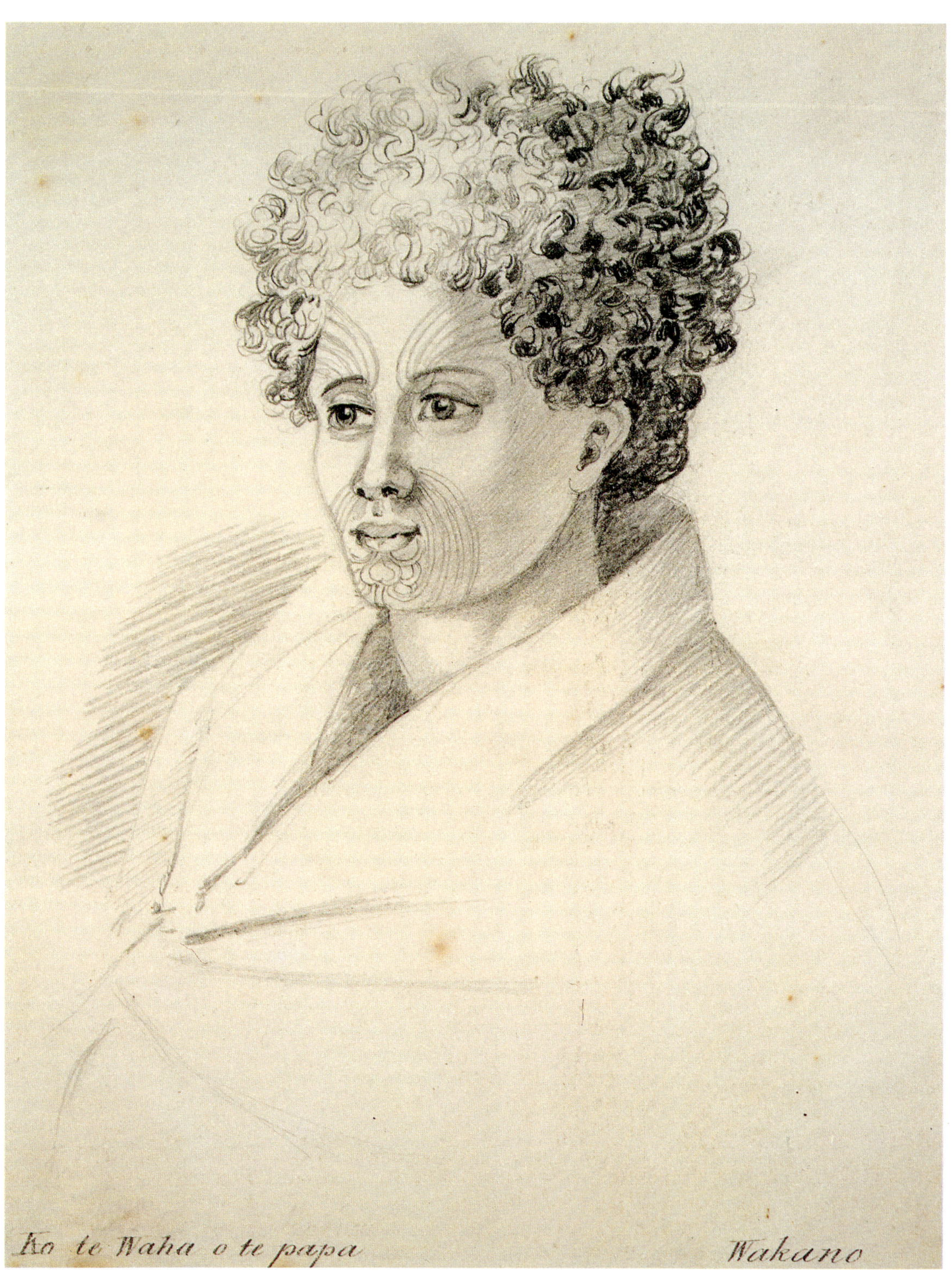

25 [*Album page 55, bottom*

Kino Kino.
Ohuia

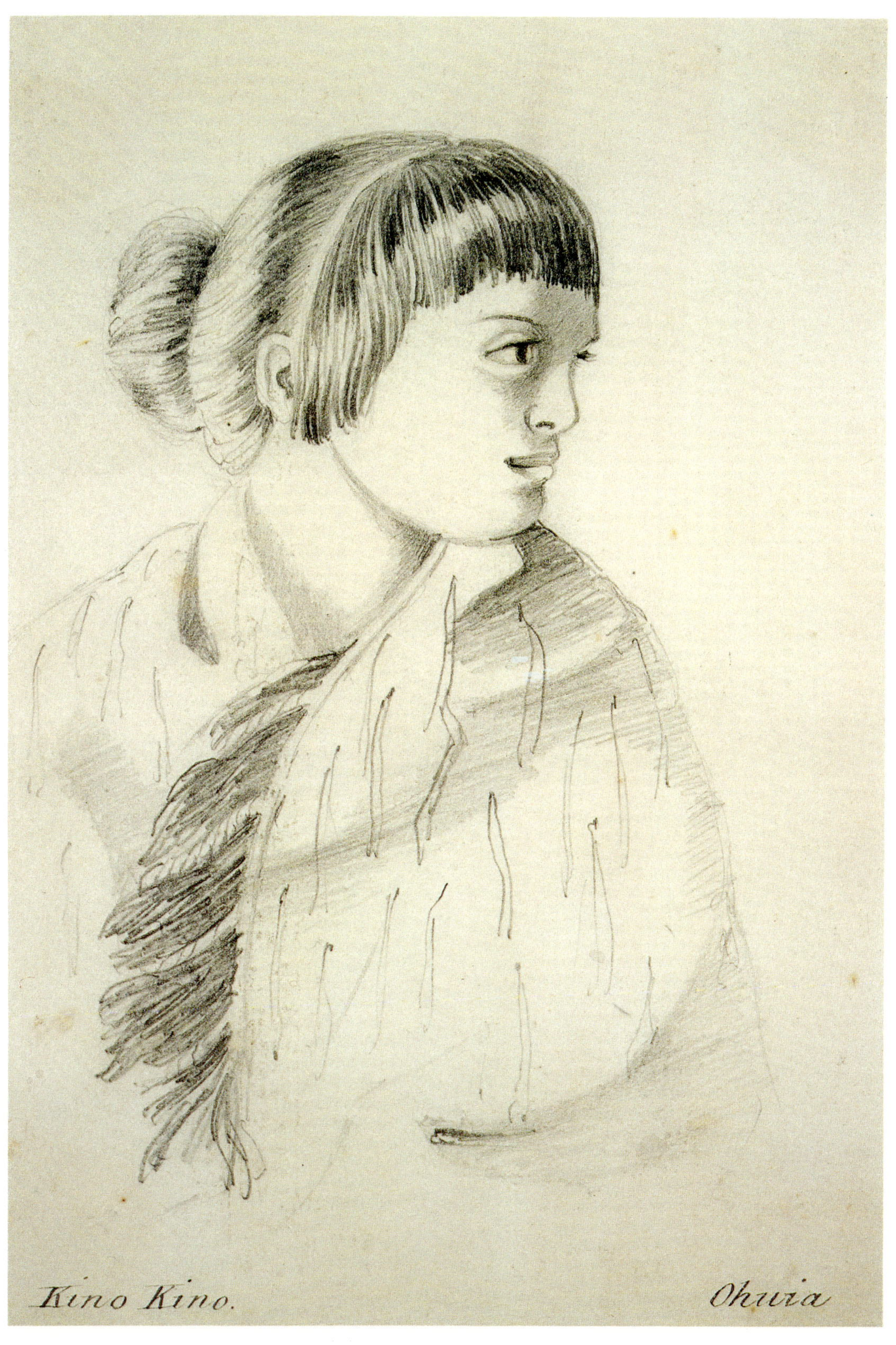

26 [*Album page* 57

[Two Maori Girls]

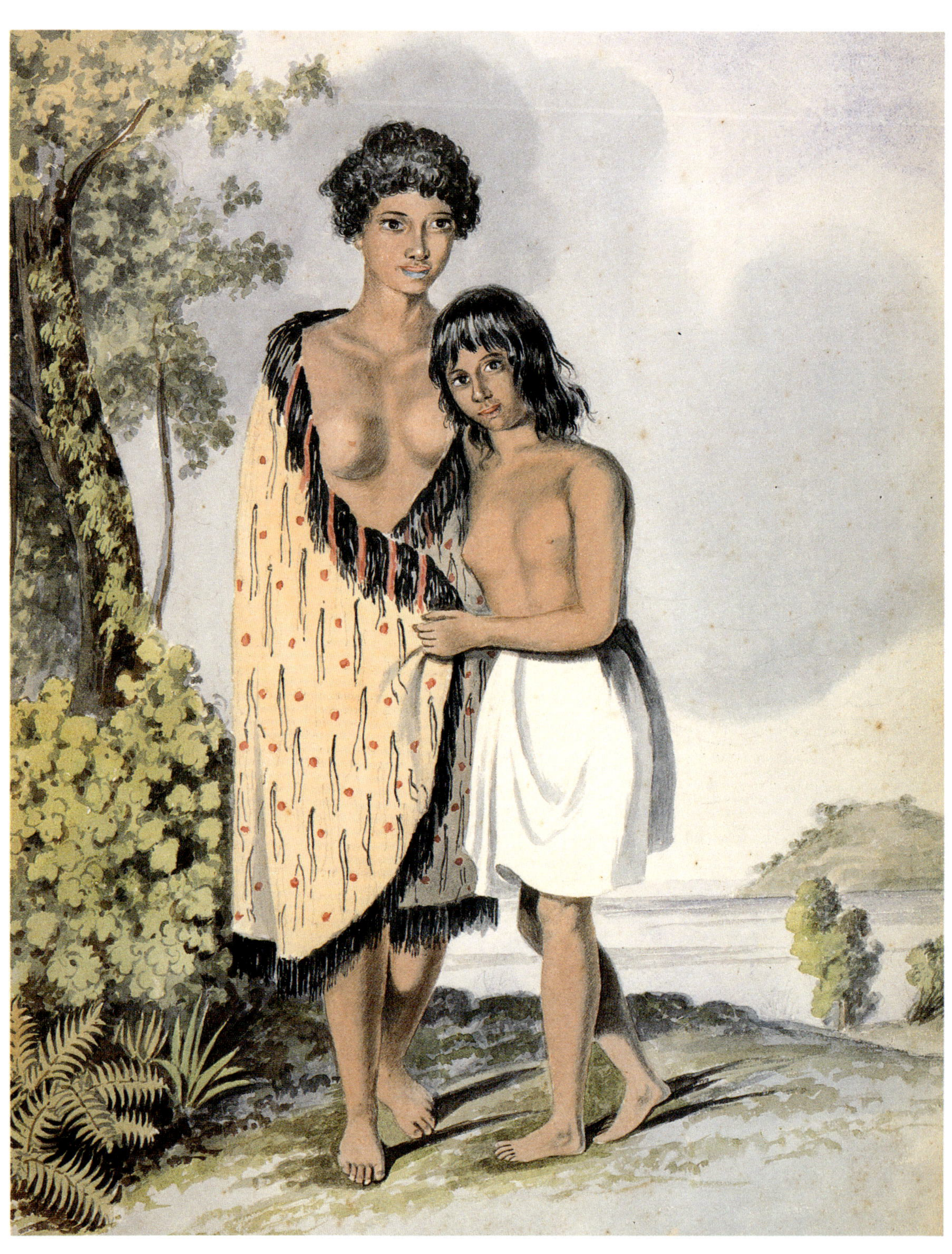

27 [*Album page* 59

View on the lake of Rotorua. The island of Mo Koia in the Centre of the Lake

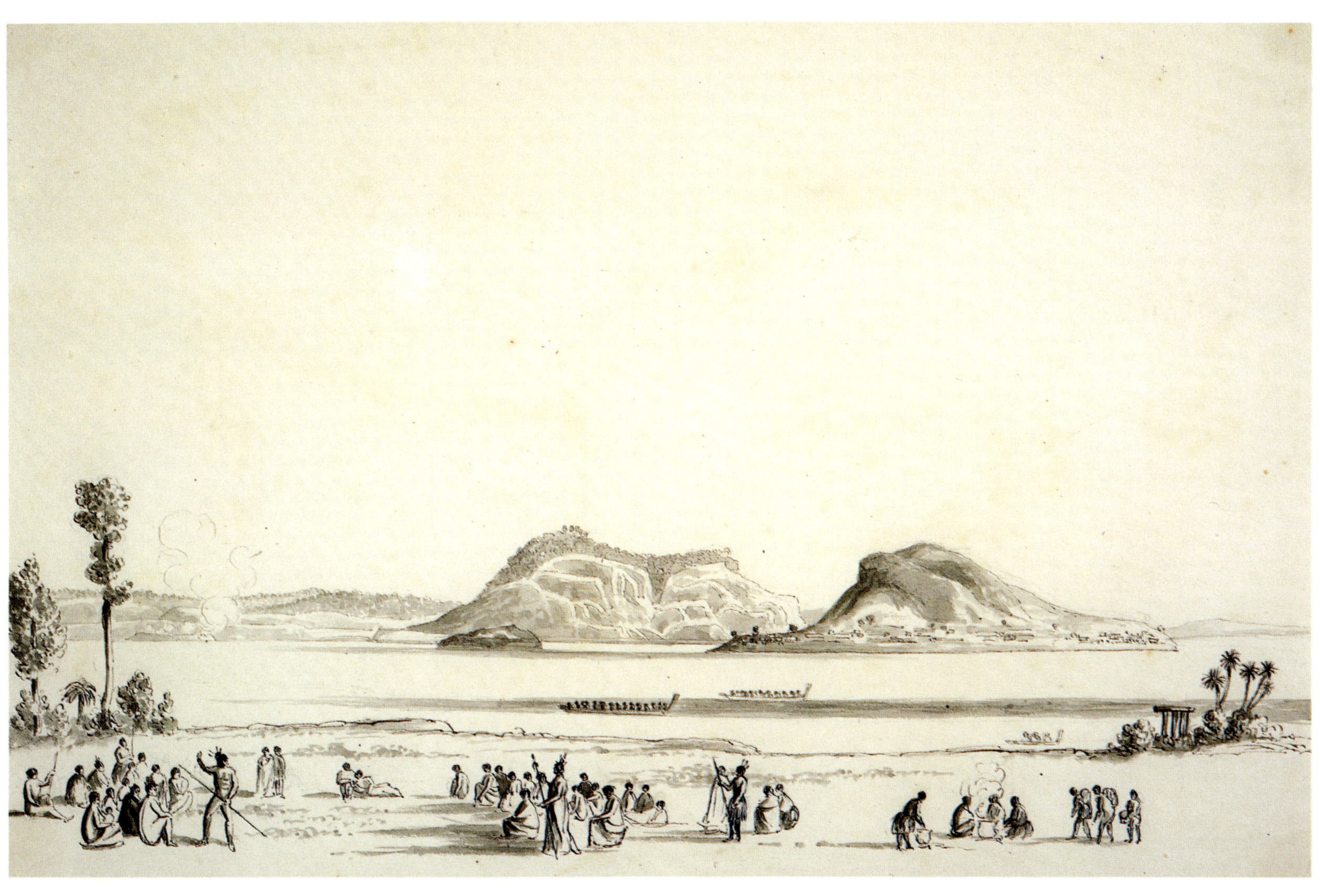

28 [*Album page* 51

"And the Wilderness shall become the fruitful Field"

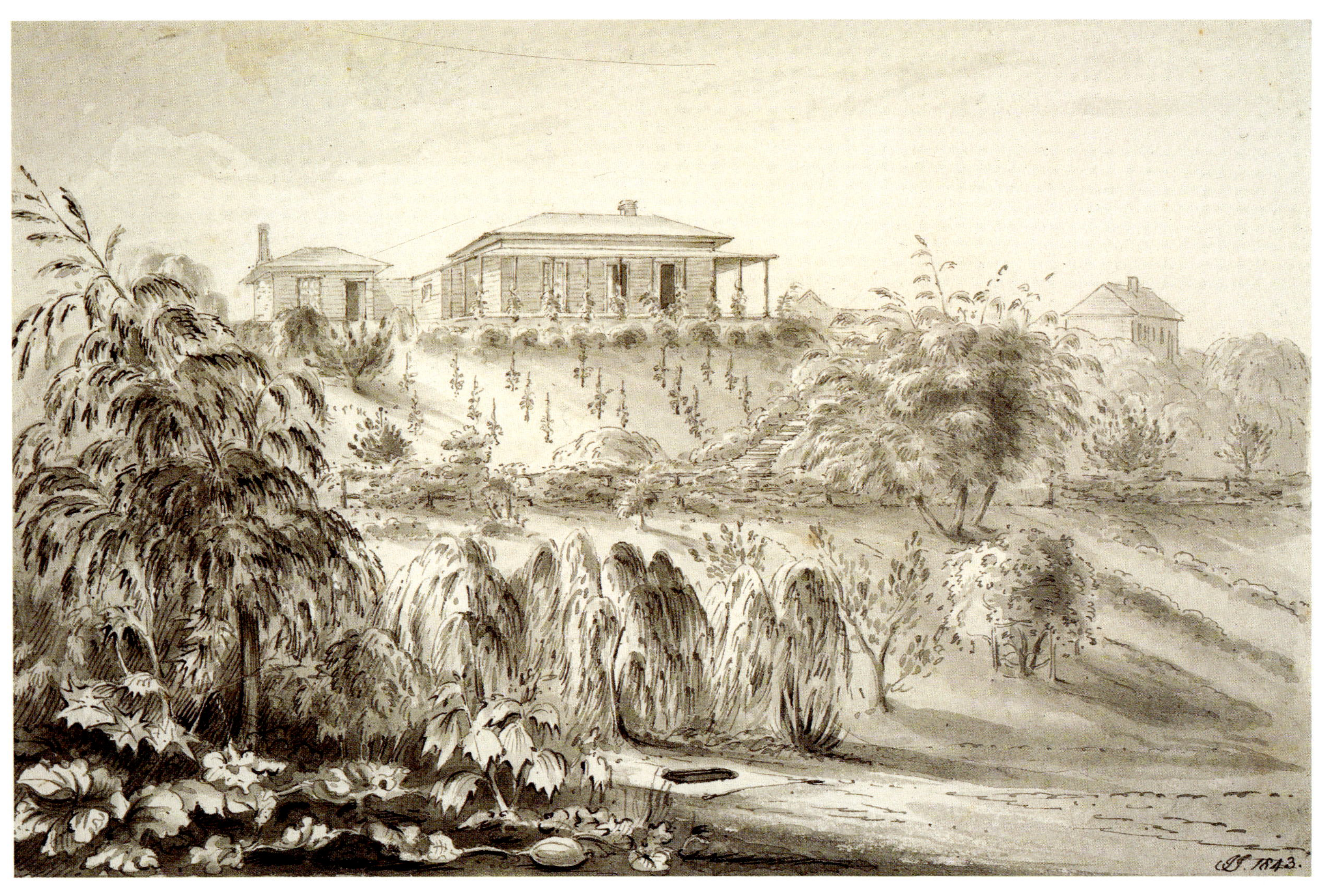

29 [*Album page* 73

"And the solitary places shall be made glad"

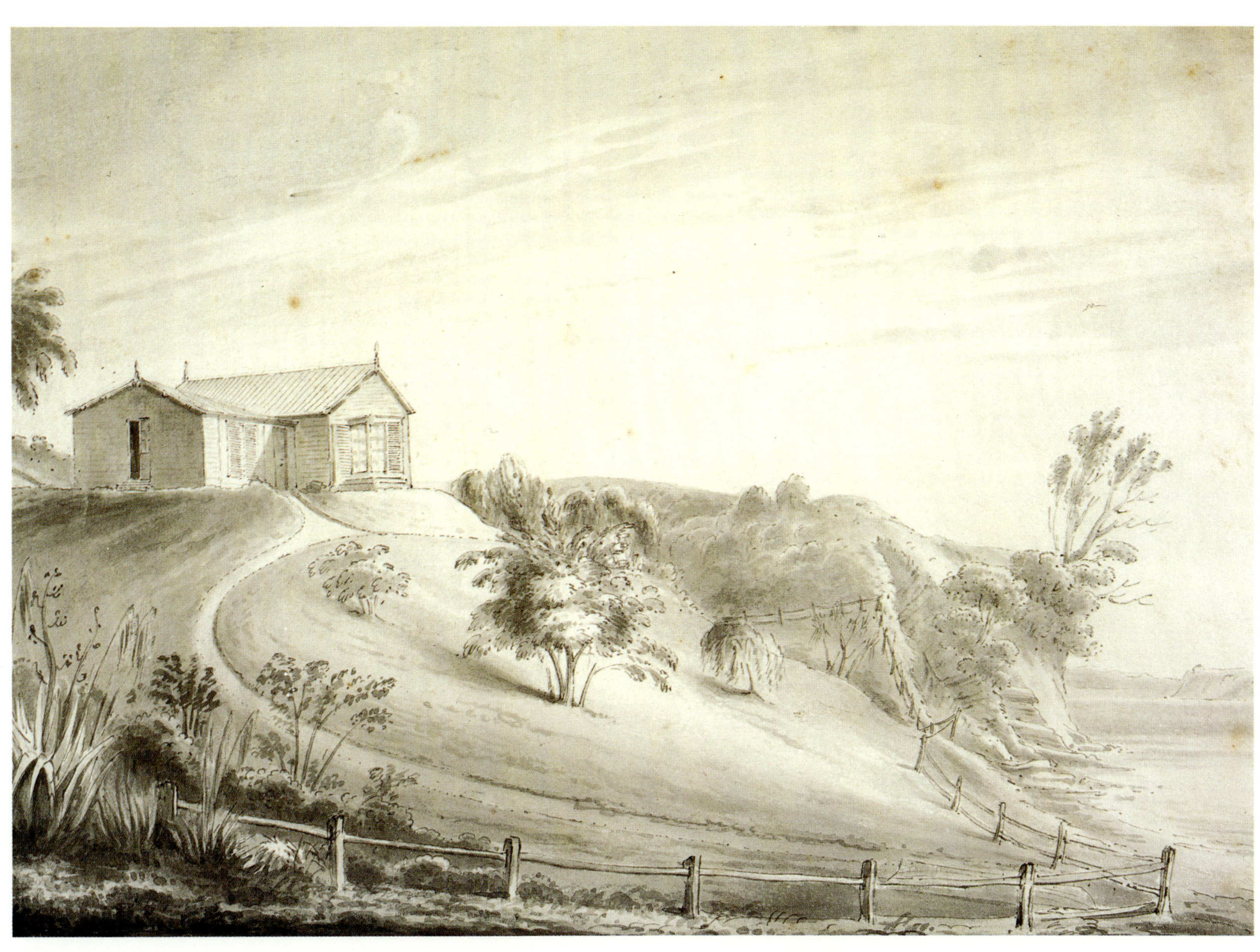

30 [*Album page* 69

Wellington from the 'London'

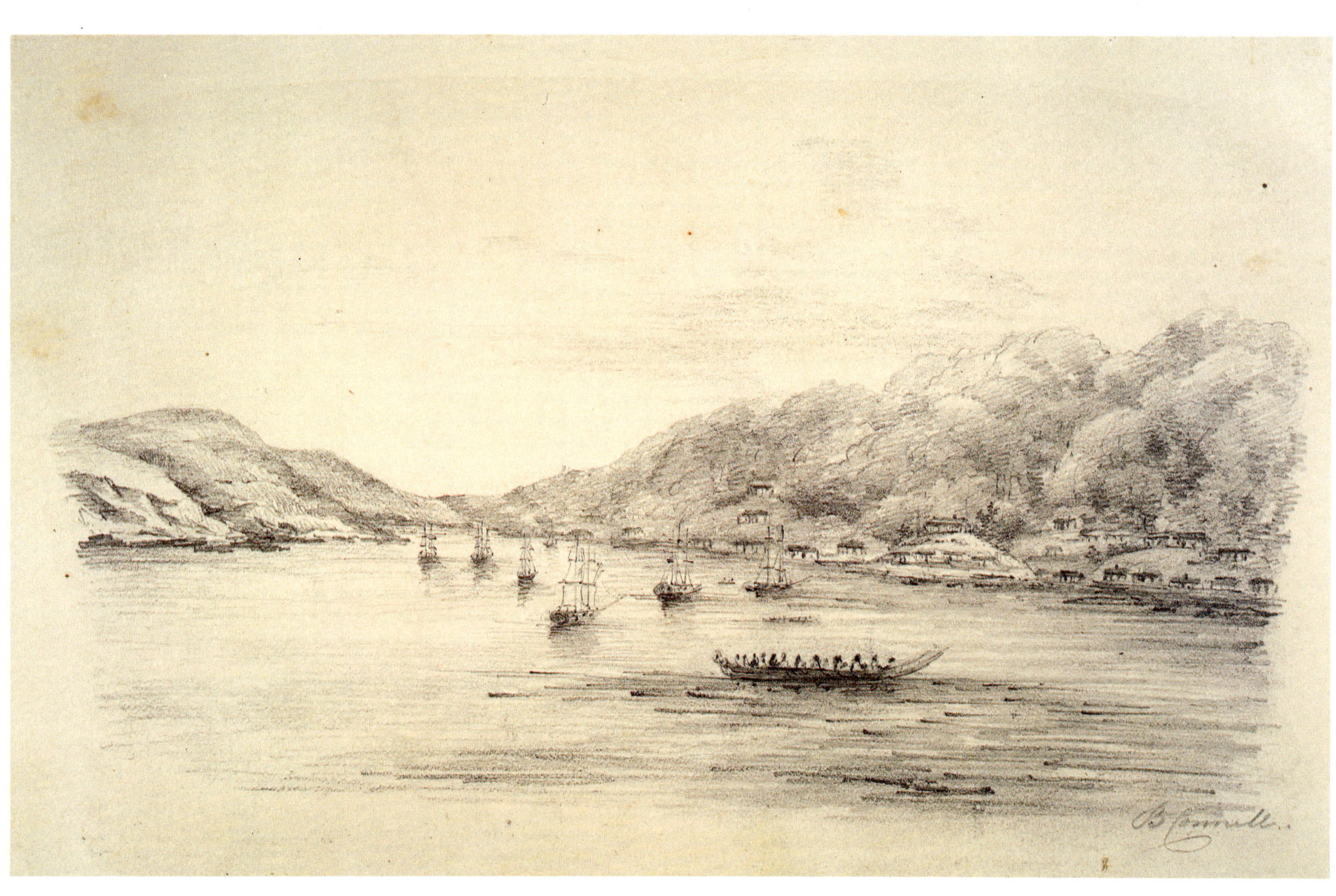

31 [*Album page* 71

Entrance to the Harbour Manukao from Puponga Head

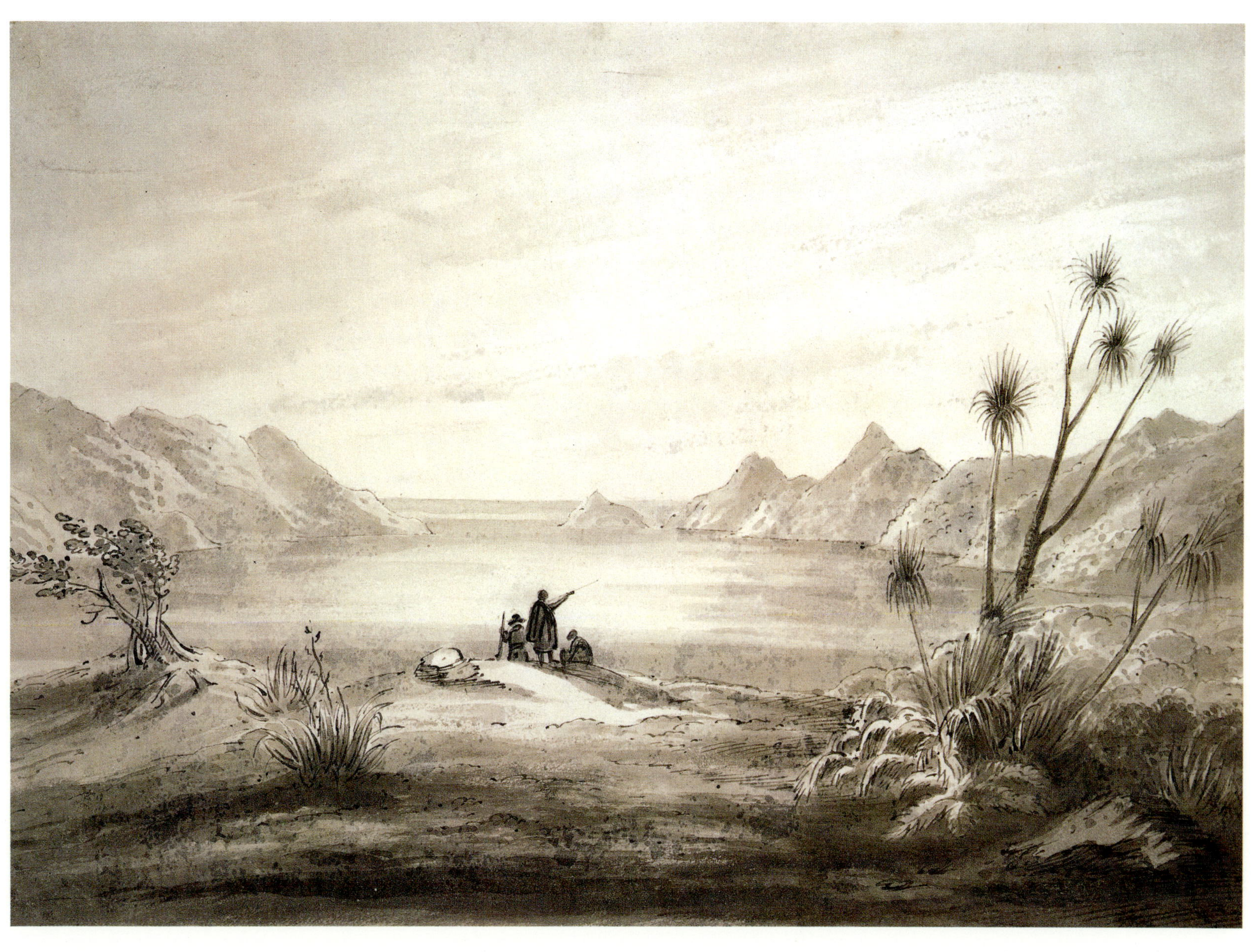

32 [*Album page* 78

Rangi Kawauw

Rangi Kawauw.

Rangi Kawauw was a Maori maid,
Born in the forests deepest shade,
Her limbs were round, her eyes were bright,
Her hair, black as the shades of night,
In rich profusion grew;
Her cheeks displayed a glowing red
Which broke throughout their darker bed,
The lashes of her eyes were long
Such as we love to praise in song
Her lips were stained with blue.

Tohunga's skill her Kauwai show'd;
In graceful lines the carving flow'd
Tis said, the artist lost his heart
When first the maidens lips did part,
They held such brilliant pearls;
The richest copper could not win,
The slightest praise, when near her skin;
Above her breasts a tiki hung,
Below the flax tatara strung,
Its leaves in waving curls.

With graceful ease she wound her way
And sang her native roundelay;
It spoke of battles, love, and food
With threats of drinking some one's blood
Twas quite a Maori song
She climbed the lofty forest trees
And plucked their fruits with greatest ease;
Her Mats were worked with nicest skill,
The richest fringe the edges fill
Its strings so black and long.

A sharks tooth dangled from her ear
A costly gem the Maori's wear,
Its root was tipt with brilliant red,
Bound to the ribbon by a thread,
A single waka kai
She was indeed a rich brunette
Her eyes in sparkling lustre set,
Yet all her charms were soon forgot,
When she put on that basilisk spot
The Dirty Kokowai.

Tohunga, a priest, a person — skilled in any craft.

Kauwai, The chin, the lines marked between lower lip and chin.

Tatara, name of the rough shaggy mat.

Tiki, an image carved in the green tale or pounamou, as the natives call the stone, which is worn as an ornament.

Kokowai, red earth which is rubbed on the body, and with which their garments are smeared.

33 [*Album page* 79

[Rangi Kawauw]

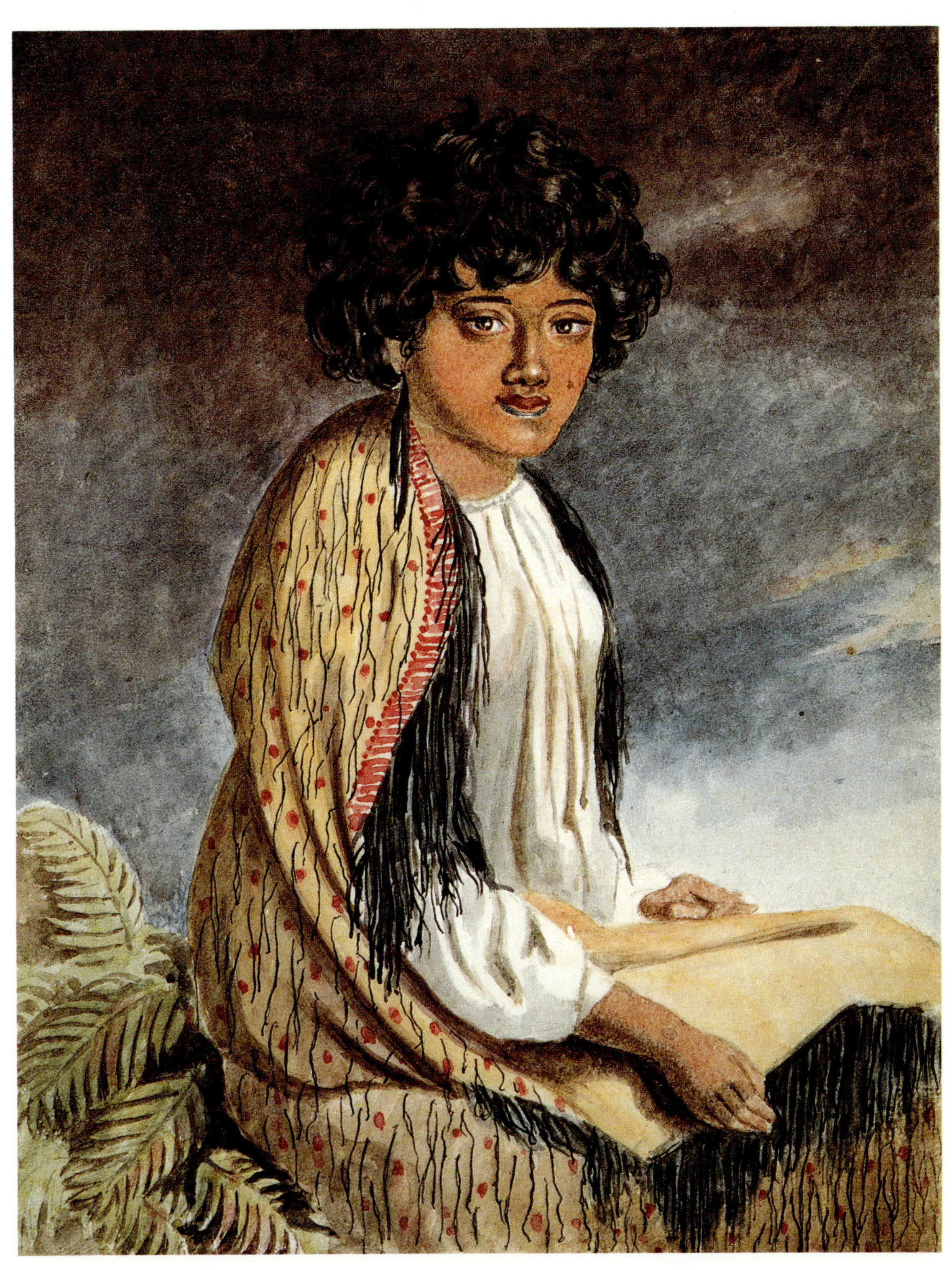

"Maori Songs."

"Maori Songs."

The "Rauiui" or "Haka" is a short sentence metrically arranged, expressive generally of some sentiment of love. It is a favourite amusement with young men and maidens to sing these catches on fine evenings or by moon light, keeping time by beating one hand on the breast, the other hand being raised aloft and made to vibrate so as to produce an effect analogous to the shake in music. When sung on board their canoes it serves to regulate the stroke of the paddles.

The following are specimens of this style of composition.

Ko to tinana ki Waitemata, ko to Wairua i haeremai, i wakaoho i taku moe - i.-

Your body is at Waitemata, your spirit has come hither to startle me in my sleep.

E hoa ma, puritia mai taku huia kia hokimai te tau o taku manawa hapakapa.

O my companions, detain my huiha, restore me the cord of my palpitating heart.

Note. The huia is a bird, whose tail feathers are highly prized as ornaments for the hair. They are black tipt with white, and are very elegant. The word is used here in the same sense as we use the word jewel.

"Puha" "Ngeri" are war songs. Some of these are very ancient, and according to tradition were in use among their ancestors in "Hawaike", the name of the Island whence they trace their origin. They appear however designed chiefly to preserve time and order in the movements of a large body of men, when assembled for the purpose of practising the war dance. The metre of the following "Ngeri" is marked in order to give some idea of the way in which it is repeated.

35 [*Album page* 82

"Maori Songs."

As this is one of antiquity it is worthy of remark that it takes notice of the seal as an inhabitant of their country.

Kia kutia | au | au |
Kia wherahia | au | au |
Kia rere | a tu te | kekeno | ke tawiti | titiro |
Mai ae | ae | ae |
Hug close au au
Fling your arms abroad, au au
Leap, the Seal stands a far off descending to
look on _ ae ae ae.

The body of fighting men which they call a taua being seated on the ground arranged three or four deep, a signal is given by one of chiefs, when they all start up, Brandishing their weapons in their right hands, while the left hand is slapt violently against the thigh, so as to preserve the time, and form an accompaniement to the song, at the words "kia rere" "leap" their action becomes furious; dancing and leaping with violent gestures, thrusting out their tongues, and rolling their eyes, they rather resemble incarnate demons that human beings.

The "Waiata" is a more regular composition. It is a song of joy, grief, or hatred, or merely serves to embody poetical fancy. If a woman is forsaken by her lover, she gives vent to her feelings, and deplores her fate in a "waiata". If a chief falls in fight, his wife, or near female relative celebrates his praise in a "waiata" denouncing curses on his enemy. The following song which breathes the deep, revengeful passion, of a New Zealander, was sung on the recent occasion of Whanake, a chief of Waitarangi, being surprised and murdered by Taraia, a chief of Nga titamatera.

Haere

36 [*Album page* 83

"Maori Songs."

Haere ra e koro-e- i tou tira ko koe Anake
Kia [1]whakairia koe ki runga i Waiwetu
Ae [2]kata ra e koro-e-, kei hoki wawe o koutou waewae

---

[3]Kore nei aku toto, te inu mai ai koe
[4]Kua pahiki au, i nui o rangi-ra-i

Mowai e ranga tou mate i te ao
Ma te [5]po tumai i runga i Tirohanga
Ma te [6]po taka mai, i runga o Kaihinu
Ae engari ra ia, tenei e hika ē.

---

7. Tenei ou roro ko te kowatu e tu ki te ahi kai
Kia reka iho ai taku kainga iho-i-

Go sir alone without a companion
To be [1]placed as a spectacle on the summit of Wairvetu.
Yes [2]laugh on sir, take care your feet return not soon

---

[3]I have no blood left, for you to drink.
[4]I am exhausted in celebrating the greatness of your fame,
Who will proclaim your death to the world?
Will the [5]mist stationary above Tirohanga,
Or the mist which gathers round Kaihinu,
Yes better let it be so, farewell sir.

---

7. May your brain be like the stone by the food fire
That sweet may be my banquet.

Notes.

(1) When an enemy is killed his head is cut off an baked,
It is then exhibited upon a pole.
(2) The lips are drawn apart so as to expose the teeth, and
give

37 [*Album page* 84

"Maori Songs."

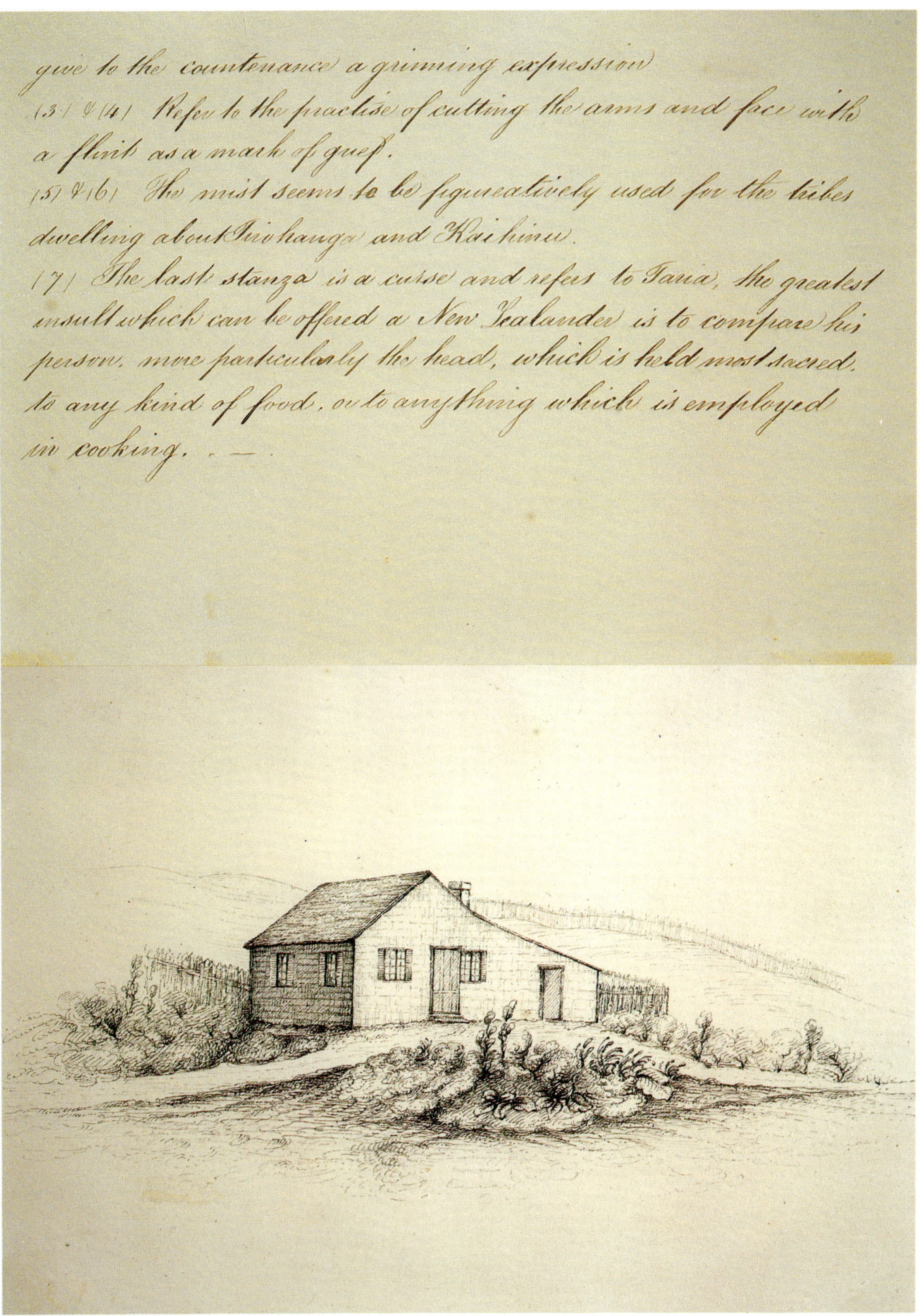

give to the countenance a grinning expression
(3) & (4) Refer to the practise of cutting the arms and face with a flint as a mark of grief.
(5) & (6) The mist seems to be figuratively used for the tribes dwelling about Tirohanga and Kaihinu.
(7) The last stanza is a curse and refers to Taria, the greatest insult which can be offered a New Zealander is to compare his person, more particularly the head, which is held most sacred, to any kind of food, or to anything which is employed in cooking. —

Major Richmond's Cottage
Auckland

38 [*Album page* 87, *top*

Kaiwarra Warra from the Petoni Road, Wellington

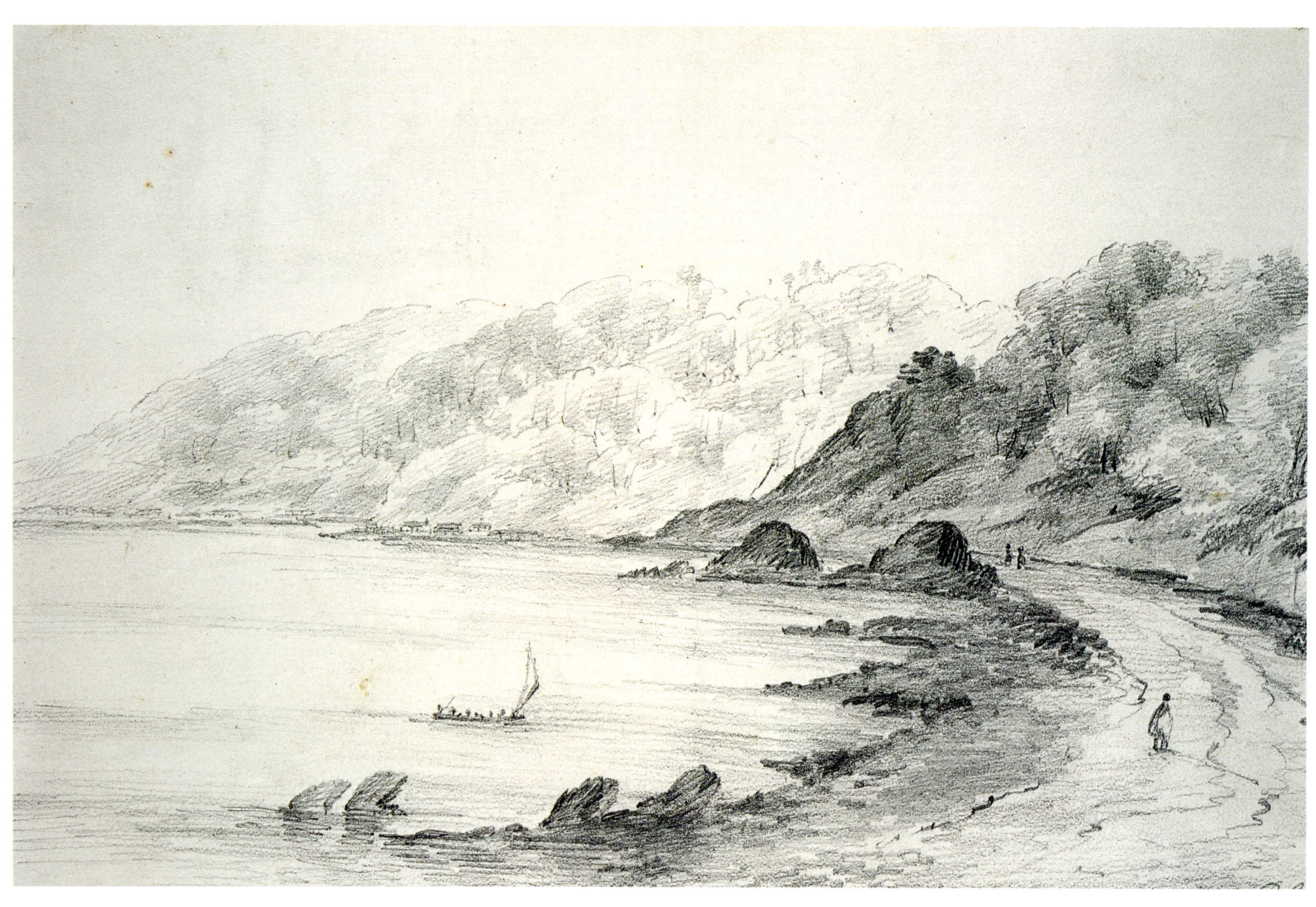

39 [*Album page* 87, *bottom*

'Te Aro' Flat, Wellington

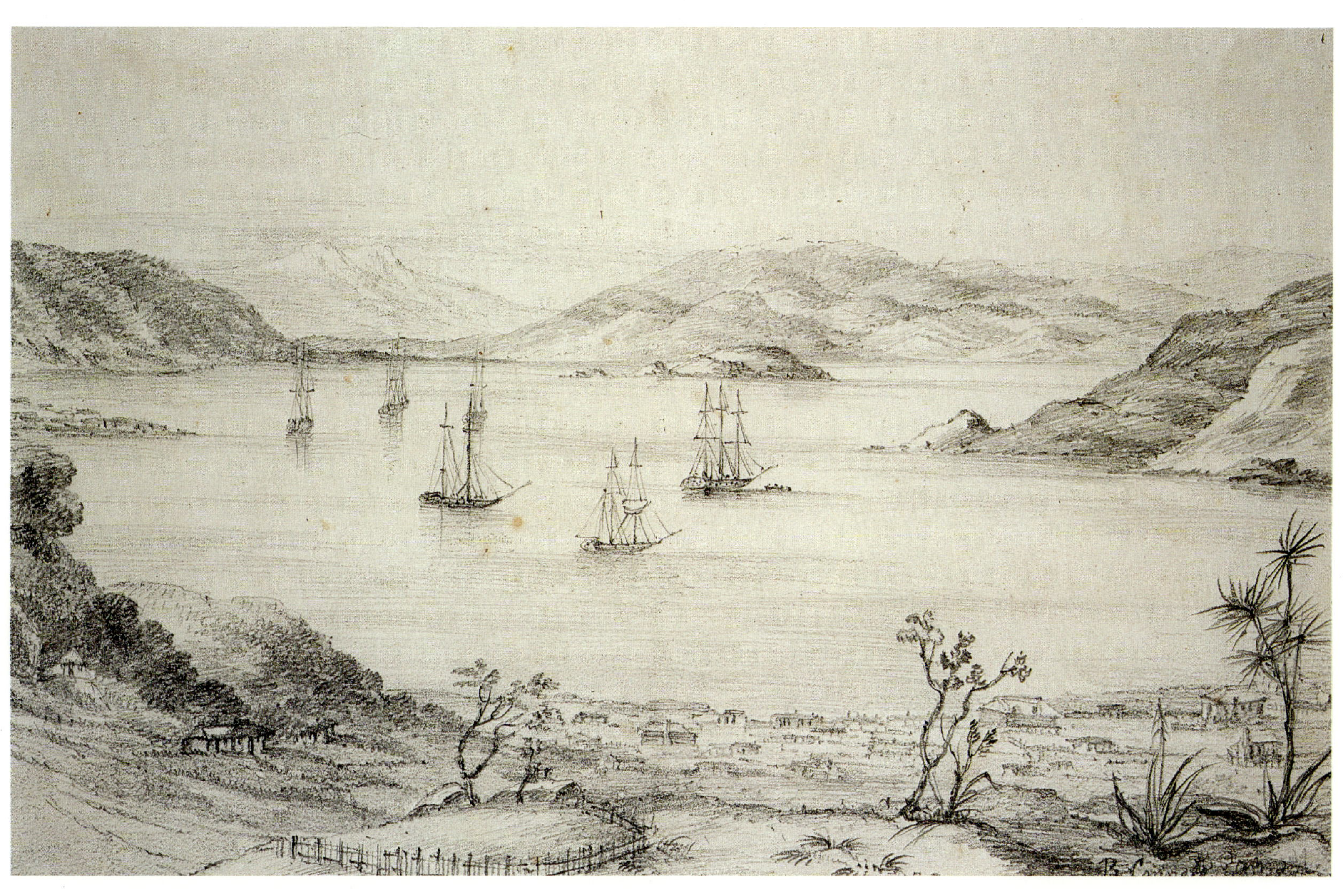

40 [*Album page* 96

[Some Maori proverbs]

Every tribe has its own Proverb which is attached to it as a motto, thus.

"Ruru ki tahi"
"The one word of Ruru"

is the motto of Naitirangi an important tribe in the Bay of Plenty. Ruru was an ancestor whose word was always law; and the present generation boast that they are ruled by the counsel of their Chiefs.

"Te uri o Te Matakapu"
"The descendants of Matakapu"

Is the motto of Ngatiwakaue another powerful tribe in the Bay of Plenty, the inveterate enemy of Naitirangi – Matakapua was an ancestor noted for being thief, Murderer &c – His decendants of the present day consider that their forefather's name is sufficient excuse for their practise of these crimes. –

Thus we may sometimes form an idea of the character of a tribe from the motto which has been assigned to them.

41 [*Album page* 97

[Some Maori proverbs]

He harihari kai.

He aha, he aha he kai ma taua.
He pipi, he aruhe, ko te aka o tawhenua
Ko te kai e ora ai te tangata
Matoetoe ana te arero i te mitikanga.
Me he arero kuri – āu.

Song of women bearing food.

What, what, shall be our food
Shell fish, fern root, the aka of the dry land
This is food which will keep a man in health
The tongue grows rough with licking
As it were a dogs tongue, – āu

Proverbs.

E mokai tapunga rua kawe ake kawe iho
O child of two growths ascending (from childhood to manhood) descending (from manhood to second childhood). –

Viz. Once a man, but twice a child.

He konanu kaki, papaka nana.
Deep throat, shallow sinews.

42 [*Album page* 85

The Raupo Cottage
of the Revd Mr Maunsell, Maratai, Waikato

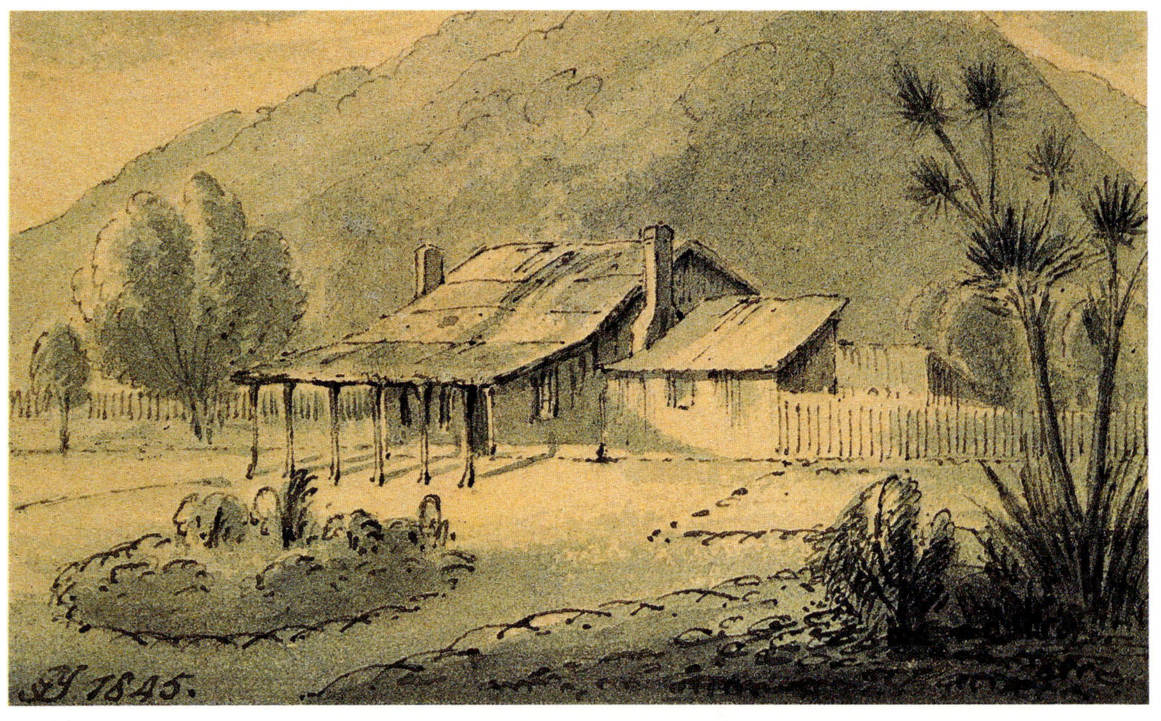

43 [*Album page 115*

The first Government Settlement on the Waitemata River. 1st October. 1840

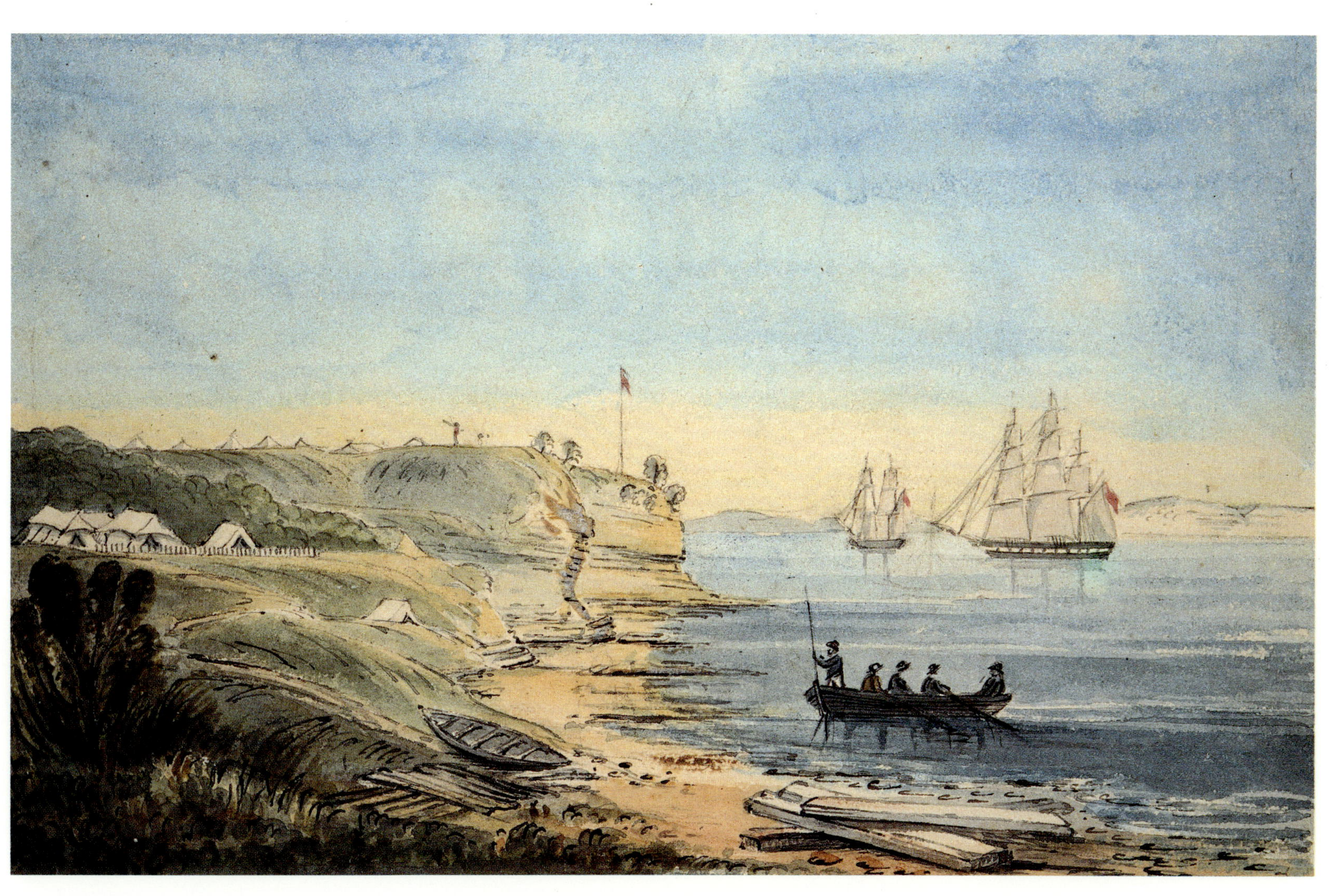

44 [*Album page* 107

Auckland looking NW

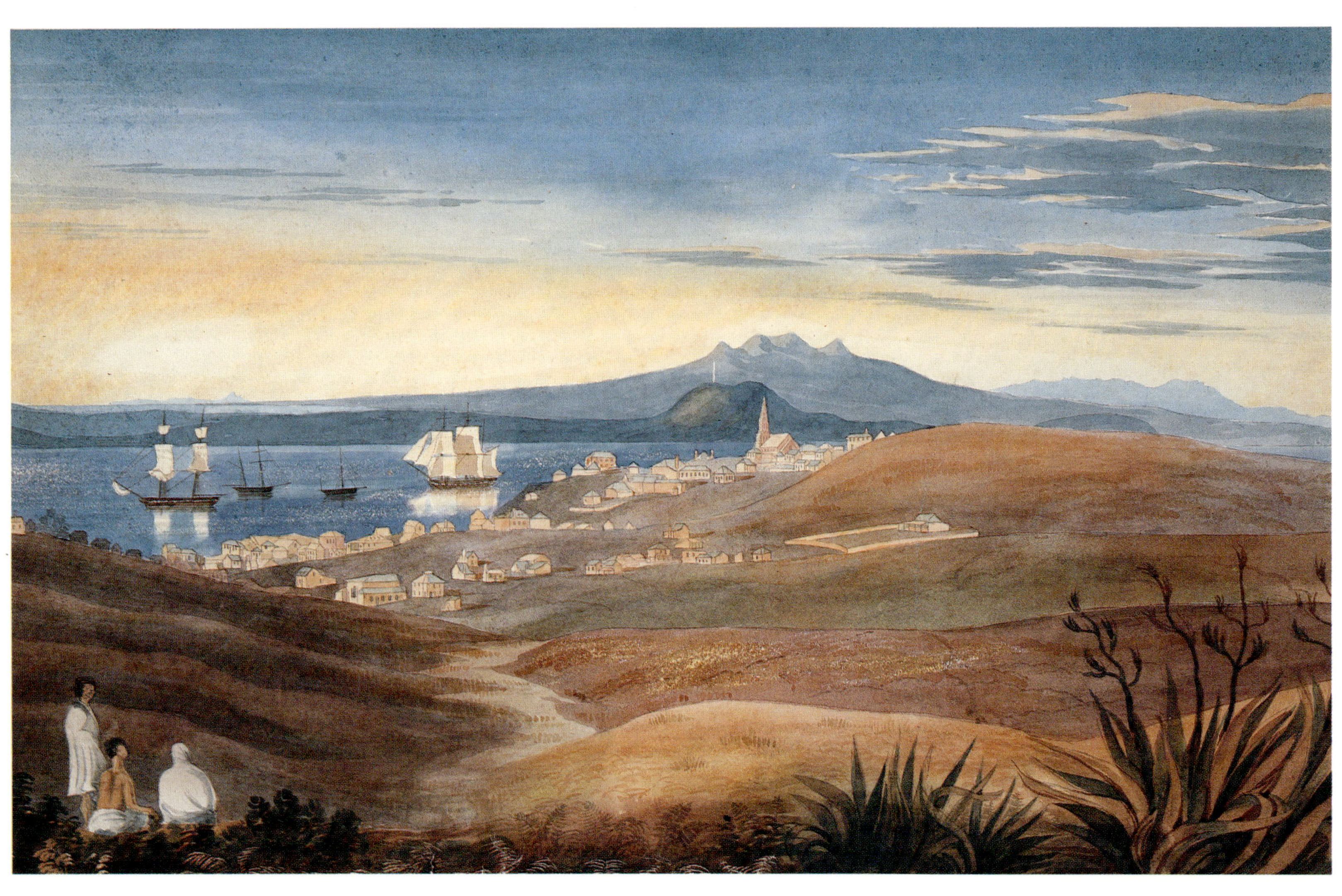

45 [*Album page* 111

[View from above Grafton Gully, showing graveyard and Government House]

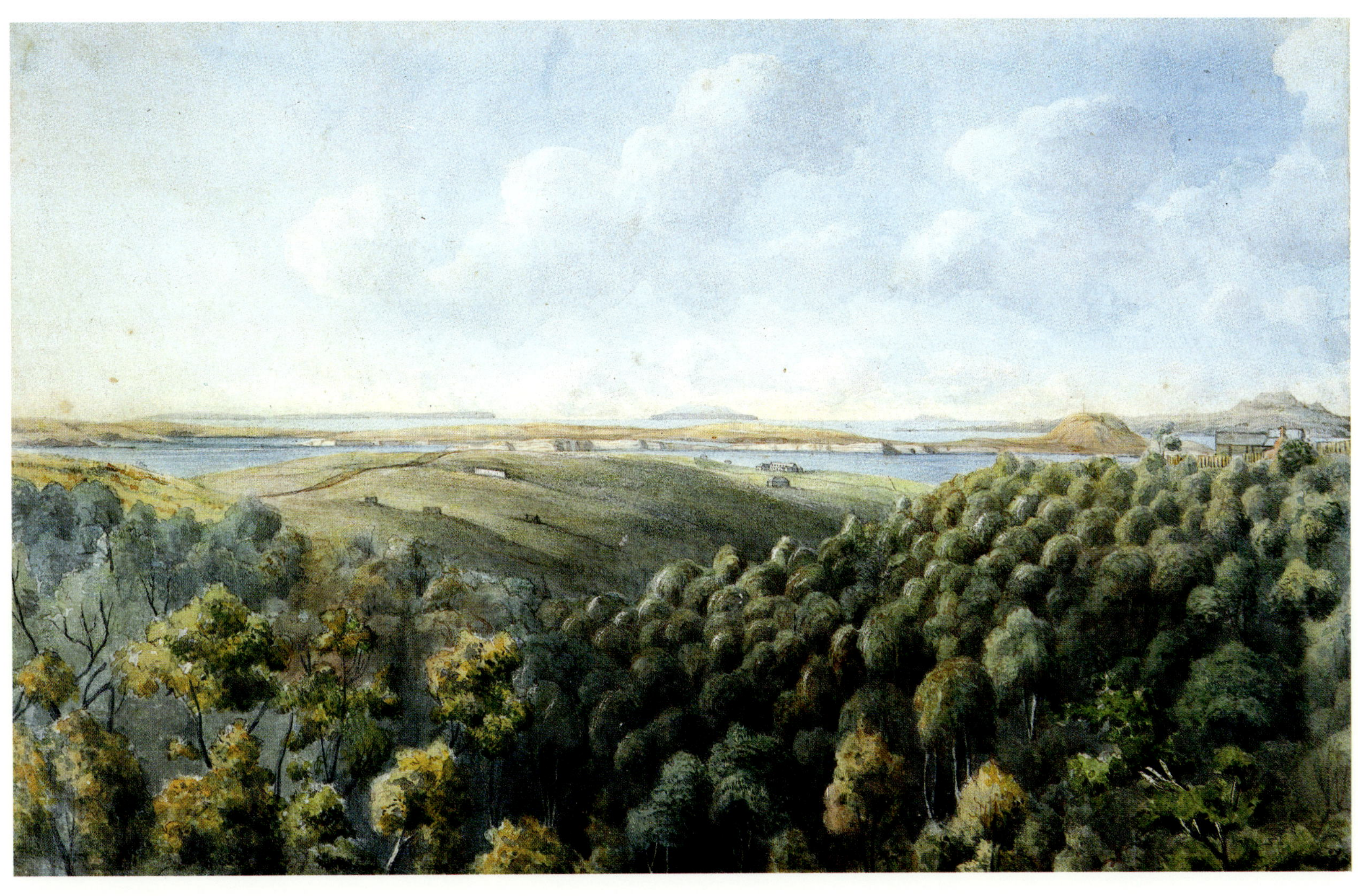

46 [*Album page* 120

1st Church at Auckland
West Front

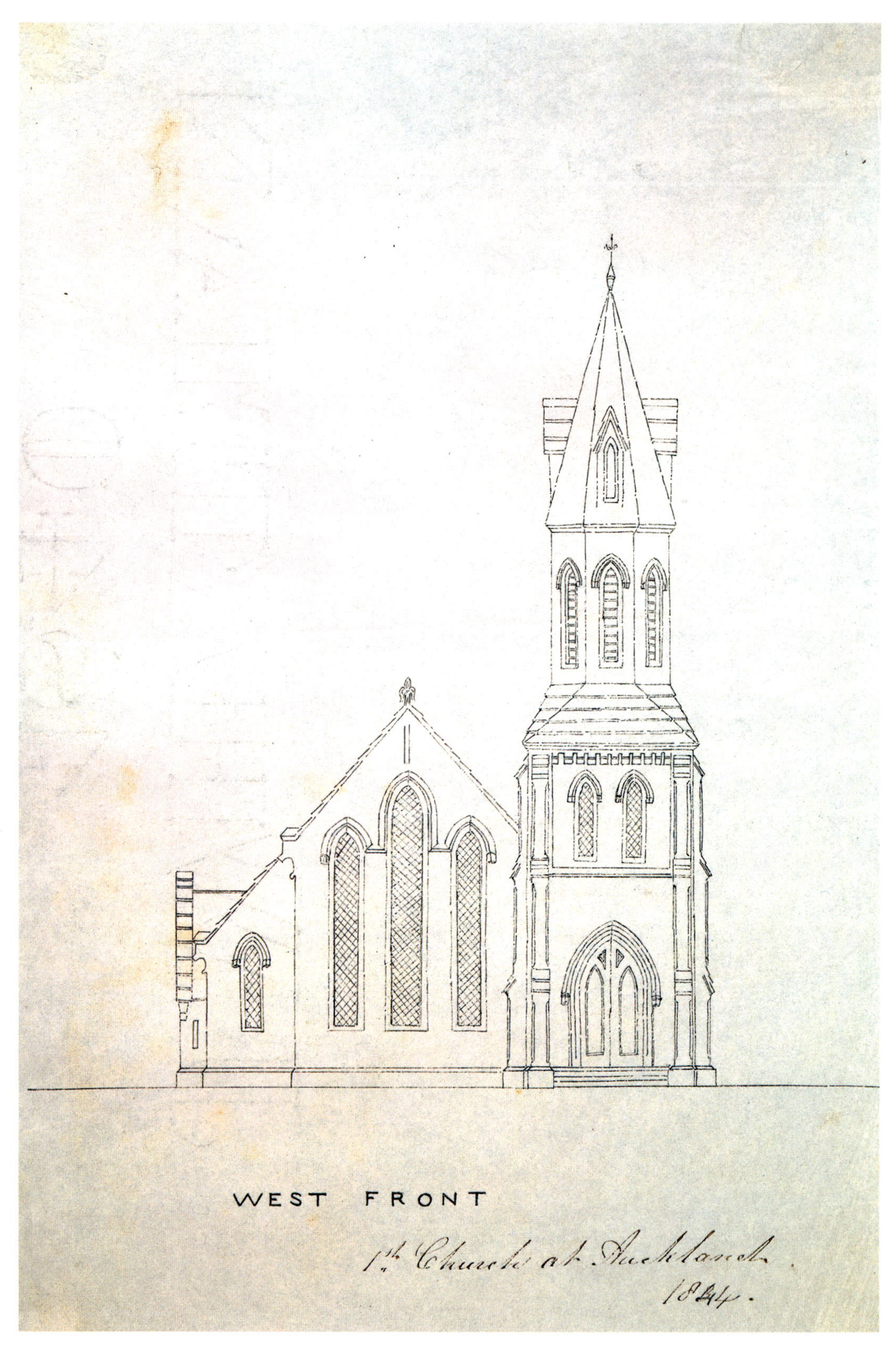

47 [*Album page 122*

East Front

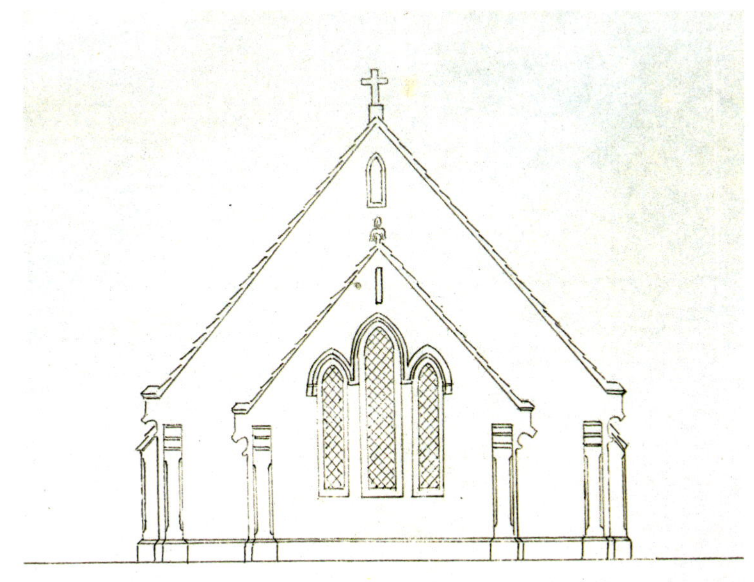

Side Elevation

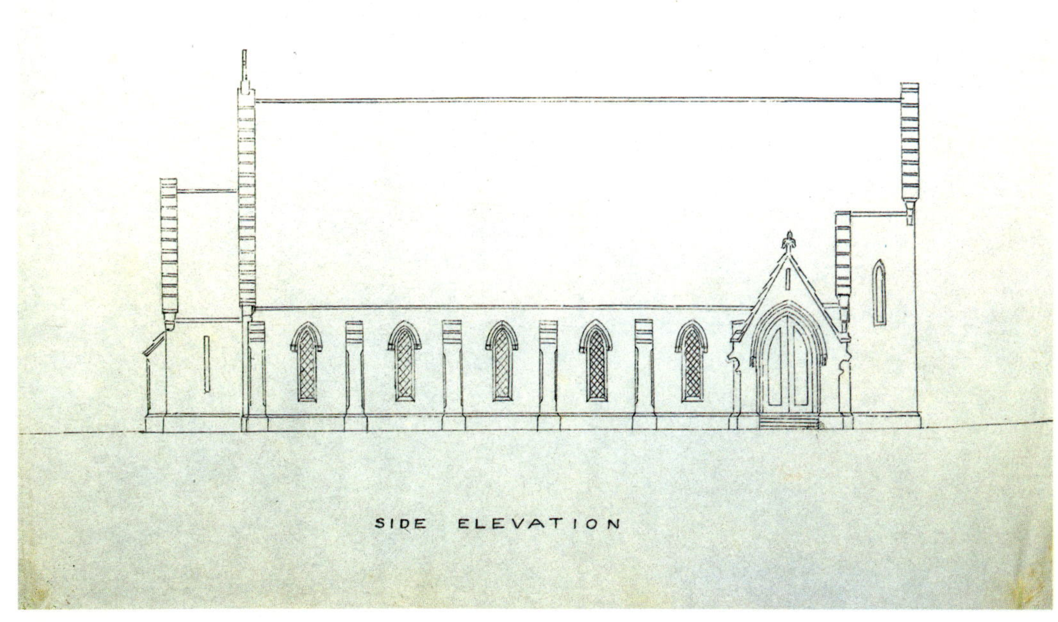

48 [*Album page 119*

A meeting of visitors Mounganui
Tauraga in the distance.

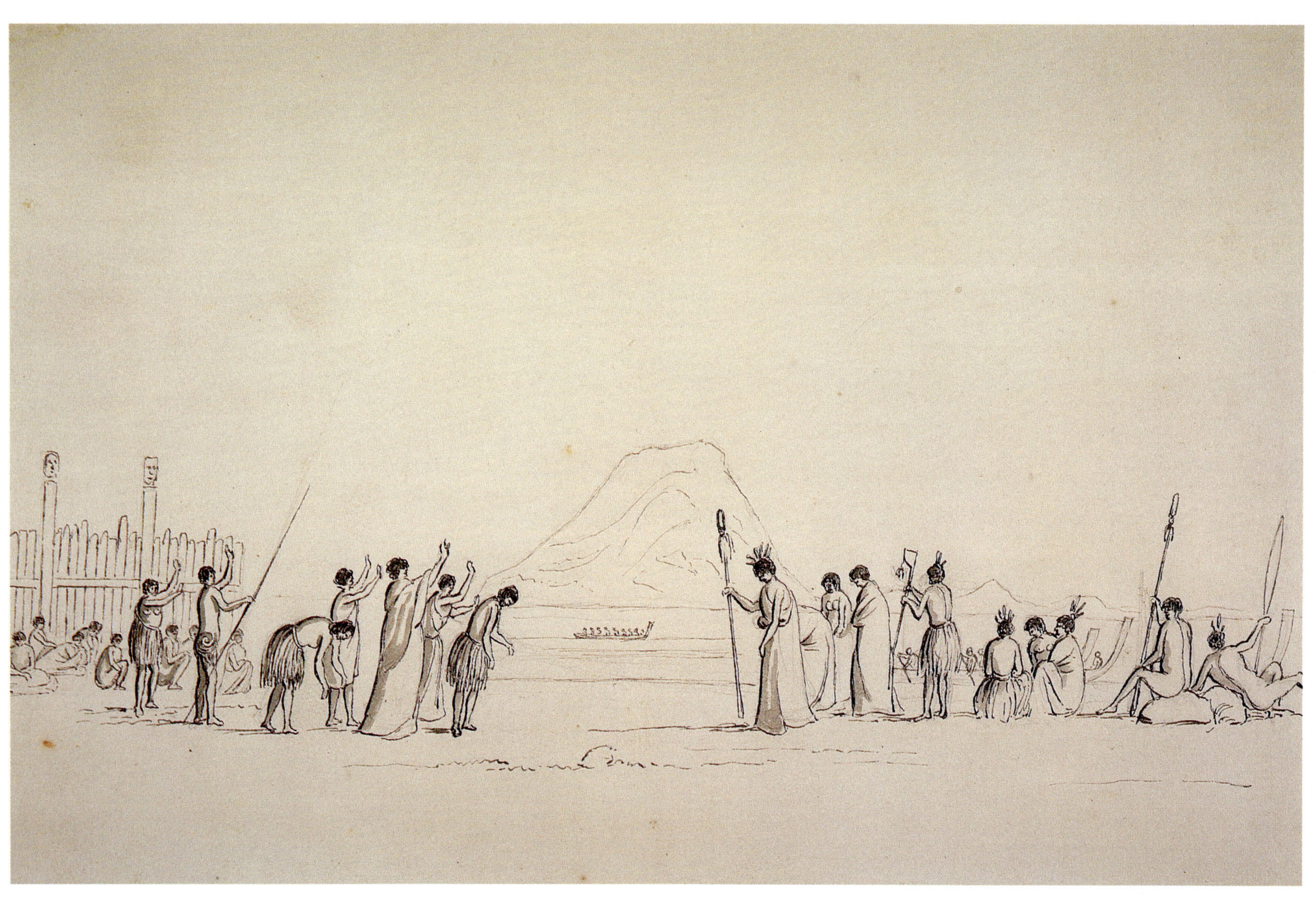

49 [*Album page* 127

The Banks of the Waiho near 'MataMata'

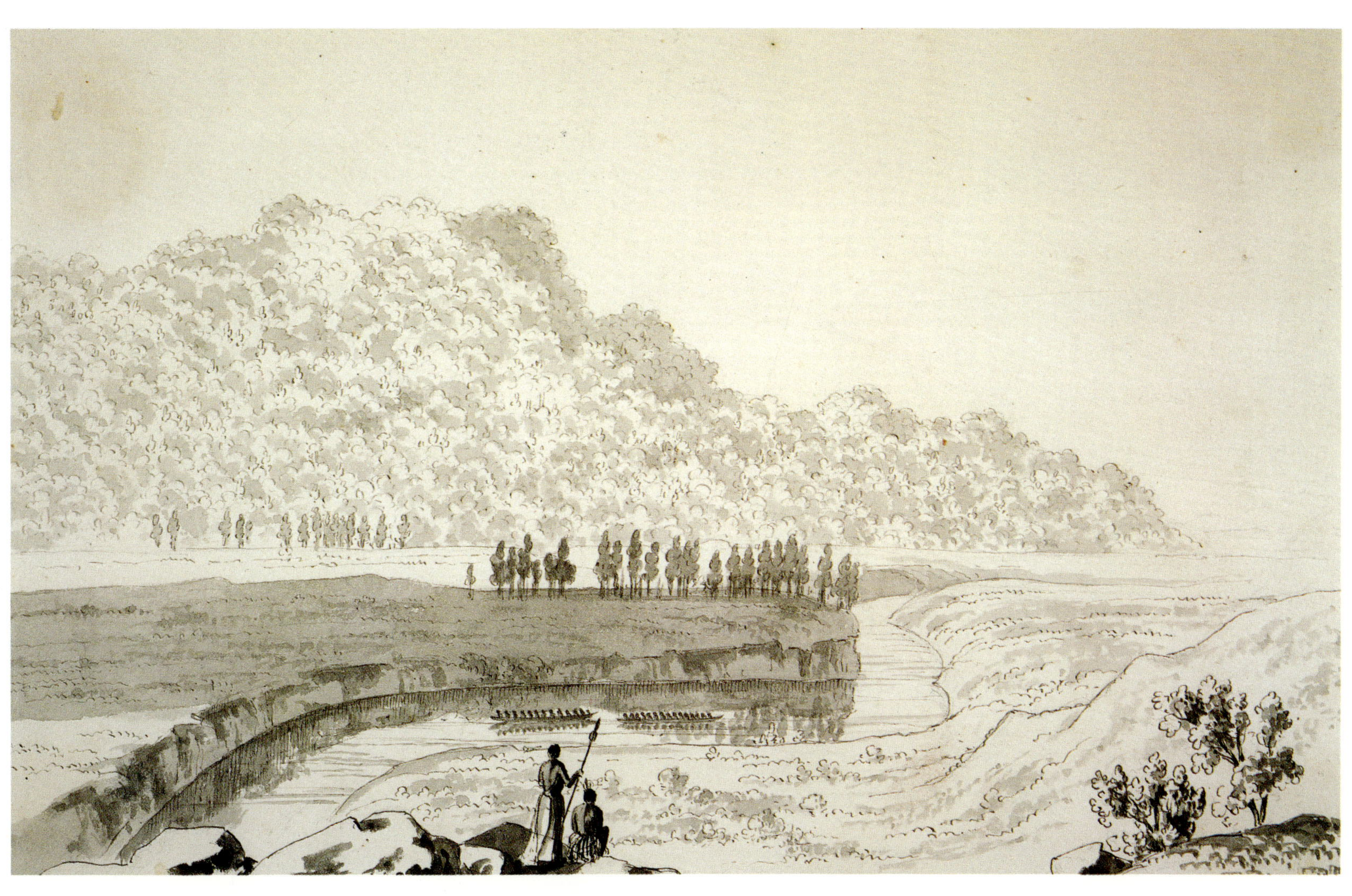

50 [*Album page 121*

The Pah of "Maketu" at Otawao in the Waipa

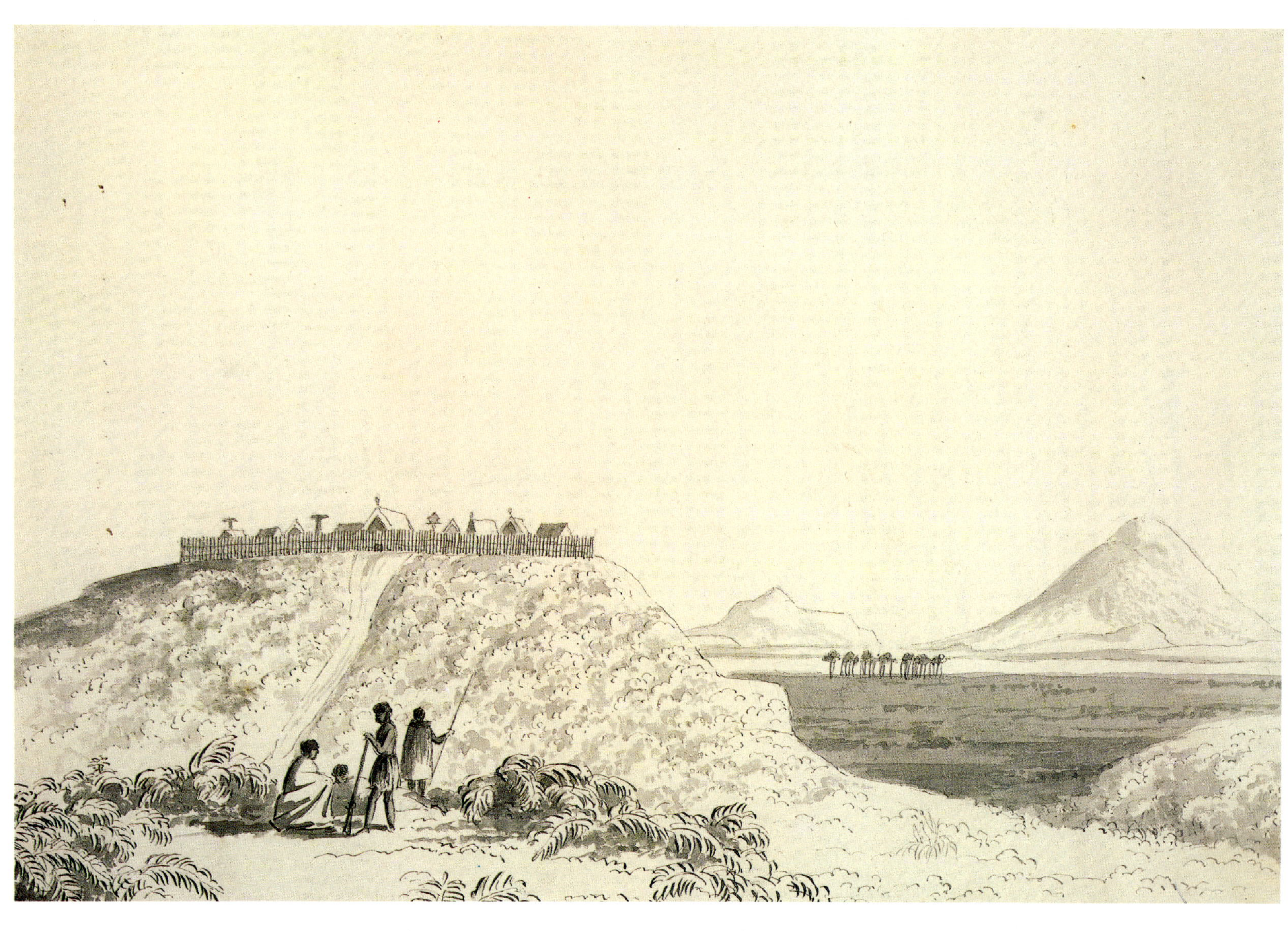

51 [*Verso of Album page* 121

'Wake, warriors, wake! there's danger in your sleep . . .'

Wake, warriors, wake! there's danger in your sleep;
Unnumber'd forms are moving in the fern,
Creeping like swine, through every wind and turn;
Rise chiefs! arise! and strike the hatchet deep,
Man the defences, and the portal keep,
The shout of blood, ring loud, in every ear,
For ruthless foes, are fast approaching near."
An aged warrior raised the battle cry;
Watchful was he, when all were slumbering by,
His practised ear, detected soon the sound,
Of rumbling feet upon the hollow ground,
Listening he stood, till near him human heads
Arose with caution, from their ferny beds;
He knew the foe, and starting from the ground,
Shouted the battle cry, which echoed round.
Th'alarm was heard, ~~and~~ the gathering bands arise
And quickly arm, to meet the dread surprise,
Mother's with haste, their children quickly lead
To cells, and rua's overgrown with weed,
Where should success, attend th'assailing blow,
These secret holes might shelter from the foe.
Near to the trenches, fierce the warriors rage,
The pah was scaled, each hand to hand engage;
The tu meri, and taia's sweeping blow
Strike through the scull, and lay the warrior low;
The long timata urged with furious thrust,
Pierces the foe, who falling, bites the dust;
Vain his attempts to wrest the pointed wood
Transfixed to earth, he welters in his blood.
Th'assaulted tribe, give way on every side
And slaughter sweeps their ranks ~~in gallant~~ with giant stride;
The shrieks of wounded, and the dying groan,
The children's scream, their mother's wailing moan
The savage curse, the muskets' rattling peal,
Fierce crackling flames, and blows on ringing steel
Complete the horrors that the victors feel,—
The chieftain leader, of th'assailing foe
Towering in height, deals death in every blow,
His hatchet quivering o'er his feather'd head,
With eyes distorted, make his presence dread;
The blazing fortress, lights him on his way,
A demon savage rushing on his prey;
With blood stain'd hands, and gory weapon flew,
~~The preying vulture of the conquered crew~~;
~~Tore out their~~
A vulture preying on the foes he slew;
Tore out their hearts, gazed on the crimson flood,
Shouted his victory, and drank their blood.

Decr. 1843. J. Merrett.

52 [*Album page 101*

Statement signed Maketu Waretotara

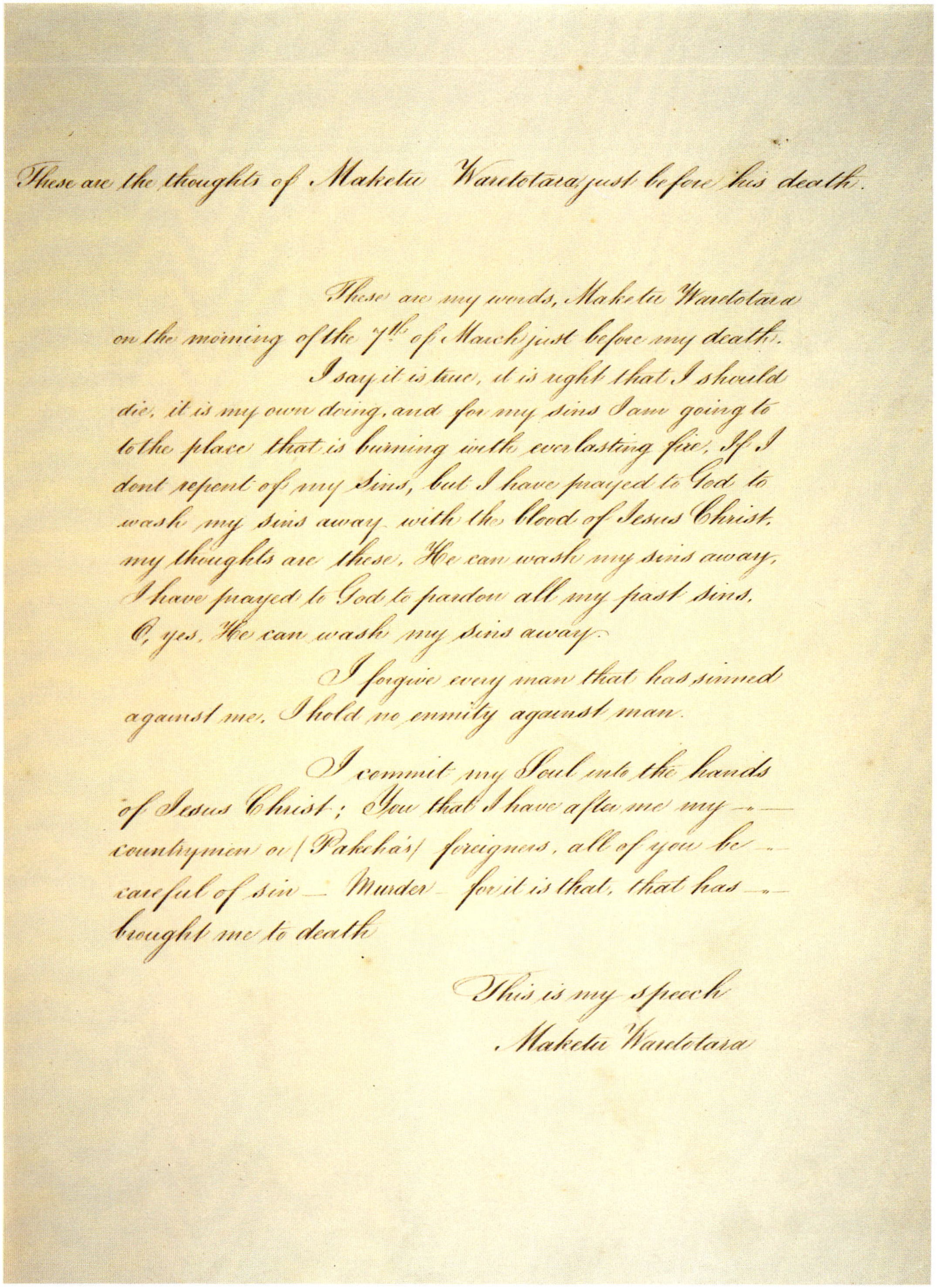

These are the thoughts of Maketu Waretotara just before his death.

These are my words, Maketu Waretotara on the morning of the 7th of March just before my death.

I say it is true, it is right that I should die, it is my own doing, and for my sins I am going to to the place that is burning with everlasting fire, If I dont repent of my Sins, but I have prayed to God to wash my sins away with the blood of Jesus Christ. my thoughts are these, He can wash my sins away, I have prayed to God to pardon all my past sins. O, yes, He can wash my sins away.

I forgive every man that has sinned against me, I hold no enmity against man.

I commit my Soul into the hands of Jesus Christ; You that I have after me my — countrymen or (Pakeha's) foreigners, all of you be — careful of sin — Murder — for it is that, that has — brought me to death

This is my speech

Maketu Waretotara

53 [*Album page* 141

Maketu

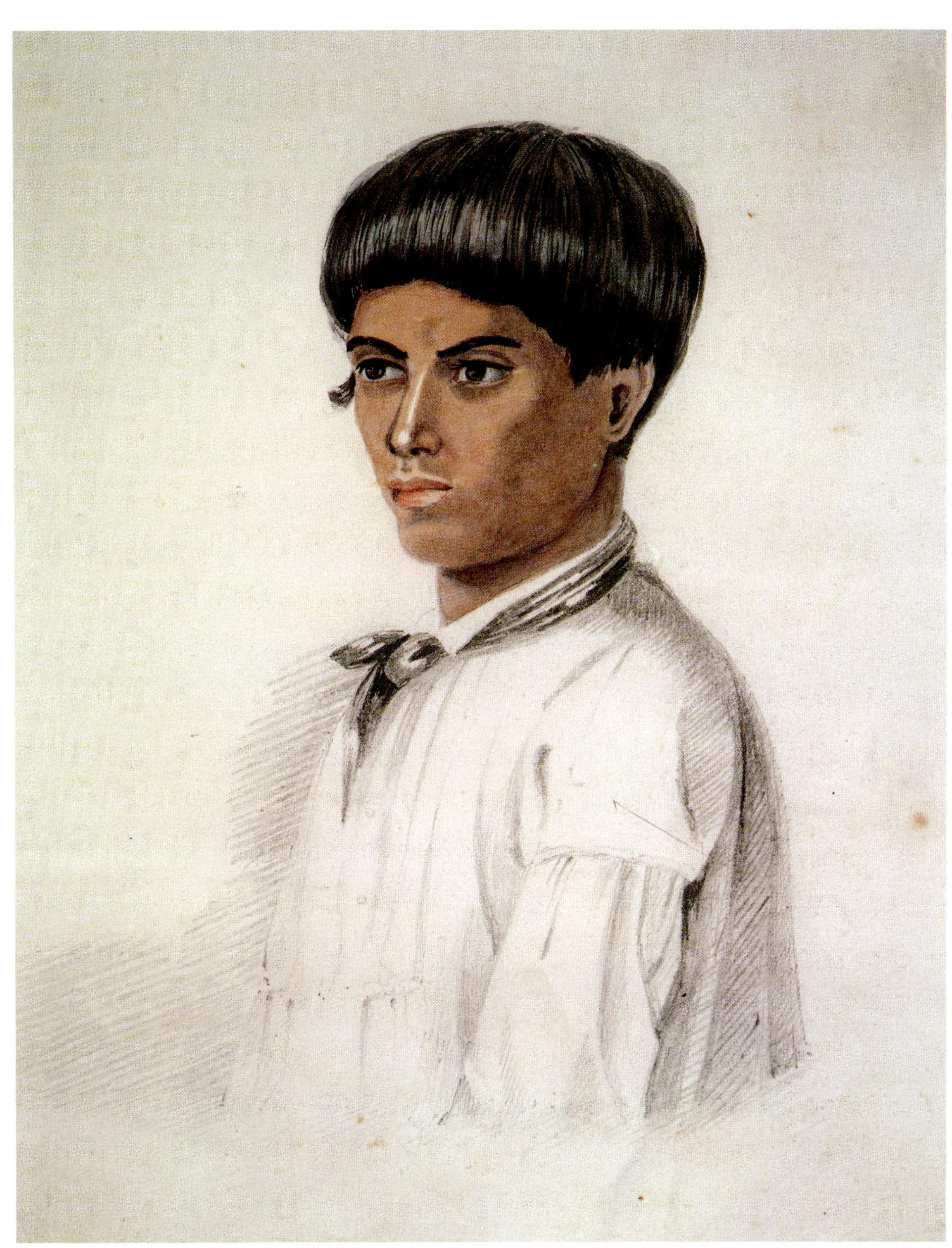

54 [*Album page* 157

To Mrs Hobson
From her friends on the day
of her departure from New Zealand.

To Mrs Hobson
From her friends on the day
of her departure from New Zealand.

The broad white sails are spreading
The gallant ship moves on.
The hour has come we're dreading
From our straining sight thou'rt gone

Our grieving souls are thinking
Of what we've lost in you
Our sadden'd hearts are sinking
As we wave a last adieu.

Graceful we've seen thee standing
First Lady of the land
Praise winning, not demanding
From all the circling band.

Playful we've seen thee smiling
Within the festive hall
Unwittingly beguiling
The yielding hearts of all.

We've seen thy gentle bearing
Thy offices of love
We've heard thy voice endearing,
Like an Angel, from above.

The bed of sickness soothing
Its sufferings, to heal
The deathbed pillow smoothing
With more than human Zeal.

We've.

55 [*Album page* 158

To Mrs Hobson . . .

We've seen thee unrepining.
With meekness bear the blow,
From Providence, untwining
The closest bonds below.

Admiring we could watch thee,
Can we but mourn the ties!
That from our sight must snatch thee
No more to glad our eyes.

Friends sincere may meet thee,
When thou'lt reach fair Englands strand.
Kindly looks may greet thee,
With friendships open hand.

Yes, other friends may prize thee
By voice and gesture kind
But none can idolize thee
Like some thou'lt leave behind

Yet since thy duties call thee
We could not bid thee stay
Kindred and station hail thee
Their voice thou must obey.

Then, fare thee well! Dear Lady.
May choicest blessings dwell
Around thy home and family
Dear Lady, fare thee well.

56 [*Album page* 165

Government House — Russell — Bay of Islands, New Zealand

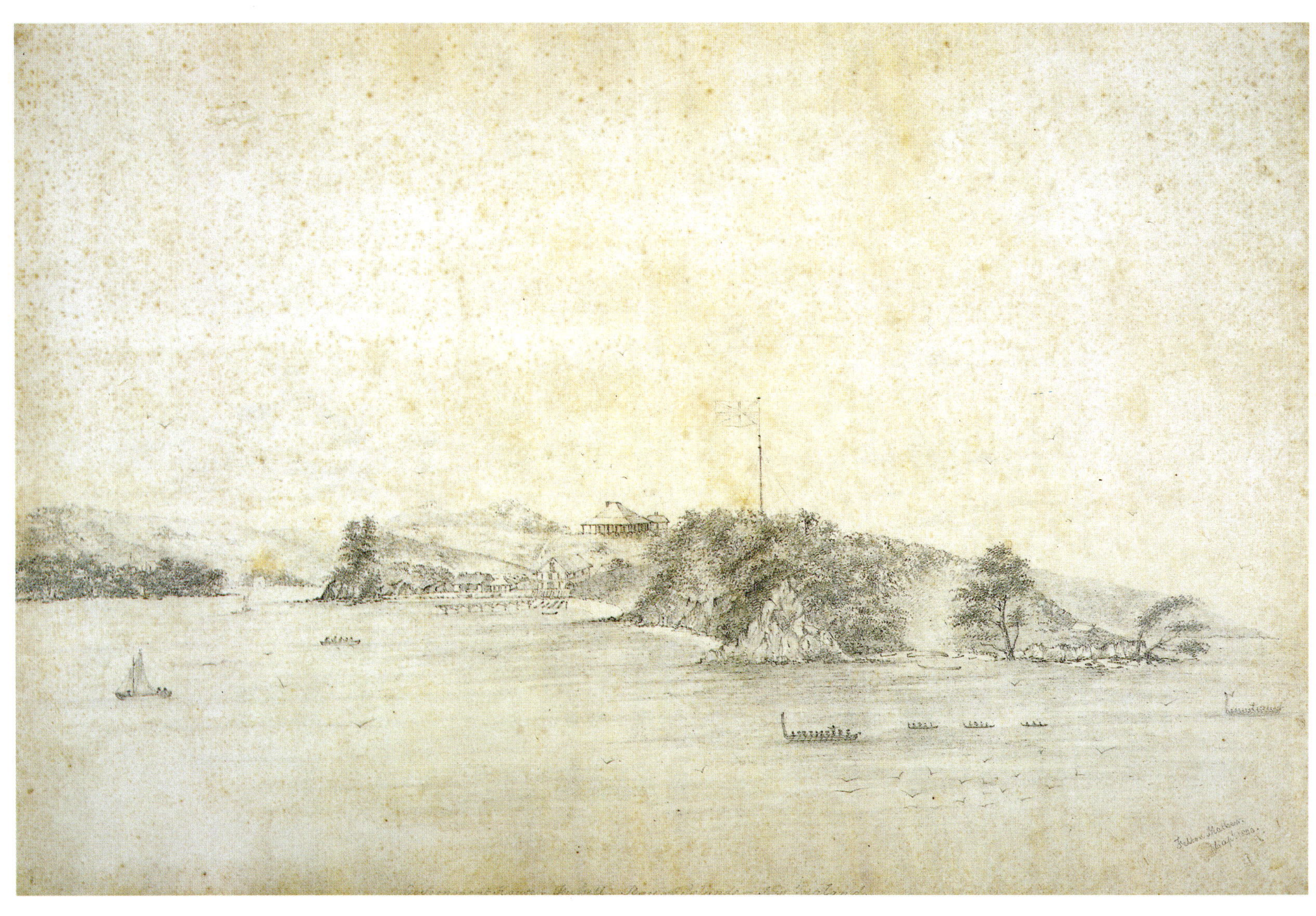

57 [*Album page* 167

[?Mount Eden or Mount St John or Mt Hobson]

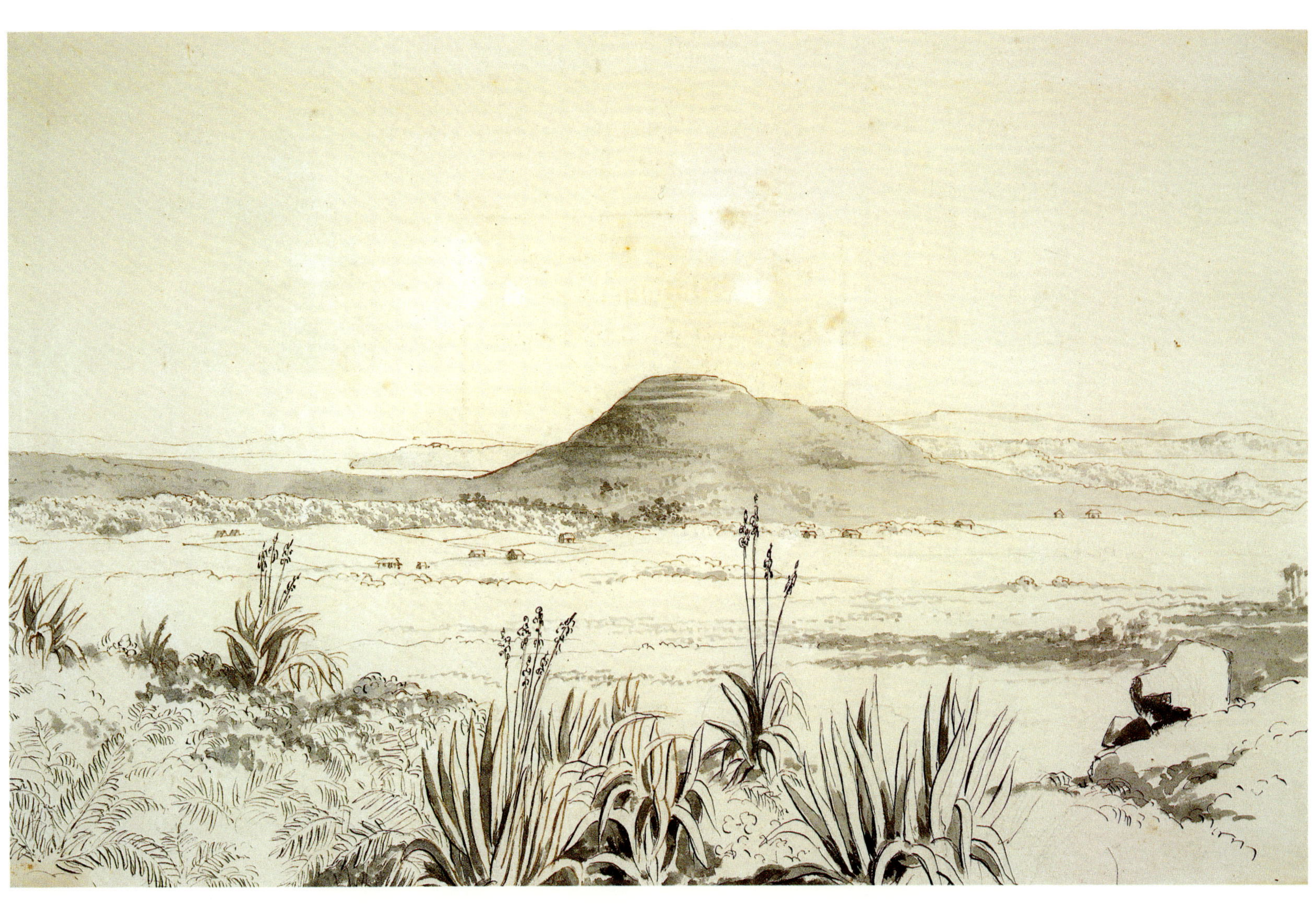

58 [*Album page* 129

The Waipa near its source at 'Rangitoto'

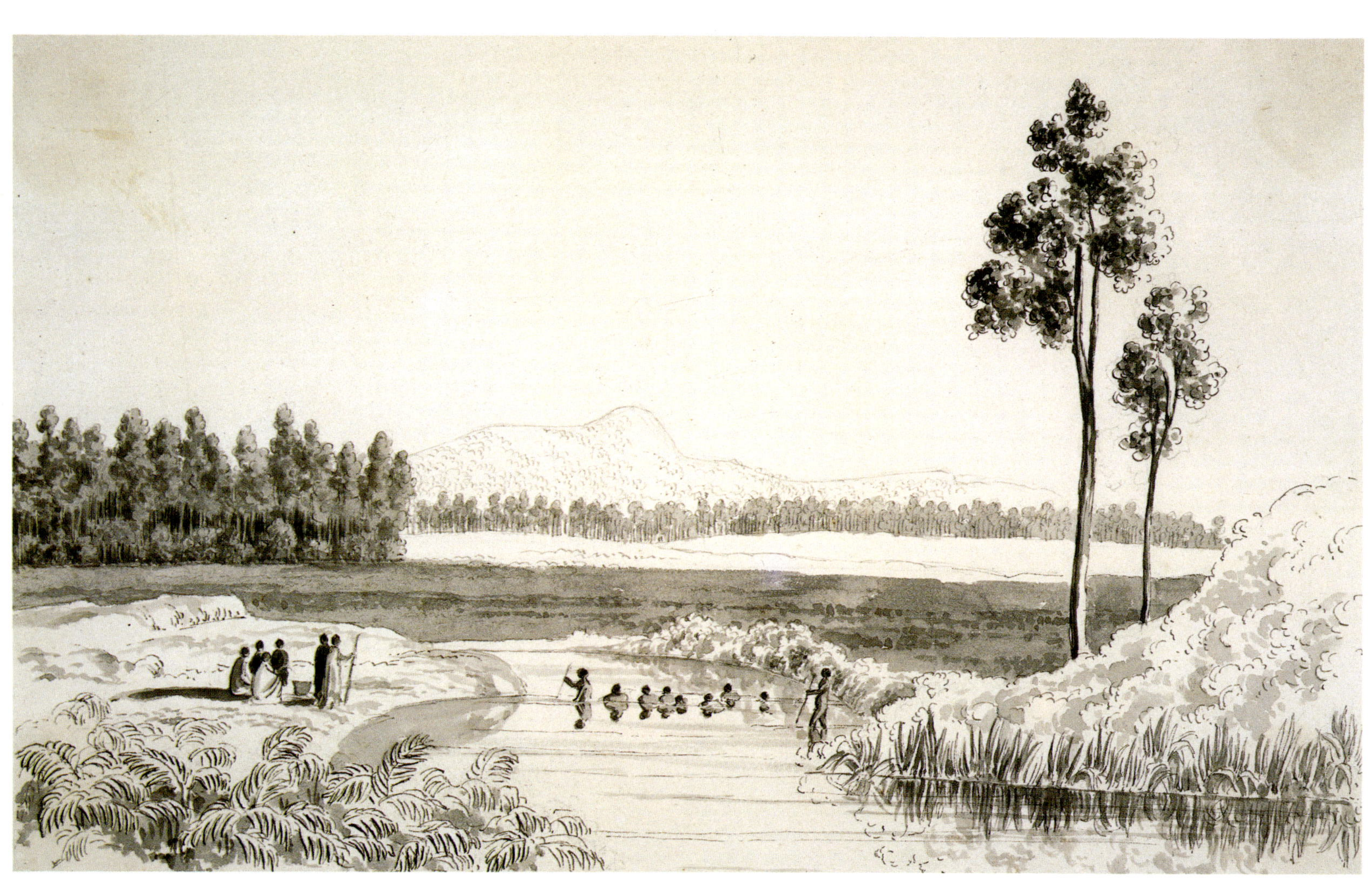

59 [*Album page* 171

'Perongia' from 'Maungatautur'

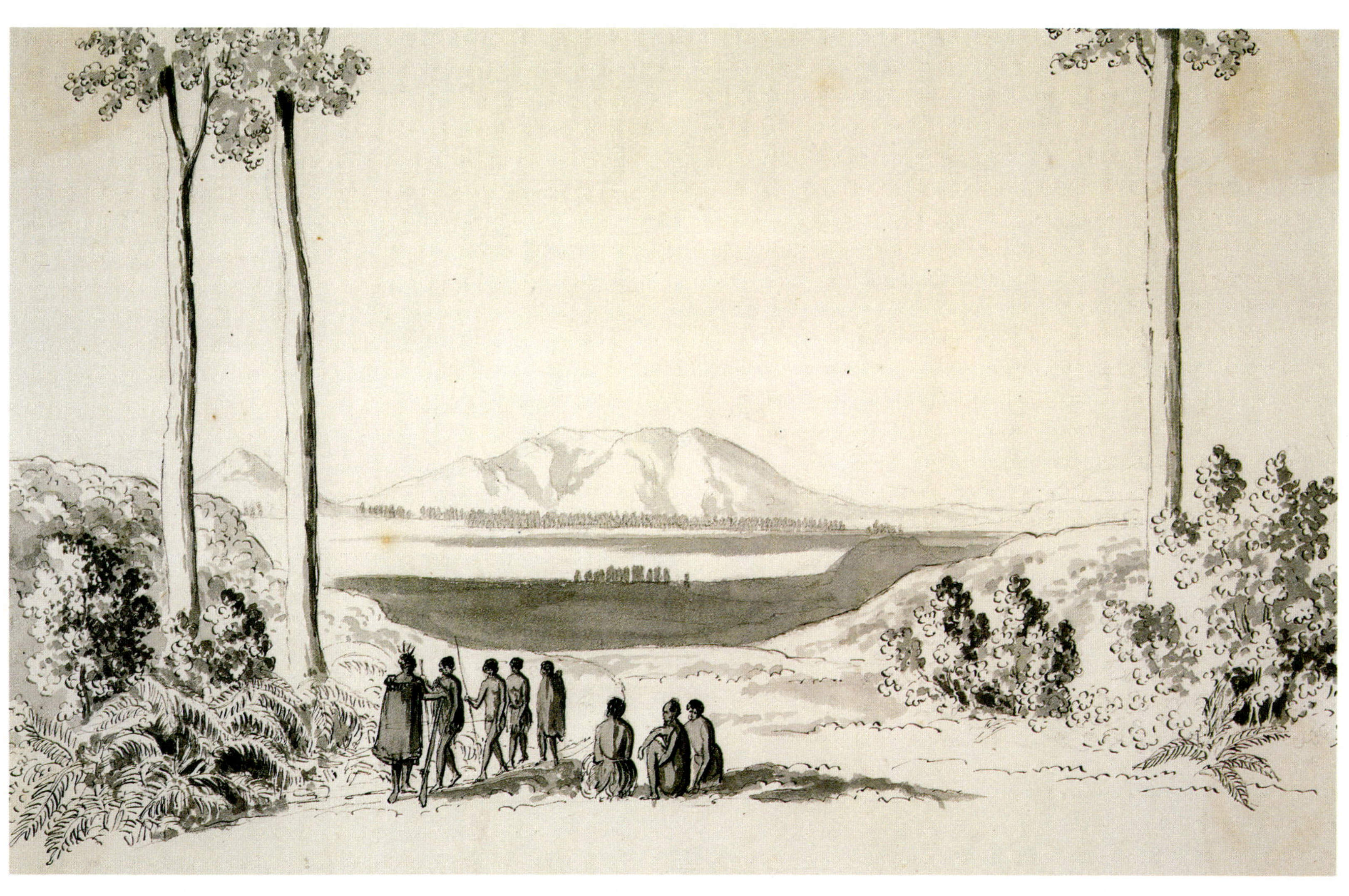

The Waré of Te Whero Whero,
Chief of the Waikato
Onahonga.

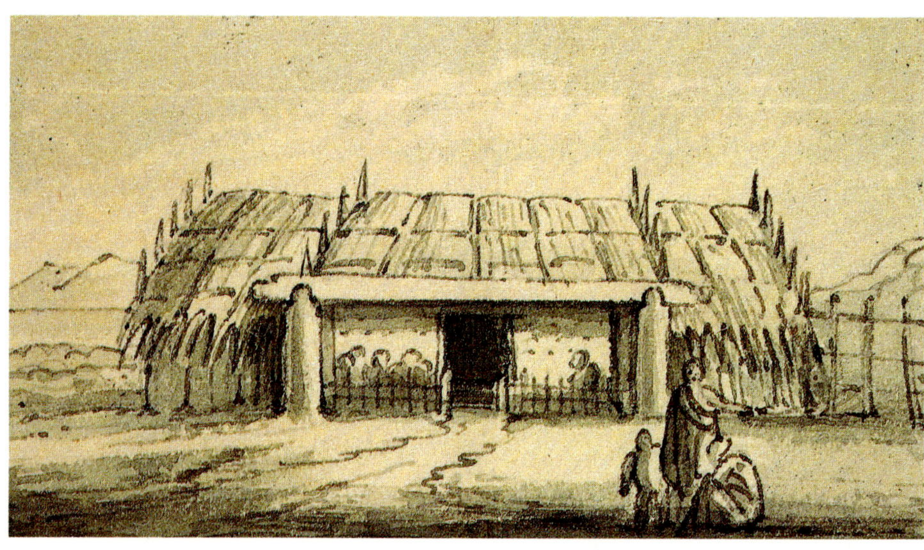

The Waré of Weremu Hoete
Chief of the Ngatepaua
Putiki

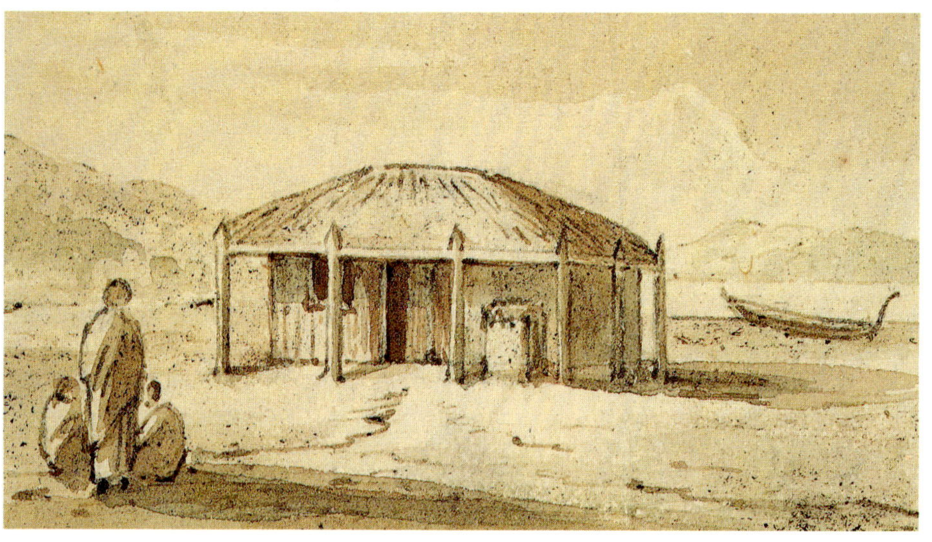

61 [*Album page 177*

View of 'Perongia' and 'Koka Puka' from 'Rarowera'

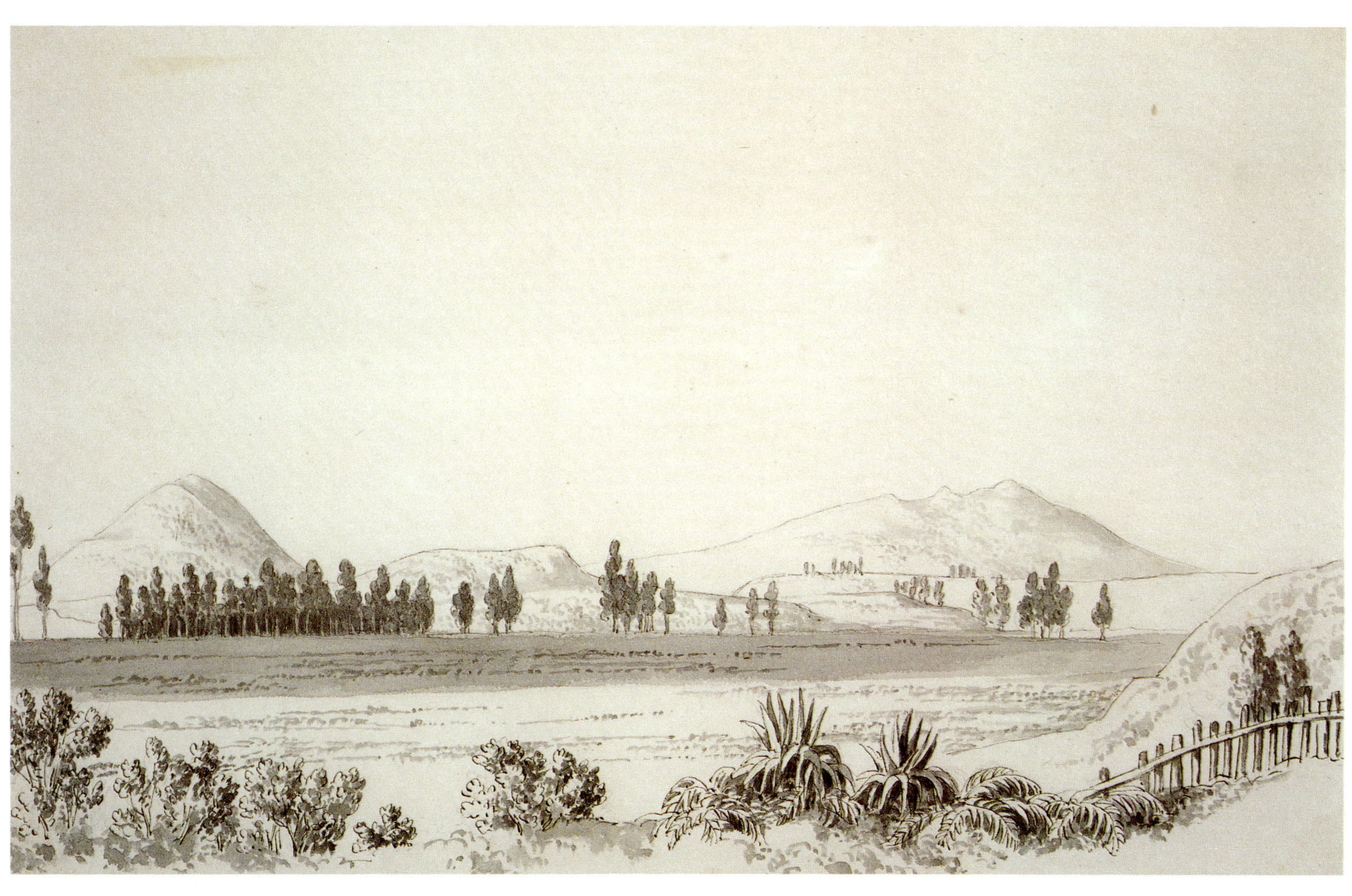

62 [*Album page 179*

The Pah of Okatina on the Lake of Name
(taken by Pomare from the Bay of Islands)
in the Taua of Hungi
16 years ago

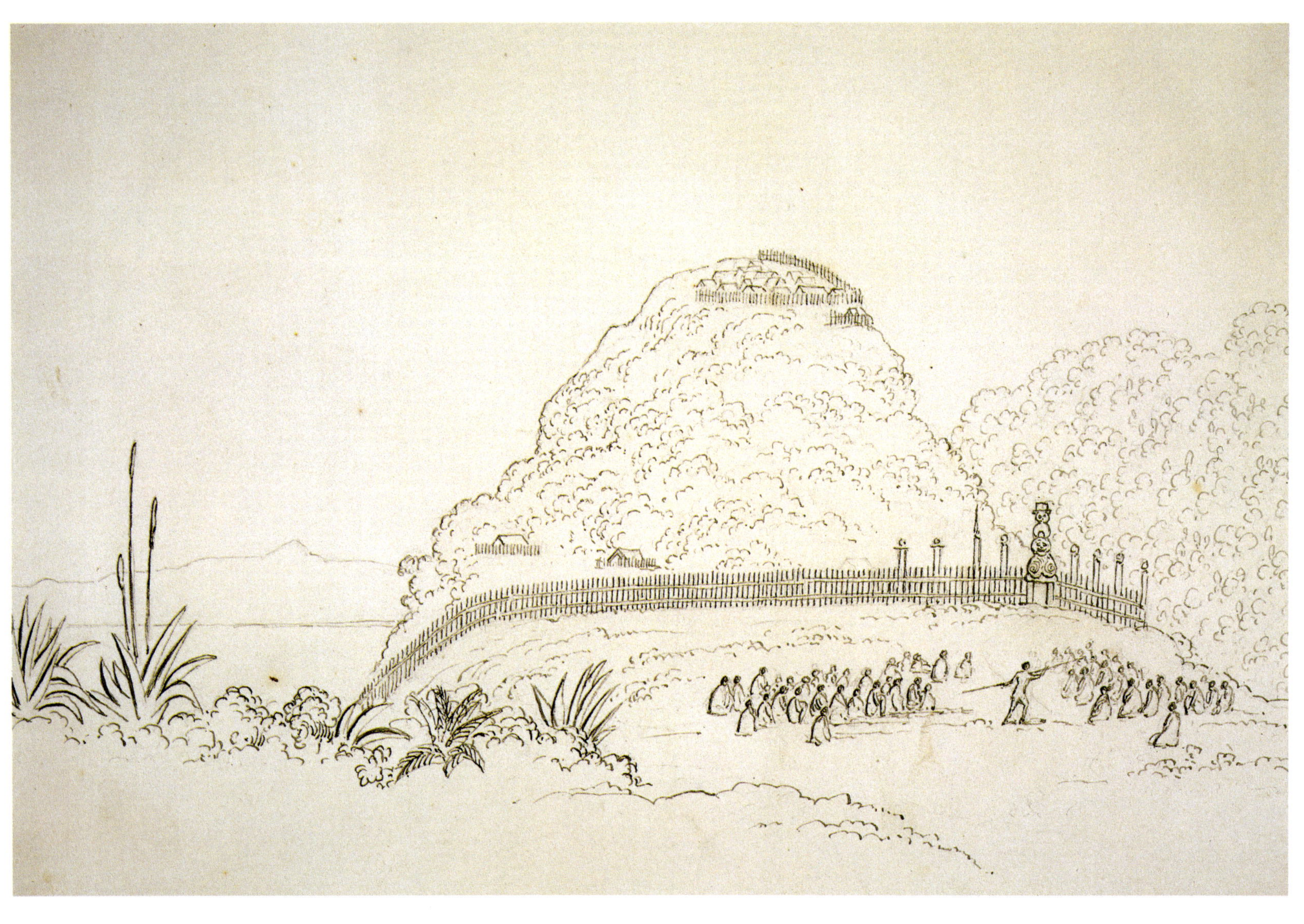

63 [*Album page* 181

View of Koka Puka from Waipa and Otawau

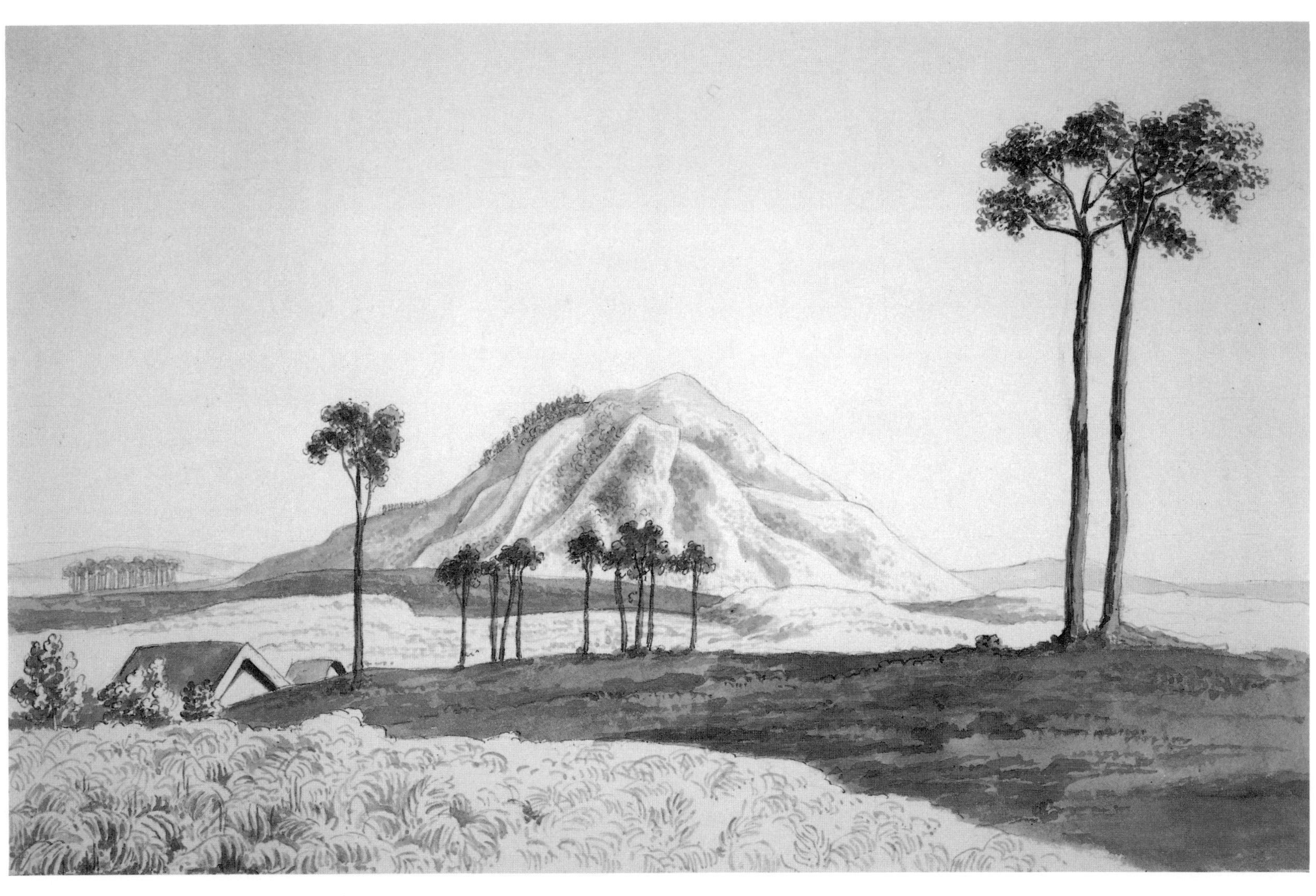

Index of Contributors

Album Plates & corresponding Catalogue entries in large bold numerals; small bold numerals indicate supporting illustrations.

Picture Collections

Auckland City Art Gallery
Auckland Institute and Museum
Auckland Public Library
Alexander Turnbull Library, Wellington
Australian National Library, Canberra
(including Rex Nan Kivell collection)
British Library, London
Hocken Library, Dunedin
Mitchell and Dixson State Libraries of
New South Wales

Catalogue Explanation

PAGINATION In the album given to Mrs Hobson items were pasted or written on unnumbered pages. The Alexander Turnbull Library numbered all pages (including blanks) and gave items their non-sequential page numbers. We have renumbered and sometimes rearranged items to make a logical sequence. These new numbers are printed in bold, the Turnbull Library page numbers follow in italic. In the text bold numerals refer to Album plates or corresponding catalogue entries.

ATTRIBUTION Only six works carry signatures or initials. The others have had to be attributed on historical or stylistic evidence. Square brackets around an artist's name indicate attribution. Where insufficient evidence has been found a question mark precedes the artist's name.

TITLE/SUBJECT Where the title is known from inscription on the album page, or on the front or back of the work itself, it appears without brackets and in the form and spelling of the original. Square brackets indicate editorial insertion to show modern spelling or supply a title. A list of plates giving the titles as inscribed is printed on pp.41-42.

INSCRIPTIONS Inscriptions appear in the works or on the Album pages in a variety of hands. Where inscriptions or other material are on the back of works these have been lifted from the Album and photographed in the Conservation Laboratory of the National Library of New Zealand. Descriptions of these follow the title/subject entry and are reproduced in the catalogue notes.

SIZE Dimensions are given in millimetres, height before width. They refer to the actual size of the image.

SIGNATURE & DATE Signatures are noted. Otherwise the entry is shown as 'unsigned'. Dates which are known from the artist's inscription on the work appear without brackets; dates in square brackets have been supplied. Where a single year has been given this has been based on documentary evidence. Where work appears to have been done later than Mrs Hobson's departure in June 1843 this is recorded in the notes.

SUPPORT The thickness of the support is given in millimetres and the nature of the paper noted. The nature of support has been evidence in checking attribution of certain works.

MEDIUM Ink is black unless otherwise stated. Grey or sepia 'wash' indicates the use of a monotone watercolour.

NOTES Where possible, background references to the subject matter of these works have been given from contemporary published and manuscript sources listed in the Bibliography; brief references only are given here. The significant unpublished source is referred to as the 'Grey Album'. This collection of early New Zealand visual records was given by Sir George Grey to the British Museum in 1853, and is now held in the manuscript section of the British Library.

Catalogue to the Album

Janet Paul

with new translations
& notes to Maori texts by
Christine Tremewan

1 [*Album page 1*

MRS HOBSON/GOVERNMENT HOUSE/AUCKLAND, NEW ZEALAND/*March* 184 [3]

[ASHWORTH, Edward 1814-1896]

Unsigned March 184 [3]
Lithographed design (W. & H. Rock, London) mounted as title page on first page of Album
Hand-lettered and hand-coloured with gilt highlights and gold leaf border
252 x 179 mm
Cream wove paper, no visible watermark

This album was presented to Mrs Hobson but no reference could be found as to exactly when. It could have been when she left New Zealand; it could have been as much as two years later. The inscription is lettered in brown ink. The date under this inscription reads 'March 1843' but the final numeral has been altered. In (now faded) blue ink the '3' is obscured with a squiggle like a Greek 'δ'. It is possible that this figure is meant to read as a '5'. Mrs Hobson left Auckland in June 1843 and most of the material in the Album was prepared to mark that event. But one drawing (Plate **42**) is inscribed 'J. J. 1845'. The drawing of the East Front of St Paul's (Plate **47**, top) is dated in ink '1844', and on the verso of another (Plate **51**) is most of a handwritten poem signed 'J. Merrett' and dated 'Decr 1843'. Because all these were done after Mrs Hobson's departure, it seems that the Album had been presented to her in an unfinished condition and that either it was retained for further additions, or these were afterwards taken to England and inserted there. It may have been hoped that the blank pages would eventually be filled.

The frontispiece of the Album explains its contents: 'Costumes, Scenery, Specimens of Literature etc. of the North Island of New Zealand' and gives dates '1841, 1842, 1843'. We now know (see p. 34) that this was painted by Edward Ashworth, a young architect who in 1843 tutored Eliza Hobson's children. It is likely that it was Ashworth who also began compiling a memento for the woman her friends so greatly admired. Since he had come well equipped with drawing and survey materials, he could have brought a pristine gift album with its uncoloured lithograph for title page. When he left the country in January 1844 he may have handed on the work to someone else.

If an editor is allowed a guess, I would suggest that either Shortland or Johnson could well have employed Merrett to make the final drawings (Plates **49, 57, 58, 61, 62** and **63** are all in the same hand), and that Dr Johnson could have delivered the Album personally to Eliza Hobson, in 1845, when he visited England.

ASHWORTH *Native New Zealander,* ink and watercolour, 176 x 110 mm
ATL MS 'Journal of a voyage from London 1842, 1844' p.3a

COSTUMES, SCENERY, SPECIMENS OF LITERATURE ETC./OF THE NORTH ISLAND OF/NEW ZEALAND/1841 1842 1843.

[ASHWORTH, Edward 1814-1896]

Unsigned [1843 or January 1844]
Frontispiece
Sepia watercolour 313 x 199 mm
.21 mm cream wove paper, no visible watermark

The evidence on which this attribution is based lies in the material and style of Ashworth's notebooks and 'Journey to the Waikato' (December 1843) in the Alexander Turnbull Library manuscript and picture collections. The text on the lower left of the drawing is from *The Merchant of Venice,* Act 2 Scene 1. Morochus, a 'tawny Moor', speaks:

> Mislike me not for my complexion,
> The Shadowed livery of the burnished sun
> To whom I am a neighbour and near bred.
> Bring me the fairest creature northward born
> [Where Phoebus fire scarce thaws the ysicles,]
> And let us make incision for your love,
> To prove whose blood is reddest, his or mine.
> I tell thee Ladie, this aspect of mine
> Hath feared the valiant . . . .

Ashworth, in his entry for 8 December 1843, used lines from the same quotation: 'While we halted for breakfast on the river's bank, a large canoe came up to hail us. There were 30 or 40 natives in it and several dogs. The bright sun set off to great advantage their sleek and at the same time muscular forms and reminded me of Shakespear's Moorish prince, "Mislike me not for my complexion . . . . "'

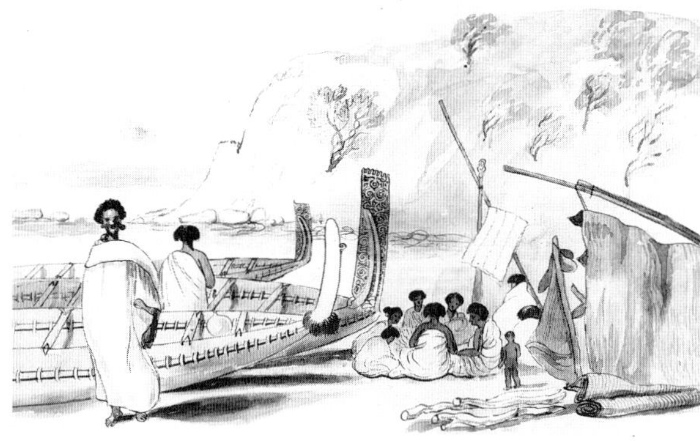

ASHWORTH *New Zealand navigators ashore 1842,* sepia ink and wash, 183 x 244 mm
ATL A208/11

Four of the artists contributing to Mrs Hobson's Album worked in monotone watercolour, sometimes with black or brown ink, but only Ashworth and Merrett used this medium for groups of figures in landscape. If we compare Ashworth's 'New Zealand navigators ashore, 1842' and 'Native New Zealander', 1843, with the frontispiece figures, there are striking similarities:
1. Chinese white is used on forehead, nose and limbs to highlight form, and the limbs themselves are sturdy;
2. The bulk of figures is emphasised and given a classical air by thick folds of cloth worn like Roman togas;
3. Hairstyles are given sideways emphasis.
More conclusively, his Sketchbook E42 has, on p.11, a prototype drawing for the ponga fern at the top left, and also the tree fern in silhouette on a dark background.

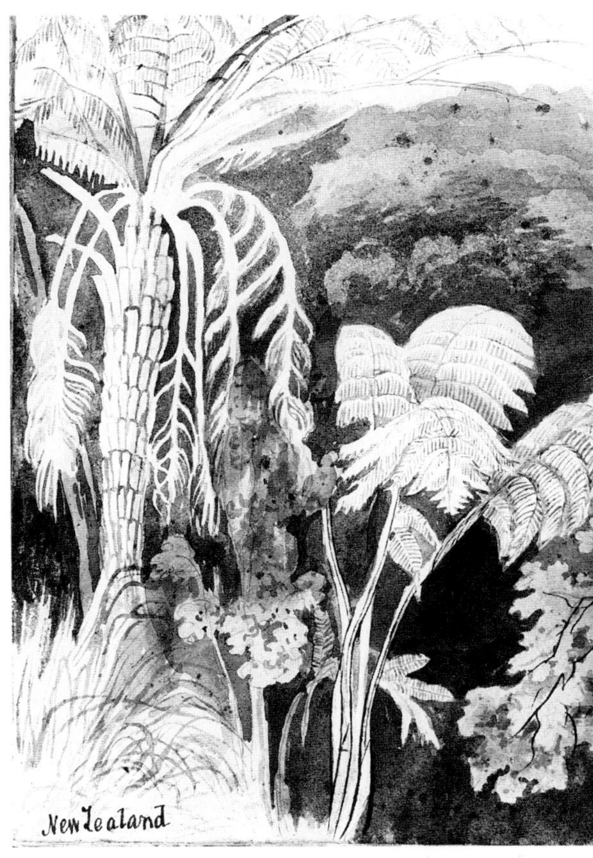

ASHWORTH *New Zealand,* ink and wash, 240 x 140 mm
ATL E42 Sketchbook p.11

The artist has printed his description on a triangularly woven Polynesian sail. Such a sprit sail was put up to assist or to rest the paddlers and was held up by two angled poles turning on a bass pivot.

Ashworth's extraordinary rendering of carved figures on the three canoes has an individual distortion which echoes his first written description of Auckland's main street: '. . . here and there a long red canoe with a frontispiece of human deformity boasting a splendid wig of split feathers and glaring fiercely and fixed with mother of pearl eyes'.

3 [*Album page 5*

Government House Auckland NW view.

[ASHWORTH, Edward 1814-1896]

Unsigned [1842 or 1843]
Pencil and watercolour 122 x 283 mm
Mediumweight cream wove paper, no visible watermark
Title inscribed on Album page

Auckland's first Government House was prefabricated in London. 'Captain Hobson's Mansion', as it was called, was much discussed and its cost deplored. The *New Zealand Gazette* (4 July 1840, p.3 col. 2) printed a detailed history:

> On Friday January 3rd 1840 the surveyors of the Board of Ordinance inspected a splendid house, now constructing by Mr Manning, of High Holborn. The house is wholly of wood and will shortly be taken to pieces and transported to New Zealand where, when set up, it will form the government house of the colony. . . . Its dimensions are 120 feet in length, 50 feet in breadth, and 24 in height. The best Norway deals are used in the building, the massive framework, upright posts, and roof of which are all bolted and screwed together in such a manner that . . . every portion of it may be disconnected and again connected . . . when painted the walls will have the appearance of massive masonry. The roof has two coverings, one of fir plank furnished here, and the other of shingle to be provided in the colony.

This house of 6,000 sq ft was modelled on one built twenty years earlier for Napoleon at St Helena. Fitted with twenty already glazed french casements, its rooms furnished at a cost of £600, the whole weighed 250 tons when packed. It was shipped on the *Platina,* 26 February 1840, and arrived at Port Nicholson on 6 July. There, the settlers hoped to keep both house and Governor, but the ship went on to Auckland on 2 September.

From a second painting (Plate **8**) we can see that Government House was placed on an elevated site and faced towards Rangitoto. The 'Plan of Auckland as it stood in January, 1842' (see p.20) shows Government House in wide grounds on the eastern slope of

Princes Street, its gateway at the south-east extremity where Princes Street is met by the then unnamed Waterloo Quadrant.

This painting of the north-west view gives in more detail the domestic end of the house and its smaller side verandah. Rising behind the house, with a suggestion of terraced earthworks, is Mt Eden. The barracks are on the far left of the distant group of buildings. A small row of shrubs and the elaborate detail of a new paling fence are additions not in Ashworth's sketch.

Ashworth in a sketchbook has drawn a small sepia watercolour showing the long front elevation with its ten-foot-deep ceremonial verandah, and beneath, the oval *oeil de boeuf* windows of an excavated cellar.

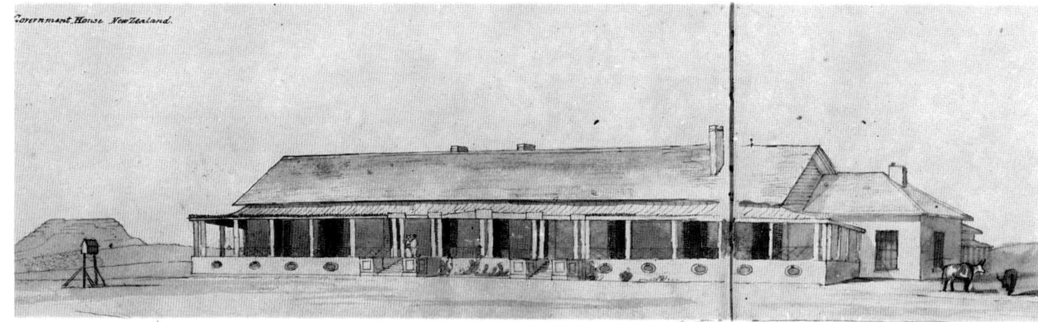

ASHWORTH *Government House, New Zealand* [?1843], sepia ink and wash, 180 x 80 mm
ATL E42 Sketchbook pp.30-31

4 [*Album page* 7

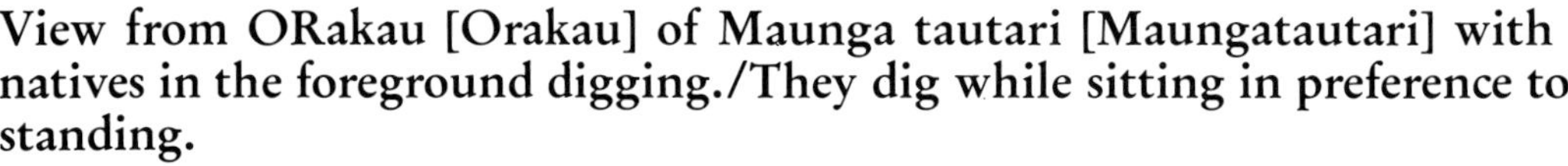

View from ORakau [Orakau] of Maunga tautari [Maungatautari] with natives in the foreground digging./They dig while sitting in preference to standing.

[MERRETT, Joseph Jenner 1816-1854]

Unsigned [1843-1844]
Black ink, pencil, grey watercolour 166 x 240 mm
Mediumweight .18 mm cream wove paper, no visible watermark
Title inscribed in black ink on Album page

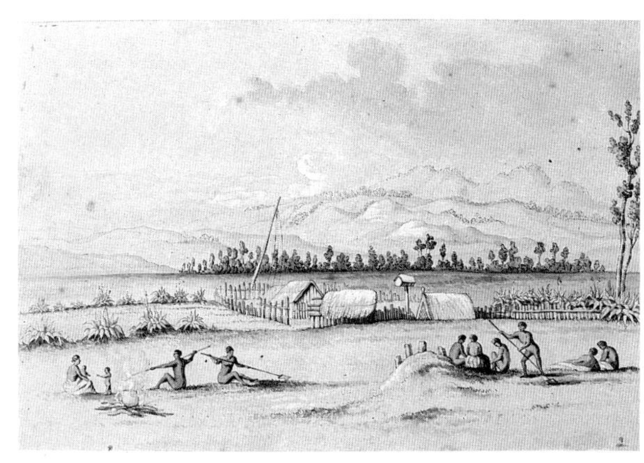

MERRETT *View from Orakau with Natives in the foreground digging* [1843-4], pencil wash and china white, 165 x 249 mm
HOCKEN LIBRARY HO neg 720

Maungatautari Mountain (815 m) is in the south-western Waikato district and lies 15 to 20 kms to the east of Te Awamutu. This view of Maungatautari appears to have been taken from flat ground facing towards Kihikihi, just south of the present Te Awamutu. It is a view which the painter Merrett knew well. He frequently stayed with his friend John Edwards, a trader at Rarowera, a short walk from the Orakau Pa. Maungatautari has been described as one of the resting places of sacred earth from Ra'iatea (Rangiatea near Tahiti) hidden by ancestors of the Tainui tribes when they spread inland from Kawhia (Ramsden 1951, pp.42-43).

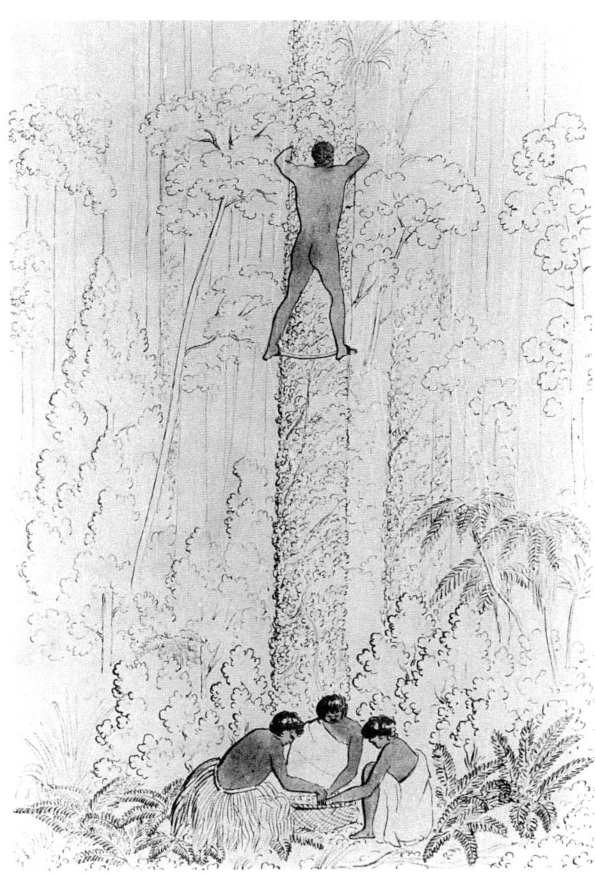

MERRETT [*Maori climbing a tree to gather the fruit of the kiekie*], ink and wash, 120 x 79 mm (an example of Merrett's style of drawing figures and foliage).
BL ADD. MS 19953 p.111 plate 281

Orakau is memorable for the heroic resistance made by 300 Waikato, Ngati Maniapoto and Tuhoe men and women against a British force of 1474 on 2 April 1864. Edward Shortland described the village of Orakau in his 'Journal of an Expedition through the Waikato with Governor Hobson in April 1842' (Hocken MS21) entry for 18-19 April.

> The country is the most lovely I have seen yet in New Zealand; fields of corn cultivated for more than a mile. Enclosures are well fenced — pig proof. . . . The kumara gardens would not disgrace an English nurseryman; not a weed was here to be seen, and the low screens of brushwood, which were set up at short distances from each other to protect the young plants from blighting winds, formed very neat fences. It seemed a favourite custom in this district to plant rows of flax bushes for this purpose.

In this drawing Merrett shows a whanau, or family settlement, its dwellings protected against the rooting of pigs by paling fences, the uprights lashed to the cross-pieces of flax rope. On both sides are cultivations of flax, making desirable varieties easily accessible. Flax provided the 'nuts and bolts' of Maori culture, and this whanau's access to the Waipa River would allow vigorous participation in European flax trade.

Reading this picture forwards from the clear bottom slopes of the mountain we see a line of tall trees, the kahikatea or white pine. On their near side a river flat; the suggestion of water is reinforced by the tall sloping post with pendant ropes of a moari, or swing. In other drawings Merrett has shown young people swinging out over a river and jumping into water (see Plate **9**, 'A Native Game').

There are two taller buildings inside an enclosure. The one furthest from our view is likely to have been the wharemoe where the family slept and has a suggestion of soil built up around it. The wharepuni facing the viewer appears to have a porch. The smooth roof may have been made from big sheets of kanuka or totara bark removed from living trees, which were not killed in the process.

In the middle ground and separated by a fence from the wharepuni are three structures. The roofed pit with a triangular opening and the other to its left, also roofed with rushes, may both have been used to store kumara underground. Between them is a small pataka, a house for food storage, protected from rats by being held aloft on a central pole. In the centre foreground we see the mound of a rua, another pit for the storage of kumara, its entrance strengthened by posts.

The foreground figures are all concerned with the business of living, although we cannot see what the seated groups of women on the right are doing. Between them a standing figure uses a ko to break up the ground. The two seated women on the left are hoeing or mounding kumara with a long-handled tool. (The Museum at Te Awamutu has a fine example of such a kaheru.) The woman on the far left appears to be keeping an eye on two small children and the round iron cooking pot on the fire. It is a kohua, one of the earliest pieces of European equipment to be readily used in the whanau.

Drawings in the Grey Album, inscribed in Merrett's hand, are also done in ink with a fine pen, and in similar style to this 'View from ORakau'. The same curled outline of foliage is present on p.33 plate 84, 'Kaekatea' [Kahikatea] and p.9 plate 19, 'The Waikato near Maungatautari'. The variety of these inscribed drawings shows that Merrett was very familiar with the Waikato landscape between Maungatautari and Pirongia.

A close copy of this drawing, in the Hocken Library, has been attributed to Edward Shortland (see p.112). It is in ink, sepia wash and chinese white; title and presumed artist are supplied by Dr Hocken and inscribed in his hand on the original mount 'Given to me by Dr Shortland and probably drawn by him'. The Hocken drawing lacks vitality of line and has that more careful and stilted approach which even an originating artist can give to a copy. It is one of four drawings with the provenance of Shortland papers which are copies of originals in the Hobson Album (see pp.36-7). Both these versions are characterised by the same stylistic features which define Merrett's work: fine ink outline, thickened uniformly on the right to indicate substance. Figures are not well articulated and children, particularly, are depicted with noticeably small heads in relation to their bodies. Repetitive symbols are used for trees and flax, the former given bulk with grey wash, the latter shaped by use of dark ground behind leaf forms. All these details have correspondence in style to work signed 'J. J. Merrett'. They are also characteristic of a number of sketches in the Grey Album which are so closely related that they must be recognised as the source from which these finished drawings were compiled.

He moko
1 Tiwhana
2 Repha
3 Ngu
4 Pongiangia
5 Wakatara
6 Kumekume
7 Rerepehi
8 Wero
9 Pukaru
10 Koroaha
11. Paepae
12. Putaringa
13 Kauwae
14. Titi middle of forehead

SHORTLAND *He moko and Key,* ink, 265 x 93 mm
HOCKEN MS 21 pp 44-45

5 [*Album page 9*

Wakatani. (left)
[Young Maori man of high rank] (right)

[MERRETT, Joseph Jenner 1816-1854]

Unsigned [1843]
Pencil and watercolour (left) 174 x 120 mm
(right) 173 x 120 mm
.21 mm cream wove paper, no visible watermark
'Wakatani' inscribed in black ink, lower right

Both portraits of these unidentified young people are drawn by the same hand. The clothing is drawn in pencil; the face, neck and hair are given form with grey underpainting and red-brown wash superimposed. The expressive eyes and use of cerulean blue on the girl's lips are all consistent with Merrett's style. The girl wears a ngutukaka (kakabeak flower) as an earring, having obviously dressed for her portrait. Two lines from Merrett's poem (Plate **32**) could equally describe this girl's moko tattooed between lower lip and chin:

> Tohunga's skill her kauwau show'd
> In graceful lines the carving flowed . . .

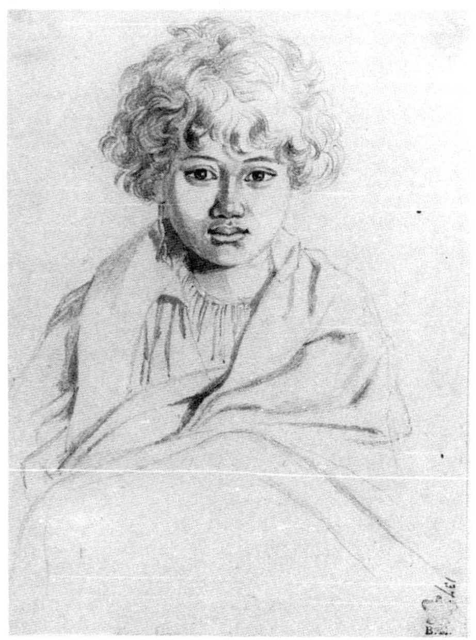

[MERRETT] [*Young woman*], pencil, 168 x 121 mm
BL ADD. MS 19953 p.47 plate 137

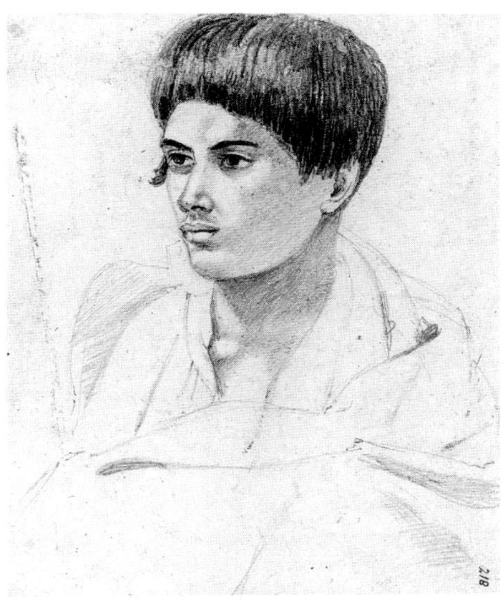

Artist unknown [*Maketu*] pencil, 150 x 110 mm
BL ADD. MS 19953 p.78 plate 218

The right-hand portrait shows by the full facial moko and the two white feathers, raukura, worn in the hair, that the young man is of high rank.

The diagrammatic numbered drawing shown and its key 'He moko' are taken from Edward Shortland's 'Journal of an Expedition through the Waikato with Governor Hobson in April 1842' (Hocken MS21, p.44). It describes a different moko, but gives names and positions applicable to the decorative elements incised on this face. It is also included here because it is a rare example of a drawing made by Edward Shortland.

Related drawings in the Grey Album inscribed in Merrett's hand are: p.47 plate 137, [Young woman], pencil drawing on cream ground; p.85 plate 244, [Young woman], pencil drawing on cream ground; p.76 plate 208, 'A slave of Wakatane's, the chief of Maraenui', pencil; p.54 plate 161, 'Pari tu', pencil; p.77 plate 215, 'A young chief of Tauterei's tribe, Wakatane', pencil.

Plates 208 and 215 in the Grey Album, inscribed by Merrett, refer to 'Wakatane' both as the name of a chief and a place. It is likely that this inscription indicates the place, Whakatane.

6 [*Album page 11*

Maketu.

[MERRETT Joseph Jenner 1816-1854]
?possibly a copy by Edward Ashworth

Unsigned [1842]
Pencil and watercolour 222 x 177 mm
.18 mm cream wove paper
'Maketu.' inscribed in black ink, lower right

Maketu, the young son of a Waimate chief, Ruhe, was apprehended for multiple murder at the Bay of Islands in November 1841, tried in Auckland on 1 March and executed on 7 March 1842 (for an account of this case see pp.18-20).

There are six known portraits of Maketu. Curiously two were given to Mrs Hobson (Plates **6** and **53**). Could they be two copies done by different artists from a single original? In each of the six portraits the subject is presented in an identical position: the head turned to the left showing a three-quarter face. In all, thick black hair is shaped by a recent haircut.

It is arguable that the four derived from a sensitive and expressive pencil drawing (Grey Album, p.78 plate 218) done at Maketu's trial. There is also a small watercolour in the Grey Album (p.45 plate 132) in which Maketu wears a heavy rain cape. It is inscribed 'Maketu hanged at Auckland 1842' in an unidentified hand. A version in the Hocken Library is a close copy done by, or for, Dr Edward Shortland of the watercolour and pencil portrait on Plate **53.**

Letter from Te Whero Whero, Chief of the Waikato tribes to Queen Victoria [and translation in English]

Signed by copyist 'na to hoa na te Wherowhero'/ 'From your friend Wherowhero'.
Undated [1843]
Brown ink 360 x 260 mm
.24 mm cream wove paper, watermark 'J. WHATMAN TURKEY MILL 1837'

Governor Hobson stayed with Potatau Te Wherowhero, chief of the Ngati Mahuta tribe of Waikato, at Kaitotehe, near Taupiri, from 8 to 10 April 1842. When his party was about to leave, Te Wherowhero gathered all his people and told them: 'When muskets and powder were first brought amongst us we were pleased. When the missionaries came I consented, for I saw they were good. And now I bring you this new treasure. We have brought law, a new law, to save us from killing and robbing each other. I will take this my treasure up Waipa, through every bend of the river. Friends, do not think little of what I say.' (Shortland, *Auckland Standard*, 9 May 1842.)

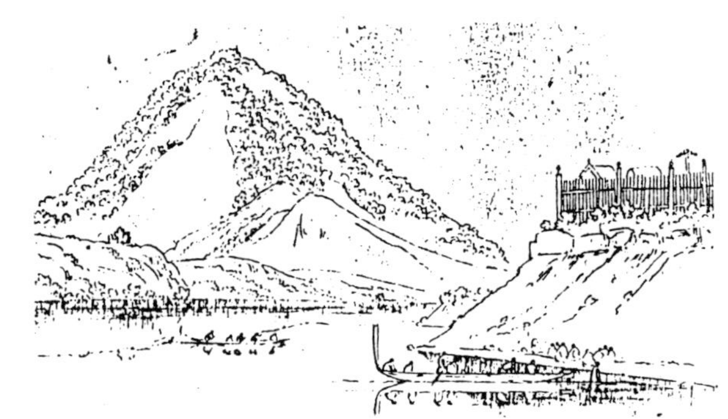

[MERRETT] *Kaitotehe, the Pah of Te wero wero,* ink, 150 x 250 mm

Te Wherowhero and others also wrote to the incoming Governor FitzRoy, expressing similar sentiments to those contained in the second paragraph of the letter (*New Zealand Journal,* 1844, p.496).

In the Grey Album is a related ink drawing (p.24 plate 55) inscribed in Merrett's hand 'Kaitotehe, the Pah of Te wero wero'.

The copyist has not been fully accurate in transcription and we give here a corrected printing with a modern translation. The letter was widely published during the nineteenth century.

E tai, e Wikitōria,

Tēnā ra ko koe. He rahi taku aroha ki a koe, e noho mai na i tōu kāinga. He mea atu nāku ki tētahi kāwana mo mātou ko ngā Pākehā o tēnei motu. Kia pai. Māu e titiro iho tētahi tangata pai whakaaro, kei haere mai ki konei te mea kori;[1] kei haere mai te mea taitamariki, te mea hīkaka, ka wehi mātou ngā tāngata Māori. Kia pēnei anō te pai me te kāwana ka mate nei.

E kui, e Wikitōria, kia pai ra tō kōrero ki te Pākehā: kia atawhai, kei haere mai ki konei patu ai i a mātou. E pai ana hoki, e āta noho ana mātou. He iwi kino mātou i mua, he iwi kōhuru, he iwi patu. Ināianei ka noho mārire; ka mahue i a mātou te kino. Māu tēnei ritenga, koia i pai ai.[2]

E kui,[3] kia atawhai.

Na tō hoa, na Te Wherowhero.

1. *Kori:* 'to move, wriggle; bestir oneself; use action in oratory' (Williams, 1971). The word is sometimes used in *waiata aroha* (love poetry) of a man or woman making improper advances (e.g. in Ngata and Te Hurinui 1961, song 120, line 25). It is here used as an adjective to describe a person who stirs up trouble.

2. The original translator has rendered this sentence as if in the past: *Nāu tēnei ritenga.* Since the *māu* form conveys a sense of future rather than past time, the expression as it stands must refer to the course of action the Queen is about to follow in appointing a new governor. The other possibility is that the sentence is incorrectly copied and should indeed refer to the past.

3. *E tai, e kui* have both been translated as 'O Lady'. There is no English equivalent for these terms of address which express respect and, in the case of *kui,* a certain amount of affection.

Lady Victoria,

Greetings to you. I feel great love for you, living there at your home. I wish to speak to you about a governor for us and the Pakehas of this land. Let him be a good man. You must look around for a man of sound judgement, so that a trouble-making man does not come here; so that an immature and ill-disposed man does not come here to intimidate us, the Maori people. Let him be just as good as the governor who has recently died.

Lady Victoria, instruct the Pakeha carefully: let him be kind, so that he does not come here to harm us. For we are peaceful, and living quietly. Formerly we were an evil people, a treacherous people, a killing people. Now we live in peace; we have left our evil ways behind. You are the one who will be taking this course of action, and we approve of this.

O Lady, be kind.

From your friend, Te Wherowhero.

8 [*Album page 15*

Government House, Auckland/showing the North Head of Waitemata Harbr.

[ASHWORTH, Edward 1814-1896]

Unsigned [late 1842 or early 1843]
Pencil, sepia watercolour, grey ink 179 x 315 mm
.25 mm cream wove paper, no visible watermark
Title inscribed in black ink on Album page

In this view, more distant than the one in Plate **3**, Ashworth has shown the back of the house facing away from the harbour. French doors open onto a wide terrace; in the long roof are the dormer windows of the servants' bedrooms (see p.112). Above the roof we see the rounded silhouette of Mt Victoria (Takarunga) with a flagpole on its summit: land falls away on the right to Cheltenham beach and Narrowneck, from which rises North Head (Takapuna). Behind are the symmetrical peaks of Rangitoto Island, the most recent of Auckland's volcanoes.

William Mason, the Superintendent of Works, had overseen the building of the road we see in the foreground. On 16 November 1840, Mason reported: 'The principal employment of the men was in cutting a road to Government House and clearing the ridges for the Surveyor General.' When the Hobsons moved to Auckland in the following March the house was still unfinished. 'As late as 14 May, tenders were being

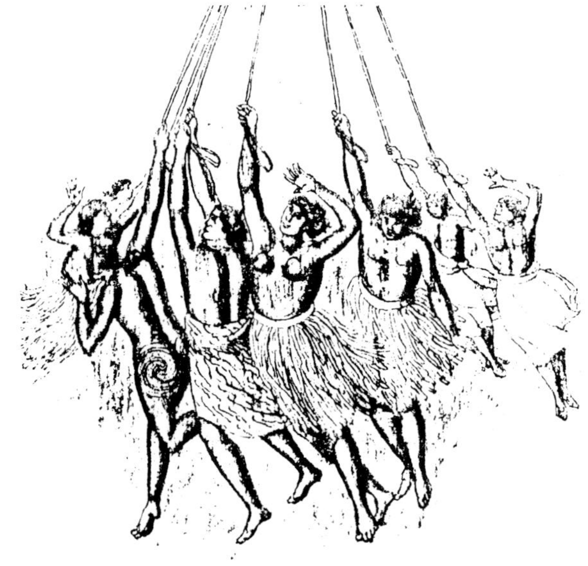

[MERRETT] [*A Morere*], ink
BL ADD. MS 19953 unnumbered drawing

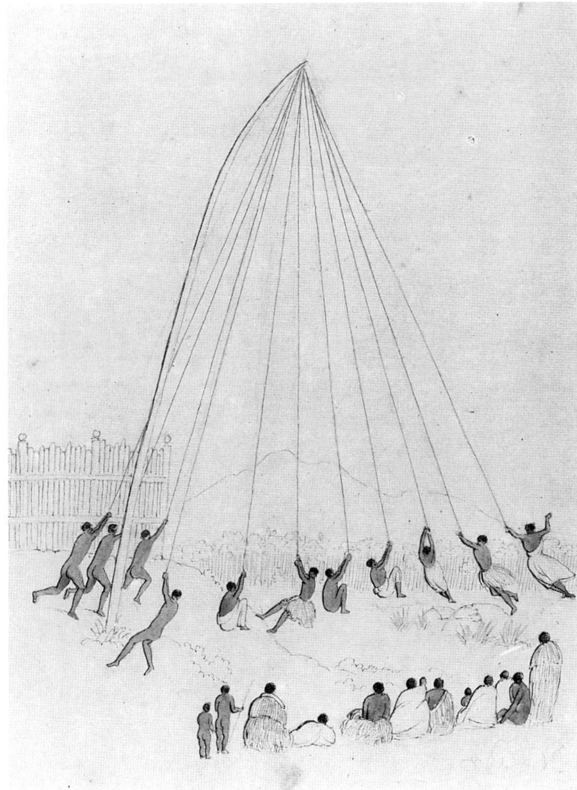

[MERRETT] *A Moari or native swing,* ink and grey wash, 190 x 311 mm
BL ADD. MS 19953 p.104 plate 273

received for a laundry, fittings for a butler's pantry and flooring to bedrooms. Government House became the main architectural feature of the new town. . . . Many of Auckland's first houses were influenced by its design, which owed much to the additions Mason made to its otherwise bald elevations' (Stacpoole 1971, p.32). By the time the house was finished with a surrounding 'terrace verandah . . . a fine promenade 2 yards wide about 100 yards long', the original cost was augmented by a further £6360. This original Government House burned down in 1848 and its replacement on the same site is now used as the Auckland University Senior Common Room.

A copy held in the Hocken Library is No.3 of a series of four watercolours previously attributed to John Johnson (*Catalogue of Pictures in the Hocken Library,* 1948, p.3). However, a sepia ink and wash drawing in Ashworth's Sketchbook (E42 pp.30-31) establishes Ashworth as the artist of both views of Government House in this Album (Plates **3** and **8**). All three are similar in style and medium.

9 [*Album page 17*

A Native Game.

[MERRETT, Joseph Jenner 1816-1854]

Unsigned [1840-1842]
Ink and grey wash 175 x 122 mm
.24 mm cream wove paper, no visible watermark
Title inscribed in black on upper right of image

'Morere' or 'moari' are alternative names for the swing. The latter form is more usual in the Waikato-Waipa area. In this lively drawing the artist shows the swing set up on the bank of a river, just outside the defences of a pa. Merrett has caught a vigorous variety of postures as the young men and women run down the slope and swing themselves by flax ropes far out over the water before jumping or falling in turn. From the Grey Album we have a closer view of the players.

Edward Shortland described such a swing set up by the Ngati Pou at Puketoi (Pukatea) on the Waikato River: ' . . . a lofty pole at least 60 feet high, rope tied to summit and at the other end a loop so that a slave could be swung out over Te Wherowhero's head: However on being questioned they denied any such intention, saying it was merely to amuse the children.'

A seated figure in the centre foreground wears a pureke (rain cape), shorter than a korowai (cloak of woven flax). It was made of muka (flax fibre) and designed to keep the upper parts of the body dry. The substructure was flax rope, and with the layers of muka, could be nearly a foot thick. The garment must have been very warm. The figure on the far left wears a kahutoi, a short waist or shoulder garment made of dyed

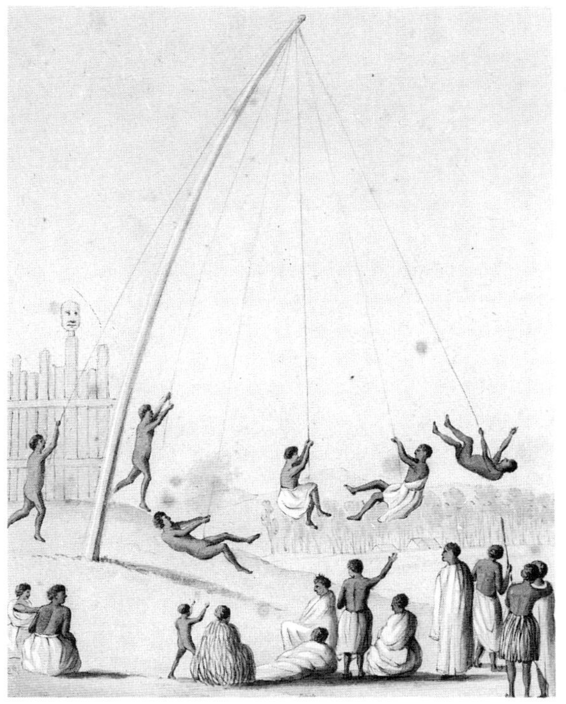

[MERRETT] *Morere or swing,* copy in ink, wash and china white, 174 x 124 mm
HOCKEN LIBRARY HO neg 721

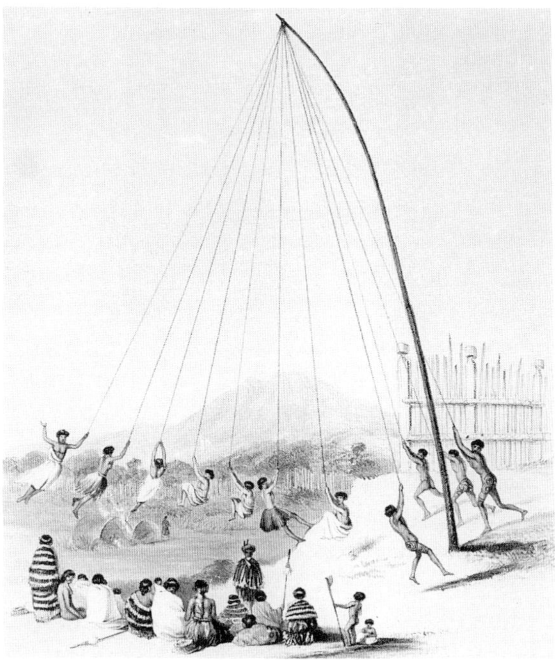

ANGAS *Native Swing,* 235 x 245 mm, lithograph (hand-coloured) top portion of plate 53 in G. F. Angas, *The New Zealanders Illustrated* (1847)
ATL

cabbage tree fibre (see M. Pendergrast, *Te Aho Tapu,* catalogue of cloaks, Auckland Museum, 1987).

A sepia, ink and chinese white version of the native game, previously attributed to Edward Shortland, is a tidy copy of this more direct drawing (see *Catalogue of Pictures in the Hocken Library,* 1948, p.52).

Related drawings in the Grey Album are: p.104 plate 273, 'A Moari or Native swing', ink; and an unnumbered drawing in ink of young people holding the ropes of a swing.

A published version is in Grey's *Polynesian Mythology* (1885), facing p.72. This engraving derives from, but uses fewer figures than, the drawing in the Grey Album.

The top portion of plate 53, entitled 'Native swing', in G. F. Angas, *The New Zealanders Illustrated,* appears to be a laterally reversed lithograph based on Merrett's drawing.

10 [*Album page 20*

[Commentary on the 'Poi']

[SHORTLAND, Edward 1812-1893]

Unsigned [1842-43]
Brown ink 360 x 260 mm
.21 mm cream wove paper, no visible watermark
Text inscribed in brown ink on Album page

In 1842 and early 1843 Edward Shortland accompanied Governor Hobson or other officials to various Maori settlements in the North Island, keeping a journal of his travels and recording songs, sayings and notes on Maori life and customs. Much of this material was later published in *Traditions and Superstitions.* The Maori songs and proverbs copied into Mrs Hobson's Album are to be found in several of Shortland's notebooks, often being copied from one to another (MSS 22, 24 and 489, Hocken Library). The exception is the poi chant and its commentary. Although the style of the latter marks it out as Shortland's work, and his presence in the official party would have given him the necessary status for viewing the tapu poi, there is no mention of the occasion and no version of the chant and commentary in the notebooks which have been preserved in the Hocken Library.

The fact that neither the chant nor the commentary was ever published (the description in Shortland 1856, p.160 is brief and quite different from the Album commentary) suggests that perhaps the original was lost before Shortland selected his items for publication. This is a pity, since this passage from Mrs Hobson's Album is perhaps the most detailed ever to have been recorded on the subject. As Elsdon Best notes (1976, p.101), 'There is but little on record concerning this pastime in the works of early writers, or any writers for that matter, and it would now be difficult to describe the purely Maori forms, so much has the exercise been influenced by the European invasion.' The brief example from Taylor which he quotes mentions, in general terms, the use of the poi as an invitation to war. In contrast, our passage gives the background to a specific event, the names of the people involved, and the chant used on the occasion. There are also new details on the use of the poi as a love-letter.

The name of the sender of the poi has been transcribed incorrectly. Chiefs mentioned by Shortland as having been in the area at the time and who had somewhat similar names are Tiwha and Te Uira, the latter name bearing a closer resemblance to the one in the Album. Taipari was well known, being mentioned by A. D. Best (1966, p.391 ff.) as the chief of Maungatapu Pa near Mount Maunganui. Descendants of these people may have more information about the incident. The chant itself contains far more transcription errors than any of the other songs recorded in the Album, and is the only one not supplied with an English translation. Most of the errors were probably made by the copyist, but some may be the result of Shortland's limited grasp of the Maori language after such a short time in the country. The song has a political and no doubt deliberately ambiguous message, and is more complex than the others copied into the Album. Since any attempt at a full corrected transcription could well be misleading, some explanations are provided on the form of the chant and some of the words or groups of words used in it.

In form, traditional poi songs were recited chants often similar to *pātere,* abusive chants which were frequently composed by women in reply to insults. The singer often begins, as here, with the words *E noho ana,* 'I am sitting' or 'I am staying', and in imagination sends her thoughts or her poi on a journey to various places where she will be honoured by famous chiefs (see McLean and Orbell 1975, songs 4, 20, 28 and 44). In the poi chant recorded here, the singer would seem to be at a place called Petoni (though the spelling and the use of *nga* are both obviously incorrect), lifting up the poi (if *hāpai* is read rather than *ka pai*) and sending it to Maketu, Te Reanuku (the syntax suggests that this was a place, though A. D. Best mentions a young chief of this name, 1966, p.388 ff.) and Te Awaho (Te Awahou). Ikairo must be Hikairo, a famous Arawa chief, but Te Wakawae has not been identified. The confusing middle section with its repetition of the word *toto* (blood) may be referring to earlier deaths which the singer is now wishing to avenge. The poi then makes its way to Tokerau or the Bay of Islands, the home of the famous chief Tareha, who is pictured as being on a ship which is yawing about (*werore* for *wherori*) at the harbour mouth at Kororarepa (Kororareka, now known as Russell). The meaning of *karau panatu ai* is uncertain. The word *Pouda* must be a transliteration of 'powder', usually written *paura.* If, as seems likely, *Nau i homai tou pouda ki Maketu* means 'You gave me your powder (i.e. lent me your support in battle) against Maketu', it suggests that this poi chant is indeed a request for military aid, made in the early days of European contact, when various power struggles were taking place among the tribes of the north with the aid of newly introduced muskets. Other words which confirm that this is a post-European composition are *kaipuke* (ship) and *pukapuka* (book, letter). The sentence *Ka* [i.e. *Ko*] *te pukapuka te kai o taku poi* probably means 'My poi is being used as a letter' (using *kai* in the sense of 'fulfil its proper function').

In more recent times the poi chant has been put to different uses, notably by the Taranaki people, who use it as a form of protest against Pakeha injustices and to proclaim the teachings of the prophets Te Whiti-o-Rongomai and Tohu Kakahi. Many public performances of Maori waiata also feature modern versions of the poi.

The long place name which follows the poi chant has not been identified.

11 [*Album page* 21

A Group of New Zealanders.

[MERRETT, Joseph Jenner 1816-1854]

Unsigned [1843]
Watercolour 254 x 359 mm full page, attached to guard
.22 mm cream wove paper, no visible watermark
Inscribed lower right, in black ink on watercolour, 'A Group of New Zealanders.'

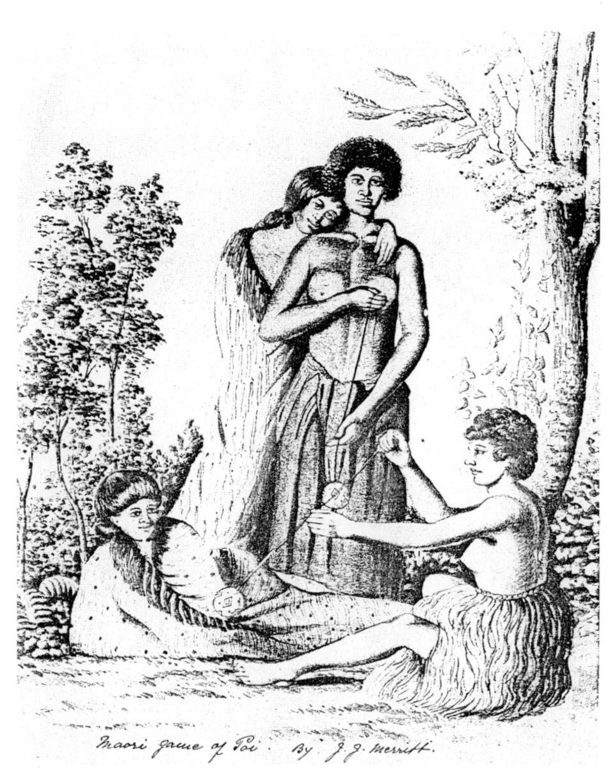

MERRETT *Maori game of poi,* watercolour and ink, 340 x 260 mm
HOCKEN LIBRARY

This painting has been done on watercolour paper exactly to fit the format of the Album, the orange-coloured paper of the Album itself being cut back to make a 20 mm hinge on which the watercolour was glued. The painting relates to Shortland's commentary on the poi, a further pointer to our conclusion that Merrett worked closely with Shortland. In the Hocken Library is another version, without the clouds and distant hill, inscribed 'Maori game of Poi. By J. J. Merrett'. These two pictures, so nearly duplicates, show that Merrett was prepared to make a very close copy of his own work; so close that it would be difficult to suggest which might be the original.

The two young women on the left of the picture are wearing the korowai, black fringed tag cloaks of woven flax fibre, typical of the period following European contact. The standing girl's cloak is ornamented with twisted thrums, hukahuka. The reclining figure is wearing a type of korowai-ngore, a cloak decorated with pompoms of coloured wool (see Mead 1969, pp.135-8). The central figure standing is wearing a blanket as a waist kilt. The seated figure on the right is wearing a traditional pākī — 'made of the cloth plant . . . the ends of the stuff of about a foot long were left out so as to form a thick covering layer over layer . . . some were tied around the neck and some around the loins' (Mead 1969, p.60).

The 'long poi' shown was in general use at this time, the short poi being a later invention. The 'poi-awe' were made by weaving or netting round bags of *Phormium* fibre, their fine mesh being ornamented with patterns or with little tufts of dogs' hair (see Best 1925, p.104).

12 [*Album page* 19

[Maori woman reading]

[MERRETT, Joseph Jenner 1816-1854]

Unsigned [1841-1843]
Watercolour 170 x 120 mm
Cream wove paper, no visible watermark
Inscribed on verso, top margin, in pencil, 'Ewaka'

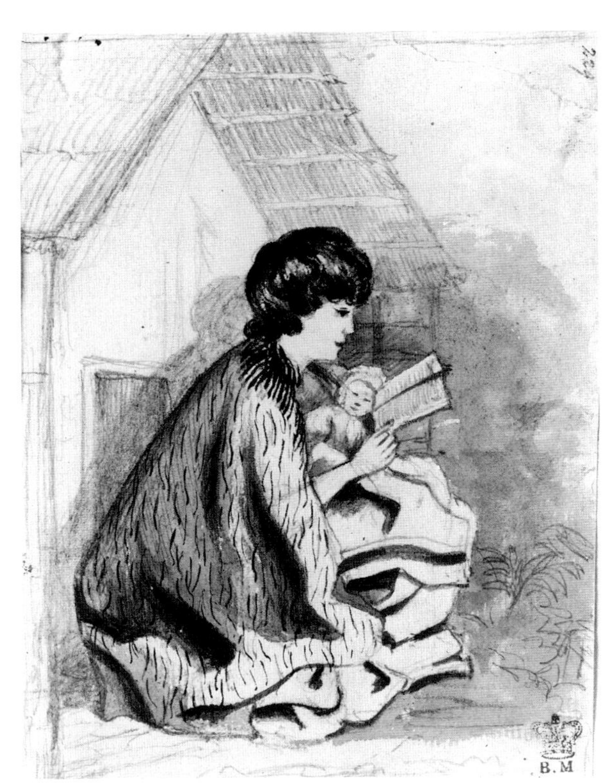

[MERRETT] [*Young Maori woman reading*], watercolour and pencil, 130 x 100 mm
BL ADD. MS 19953 p.81 plate 229

This is our first known record of a Maori woman reading. She holds a young baby wrapped in a heavy striped European blanket, a type which also appears as a cloak in G. F. Angas, *Portraits of the New Zealand Maori.* The baby is dressed in a white frilled bonnet and white gown; these garments, and the paler colour of the baby's face, suggest a European father. The mother wears a korowai-ngore (pompom cloak), the pompoms and possibly the surrounding fringe being of wool. The tags are flax. Cultivated flax appears in the foreground. The background may have been added for pictorial effect. Merrett may have seen a view of the mountain Ngauruhoe, similarly obscured by a foreground hill, on 11 May 1841, when he was with Ensign Best who wrote, 'I do not know what were Mr Merrett's thoughts, but as I sat in that lovely little bay with the waters of Taupo before me, I would not have exchanged my position with any mortal in the world. . . . To the south Tonga Ride (Tongariro) rose like a giant his crest covered with snow gilded to a dazzling brightness by the setting sun.' (Best 1966, p.308.)

What we are shown of the house in this picture resembles the description of a Pakeha-style house at Whatawhata by Edward Shortland. 'We found a hut with 2 rooms and a large porch in front like that of a native hut but which is formed by the roof and side walls of the house, the end wall being made to recede some 7 or 8 feet within. The comfort of this porch is not to be despised in the rainy season. A fire is lit in its centre round which the natives assemble to smoke and talk.' (Shortland Journal, 11 April 1842.) This final sentence suggests that we may read the round dark shape of the left foreground as indication of a recent fireplace.

The treatment of cloak, hand, flax, and fern are all consistent with elements in signed paintings by J. J. Merrett; as are the colours — umber, black, red, indigo, terra verte, and yellow-green. A related drawing in the Grey Album (p.81 plate 229) shows a woman in the same pose reading in the porch of a whare. In this Hobson Album version, the background of lake and mountains has been added.

The Pah of Oinamutu [Ohinemutu] on the Rotorua Lake:/the carvings in this pah are particularly fine

[MERRETT, Joseph Jenner 1816-1854]

Unsigned [1842-1843]
Ink and grey wash 164 x 253 mm
.18 mm cream wove paper, no visible watermark
Title inscribed in black ink on Album page

Early travellers were fascinated by this thermal area and there are many fine contemporary descriptions (see Best 1966, p.305 and Dieffenbach 1843, v. 2, pp.389-91; Wade 1842, pp.144-5; Johnson, 'Notes from a Journal' 1846-1847, pp.153-62). Dieffenbach wrote:

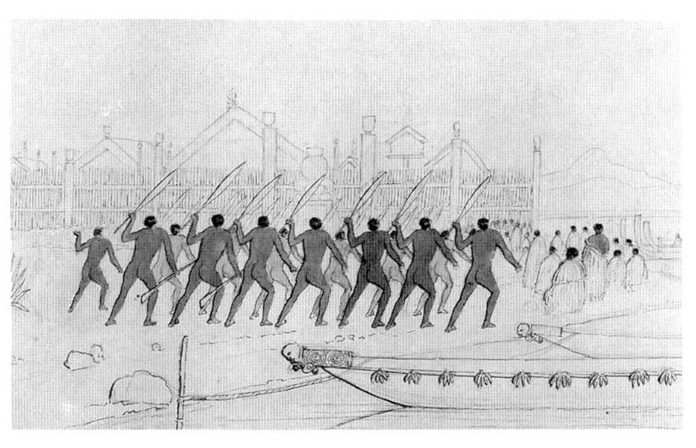

[MERRETT] *Natives launching their war canoe before the Pah of Ohinemutu at Rotorua,* ink and wash, 200 x 310 mm. Original drawing from which a lithograph in reverse was copied by G. F. Angas in *The New Zealanders Illustrated,* plate 53
BL ADD. MS 19953 p.122 plate 295

> The pa, which is the finest I have seen in New Zealand, occupies a large surface, which is intersected by crevices from which steam issues, by boiling springs, and by mud volcanoes. . . . At one time a part of the village close to the edge of the lake subsided several feet, and the water took its place. The palisades are still visible and standing upright under water. . . . The structures in this pa — the houses, doors and palisades — displayed the most ingenious pieces of native workmanship. I have nowhere seen carvings in such profusion. . . . Each of the representations of the human figure bears the name of some tupuna, or ancestor, and the whole is actually a carved history. . . . Within the pa some are busy carving, or working at canoes, whilst others enjoy the *dolce far niente.* The whole scene was complete in itself, and singularly interesting. Comparing the upstart settlements of missionary natives with this old heathen pa, the former really look extremely miserable and tame.

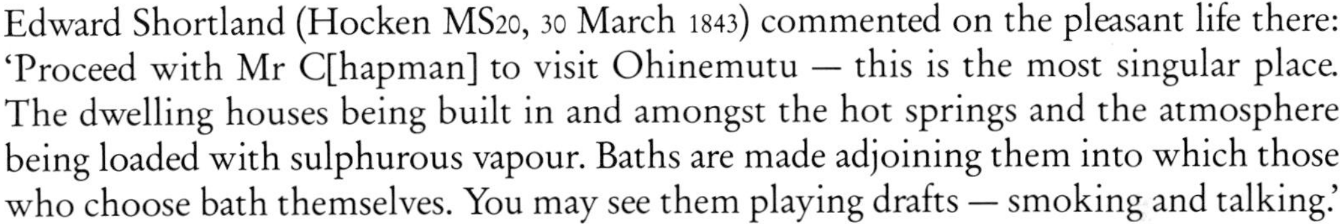

Edward Shortland (Hocken MS20, 30 March 1843) commented on the pleasant life there: 'Proceed with Mr C[hapman] to visit Ohinemutu — this is the most singular place. The dwelling houses being built in and amongst the hot springs and the atmosphere being loaded with sulphurous vapour. Baths are made adjoining them into which those who choose bath themselves. You may see them playing drafts — smoking and talking.'

Johnson, in 1846, reckoned 200 fighting men in a total population of 500. He estimated one third to be Church Missionary Society, one third Roman Catholic and one third pagan. Walking to the eastward of the pa he found: 'three springs, within two hundred yards of each other, of different temperature and qualities, one *boiling hot,* a second *warm,* and a third *preternaturally cold.* The natives make use of the latter, as if instinctively for the cure of diarrhoea and dysentery. . . .'

In the picture, a visiting party, arriving in two canoes, is acknowledging the welcome (powhiri) from the people of the place, the tangata whenua, in front of the palisades. Clouds of thermal steam rise from boiling springs within the pa.

The Hocken Library collection has a very close copy, 'Ohinemutu pa on Lake Rotorua about 1840': pencil, sepia wash and chinese white, 167 x 250 mm, title and artist supplied

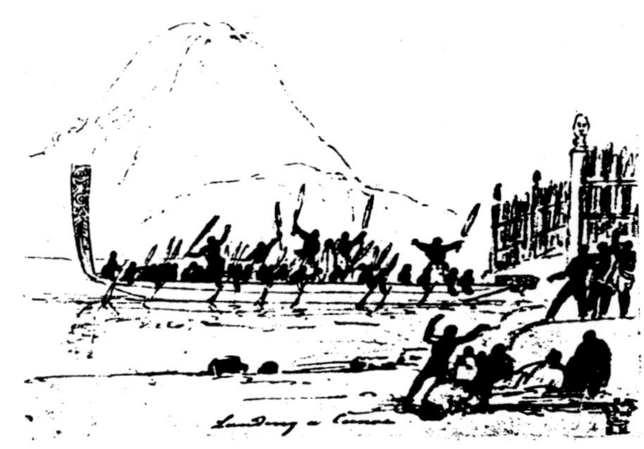

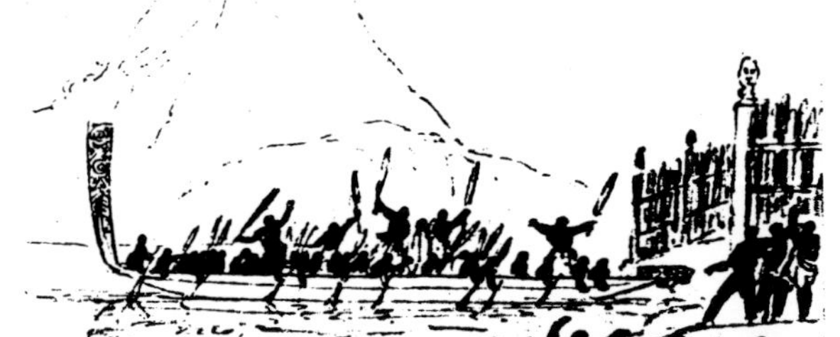

MERRETT *Landing a Canoe,* ink, 53 x 68 mm
BL ADD. MS 19953 p.15 plate 36

by T. M. Hocken and inscribed on mount. (See pp.36-37, 114 for discussion of Hocken's attributions to Edward Shortland.)

Related drawings in the Grey Album show a canoe full of waving visitors (p.15 plate 36) and give the next sequence with a back view of the visitors' haka before the palisades of Ohinemutu pa (p.122 plate 295).

Merrett had made two other earlier versions of Maori war canoes approaching a pa: 'Lake Taupo with Waitahanui Pa' (Mitchell Library watercolour) and 'Lake Taupo with pa' (RNK item 3497). In these two closely related drawings the shore welcoming party is shown waving small branches of green leaves.

14 [*Album page 31*

Russell from Paihia, Wai Keri River

[MITFORD, John Guise 1822-1854]

Unsigned [1843]
Grey watercolour 217 x 313 mm
.21 mm cream wove paper, no visible watermark
Title inscribed in black ink on Album page

John Guise Mitford's skilled and assured handling of the watercolour medium and strong sense of form and colour mark this work as different from the more linear styles of Ashworth, Johnson and Merrett. This composition pushes back into the picture plane in alternate areas of dark against light. From the high tree on the left a line of low scrub runs towards the lower right, silhouetted against an area of white; a similarly undulating diagonal runs from the hill on the left, dark against the lighter sea. The painter handles the sea so that it fills the space; it is not just a lighter gap amongst landforms. This same sense of space structures the distant hills as they recede in waves, each darkening to the summit and outlined by an air-filled valley of light. This watercolour would have been a reminder to Eliza Hobson of her first home in New Zealand on the peninsula of Okiato, seen in the centre middle distance of this watercolour.

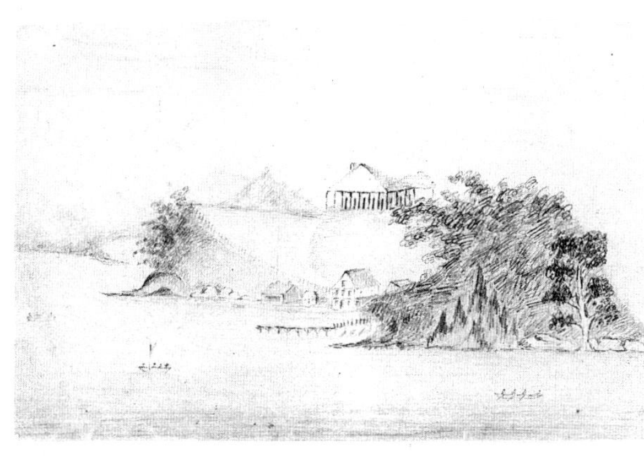

SHORT *Captain Hobson's Residence Bay of Islands*
[1840], pencil, 140 x 217 mm
HOCKEN LIBRARY HO neg 719

One primitive pencil drawing of Captain Hobson's residence and the tiny settlement at Okiato has survived. It was drawn by the Hobsons' governess, Ellery Short, in 1842.

Edward Ashworth visited Kororareka on 27 January 1844. His verbal description complements this watercolour, although his viewpoint was from the signal station behind the township:

> The general aspect is uninviting in the extreme, but a fine varied prospect may be commenced from the signal station near the town, Russell the experimental capital of Capt. Hobson and ridge upon

> ridge of wooded hills behind it. Further north Waimate church steeple and some of the farming settlements may be discerned at that prosperous seat of learning and husbandry, the picturesque indentations of the bold shore are laid out to full view with here and there in a wooded gully or on a fertile spot the residence of some retired naval adventurer, and on the dark green bosom of the Bay several large American whaling ships.

This picture was first reproduced as the frontispiece to Ruth Ross, *New Zealand's First Capital,* from which this map is taken. The names of 'the experimental capital of Capt. Hobson' are confusing. Okiato was renamed 'Russell' until January 1844, when Kororareka instead became 'Russell' (*New Zealand Government Gazette,* 13 January 1844).

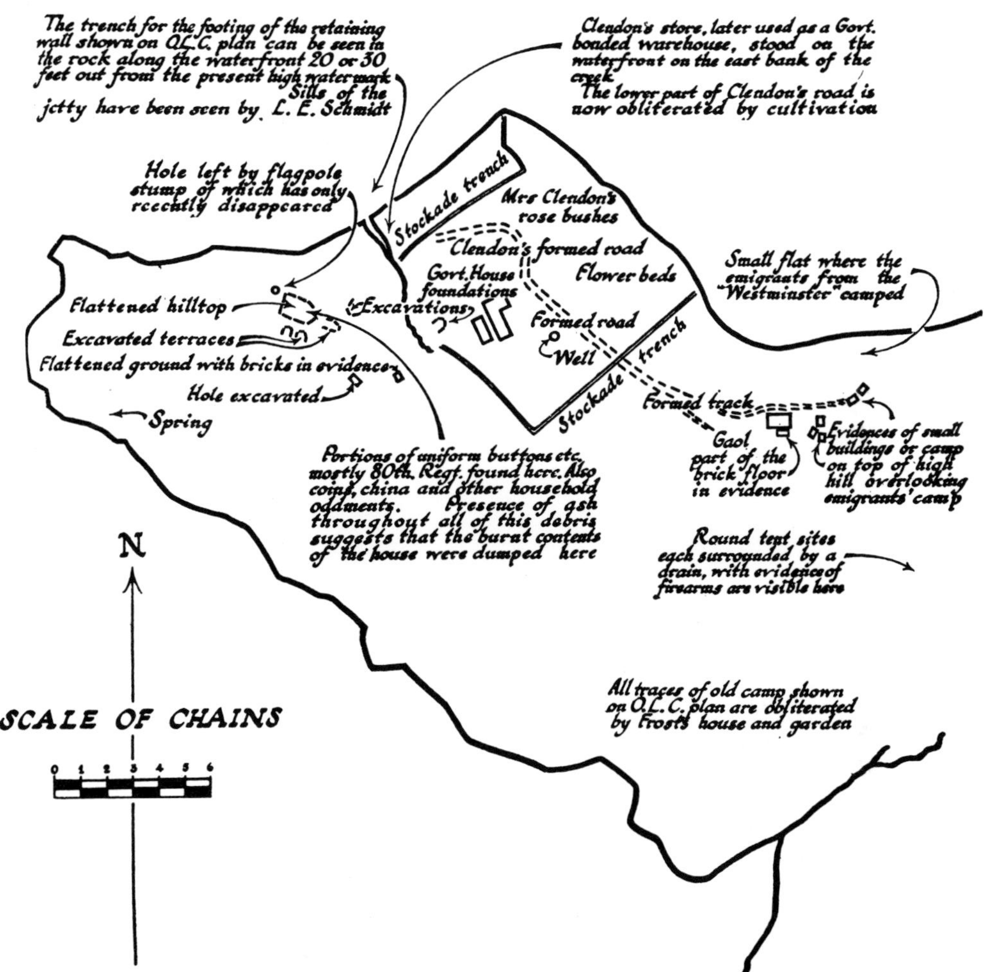

Traces of Old Russell visible in 1943, as surveyed by John R. Lee, in *New Zealand's First Capital* (1946) p.73

It is possible that one item on the next page of the Album was removed a long time ago. Evidence of adhesive on the guard and on the verso of this page suggests that an item could have covered the whole page. The time lapse is proved by foxing marks which fit the verso of this page, and the shadow of staining from pigment corresponds to large outlines offset from this landscape. The support for this item differs in weight and colour from all other papers in the Album.

---

15 [*Album page* 33

View of the town of Auckland from the opposite/shore of the Waitemata

[?MITFORD, John Guise 1822-1854]

Unsigned [1843]
Pencil, grey wash, heightened with body colour white
246 x 356 mm, entire page adhered to guard
.25 mm grey-green paper, wove texture, no visible watermark
Title inscribed in pencil on bottom margin of image

This view shows the growing town centred on Point Britomart. The larger buildings back from the Point are the Barracks and St Paul's Church. The row of buildings to the right on the cliff mark Shortland Street running down to Commercial Bay. Queen Street runs up behind the schooner on the right. To the left of Point Britomart is Official Bay, above which appears the long roof of Government House. Mechanics Bay lies to the far right of the picture. The higher and more distant volcanic hill is Mt Eden, the smaller one in front and to the left is Mt Hobson.

Without evidence of colour this is not an easy attribution to make. Merrett also made views of the town from the sea or the North Shore. The absence of any defining ink or pencil outline argues against Merrett, as does the fluent brush stroke and the handwriting of the inscription, which is not Merrett's. The attribution by Roger Blackley (1983) to John Guise Mitford is very likely correct. This work has the same treatment of alternating bands of light and dark as the opposing view of Waitemata Harbour on Plate **18** and a similar shorthand for distant buildings. Ron Brownson affirms (letter to Janet Paul 16 September 1984): 'The evidence is in the drawing of the rock outcrop on the right hand side indicating Mitford's practice of using three distinctive brush actions within one overall shape. Mitford does this in the ACAG watercolour [Auckland in the early 1840s] presented by Lt Col R. M. Rendel, April 1942 to the Old Colonist's Museum.'

For other related drawings, see views of Auckland in Charles Terry's *New Zealand*, lithographed in 1842 from originals by Merrett. The location of the originals is not known. Another view of the city of Auckland, also drawn in 1843, was published as a lithograph with a handwritten key. Here mountain ranges and volcanic cones suggest that it is an imaginative view from a height.

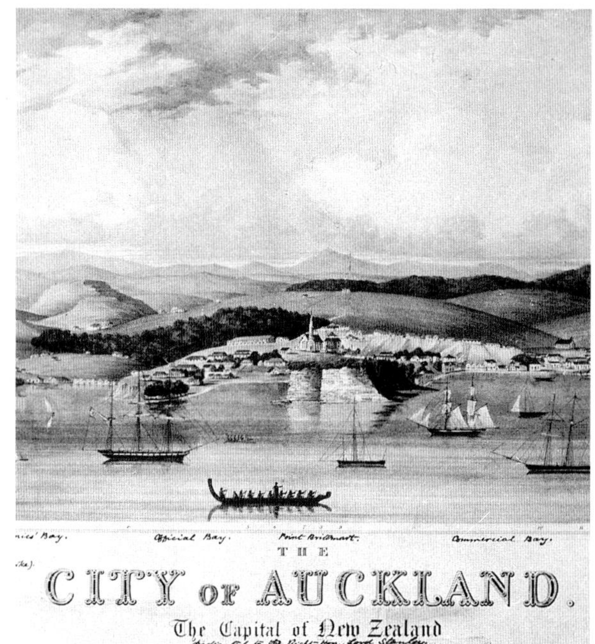

Artist unknown *City of Auckland* [1843].
Centre detail from hand-coloured lithograph with handwritten key
318 x 478 mm
HOCKEN LIBRARY HO neg 446

A Hot Spring in the Warm Lake of Rotomahana

[MERRETT, Joseph Jenner 1816-1854]

Unsigned [?1843]
Black ink, grey watercolour 160 x 249 mm
.18 mm cream wove paper
Title inscribed in brown ink on Album page. On verso, cut text of poem by Merrett inscribed in black ink, notes written in brown ink in another hand.

Joseph Merrett and Charles Heaphy are the first European artists to record the White Terrace at Rotomahana (the warm lake). Until the Tarawera eruption of 1886, the Pink and White Terraces became a focus for nineteenth-century travellers in the North Island. The Maori had used the thermal pools for medical cures. The white terraces of Te Tarata were at the north-western end of the lake. Opposite on the south-western shore were the smaller pink terraces of Otukapuarangi, with the sulphur pool Whakatarata below them. Dr Johnson wrote this vivid description:

> . . . we came in sight of the lake, and one of the most singular scenes that the imagination can picture. On the side of a hill directly opposite rose an immense cone of rock, of a dazzling white colour, shaped from base to summit in a regular graduation of steps, down which poured streams of water, while, from the highest point of the cone, which formed one side of the crater that was tinted with a variety of rich colours, from the effect of heat acting on the clay of which it was composed, rolled volumes of vapour. . . . They formed the most beautiful natural baths, quite equal to anything of the kind that art could achieve. We thus ascended step after step, each containing one or more of these basins, some having perpendicular walls, others were hollowed out at their base, and adorned by stalactites of a dazzling brightness. . . . (John Johnson, 'Notes from a Journal', ed. Nancy Taylor, pp.169–73)

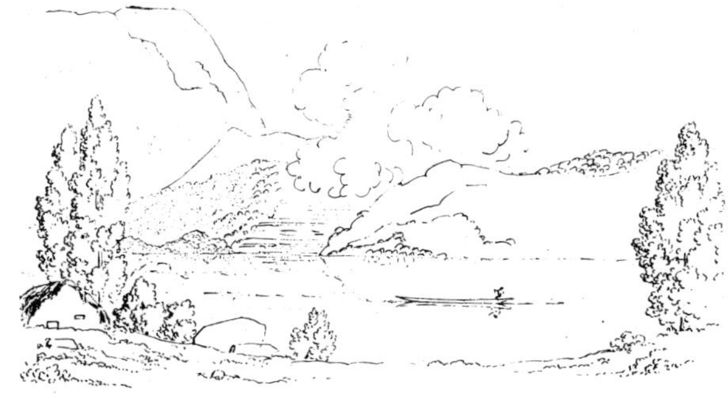

[MERRETT] *Rotomahana, one of the Rotorua Lakes with a view of the hot springs and the ascent to it by natural steps of salyx* [1842], ink and pencil, 200 x 300 mm
BL ADD. MS 19953 p.99 plate 268

This wash drawing is also important to the art historian because it gives proof that the attribution to Joseph Merrett of this style of fine ink drawing is correct. It has been painted on the same paper as part of a handwritten poem by Merrett to his wife Rangi Koa (see Plate **32**). From this paper notes explaining Maori terms in Edward Shortland's hand have also been cut. The link with Merrett is made sure by the existence of an outline drawing in the Grey Album (p.99 plate 268) titled in Merrett's writing, 'Rotomahana, one of the Rotorua lakes with a view of one of the hot springs and the ascent to it by natural steps of onyx'. The ink and watercolour version here is a more finished copy of the Grey Album drawing.

18 [*Album page* 35

Rangitoto, Mount Victoria and the North Head,/from the Government Domain, Auckland.

[MITFORD, John Guise 1822-1854]

Unsigned [1842 or early 1843]
Watercolour 165 x 313 mm
.21 mm cream wove paper, no visible watermark
Title inscribed, in ink, on Album page. On verso, in pencil, 'Rangitoto, Mount Victoria and North Head from the Epsom Road, Auckland'

This is one of the earliest paintings of Auckland's chief icon, the volcanic island of Rangitoto; because the island is circular, it presents similar profiles from many different aspects and has become for all who live about the Waitemata a most potent visual symbol. The full name is given by Johannes C. Andersen (1942) as 'Te [or Nga] Rangi-i-totongia-a Tama-te-kapua'. This name commemorates a combat in which Tama-te-kapua and his sons Tuhoro and Kahu-matamomoe engaged with older established people of the locality, the Kahui-a-marama. Although Tama-te-kapua and his sons won the battle, the chief was severely wounded and lost much blood. The battle was fought on Rangitoto Island at Oruawharu (later called Drunken Bay) towards the narrowing where Rangitoto and Motutapu almost meet. The meaning of the full name is 'the day or days of the bleeding of Tama'.

Both Mount Victoria and North Head, volcanic cones in the middle distance, were terraced Maori pa but were no longer inhabited at this date.

The inscriptions on front and back place the painter's viewpoint as 'the Government Domain' and 'the Epsom Road' respectively. Both can relate to the same point. Robert Graham, a migrant from the *Jane Gifford* first saw the suburb of Epsom on 9 October 1842, and wrote: 'A road from the top of Shortland Crescent leads on up Grafton Gully and through the present Government Domain to the Manukau, a distance of ten miles where a coach can run the whole way. Mr Gould and I went out on this road for four miles to a place called Epsom . . . saw some nice cottages and fine gardens and two farms about ten acres each under cultivation in wheat and barley.' (Quoted in *Early Epsom,* 1972, p.1.)

This watercolour has been attributed by Roger Blackley (1983) to Mitford and dated *c.*1843. This artist draws with his brush and does not use defining pencil lines. Graduation of form is suggested by small patches of warm and cool colour, in particular by contrast of cold over warm brown, or by defining dark forms against white. Such colour or tone contrasts and the appearance of whites on the sea and in the foreground, made by abrading the paper with a sharp instrument, all support this attribution.

19 [*Album page* 41

Entrance to the Harbour, Auckland

[MITFORD, John Guise 1822-1854]

Unsigned [1843]
Watercolour, brown ink 161 x 244 mm
.23 mm cream wove paper
Title inscribed on Album page. On verso, in pencil, 'Entrance to the Harbour, Auckland.'

This view is apparently seen from high ground to the left of Grafton Gully. The Auckland City Art Gallery holds a large version of this subject, a watercolour by Guise Mitford presented in 1942 by Lt. Col. R. M. Rendel, a descendant of the Hobsons. Its view looks a little further up the Waitemata Harbour and distances the houses on the hilltop at the right rather more than the present picture. Its cloudy sky is more elaborate and more closely finished; the painting of the foreground and the gum arabic overlay all suggest that it is a later studio painting, while this Album watercolour seems to have been done on the spot. Light shines on and emphasises a cleared slope to the left where a fenced corner of the cemetery protects Governor Hobson's grave. Further along that ridge, overlooking the Waitemata, is Government House. Nearer, on the right, are the houses at the top of Grafton Gully. One of these was the home of William Connell, the first Postmaster-General. The flagstaff, mid distance, marks Mt Victoria. On the right rises the triple cone of Rangitoto; the flat island in the far distance is Tiritiri.

The present painting must have been done early in 1843, before Mitford took up his appointment in Russell. That time had elapsed since Governor Hobson's funeral in November 1842 is indicated by a paling fence which surrounds the grave. A more elaborate memorial replaced it in 1885, leaving the original base intact.

20 [*Album page* 43

[Auckland Harbour]

[MITFORD, John Guise 1822-1854]

Unsigned [?1844]
Grey watercolour 216 x 308 mm
.21 mm cream wove paper, no visible watermark

This painting is done from above Mechanics Bay, now Stanley Street, looking down over scrub to the backs of a row of small cottages. The houses on the cliff beyond mark the southern end of Official Bay. To the left a flag flies on Point Britomart, and on the high ground appear the Barracks, St Paul's and the business houses at the top of Shortland Crescent. Government House lies in the sheltered hollow to the left.

The buildings are more carefully drawn than in either of the previous views by Mitford, but the rolling landforms and small round-headed trees are similar. The sense of space, of air between landforms, is that of the painter of Plates **14** and **18.** There is a similar scratched surface on foreground foliage. The tall tree, the cabbage tree, and cabbage tree branches on the left of the painting are like those on the left foreground of 'Russell from Paihia . . .', Plate **14**. Mitford here draws a complete spire on St Paul's; while in Ashworth's view of Princes Street made in 1843 or January 1844, the spire is still unfinished. This painting may have been done after Mrs Hobson left; or artistic licence may have been used. The spire was not finally completed until March 1844.

21 [*Album page 45*

A Native Chief dressed in a Dog's Skin mat,/with a weapon called wahanoghi [wahangohi]

[MERRETT, Joseph Jenner 1816-1854]

Unsigned [*c.*1843]
Pencil, black ink, grey wash 236 x 167 mm
.20 mm cream wove paper
Title inscribed in brown ink on Album page. On l.r. corner a faint pencil inscription '. . . bunch of feathers . . .'

The chief stands in full dignity for his portrait. The full facial moko; the eight white-tipped feathers of the rare bird, huia; the dogskin cloak with its ruffled edge made also of dogskin; and the weapon he carries are all signs of the highest rank. This drawing has recognisable elements of Merrett's style: stylised curls and feathers, his placement of feet and awkward drawing of arm and hand.

G. F. Angas records similar splendid cloaks worn by chiefs in the Waikato:

> The most valuable type of cloak at the time of European contact was the kahu kurī, the dogskin cloak worn only by men of the highest social status. The kaupapa or foundation is woven in single-pair twining, each weft being placed as close as possible to, and touching, the previous one, resulting in a thick, dense and very strong fabric. The whole surface is then covered with narrow strips of dogskin, arranged into patterns according to the colour of the hair. The native dog or kurī, brought from Polynesia by the Maori, was a highly valued animal, the property of chiefs. The pure breed became extinct soon after early European contact, probably through cross-breeding, and the mongrel offspring became so common that the dog was no longer in demand for its skin and kahu kurī were made no more. (Pendergrast 1987, p.9)

The National Library conservator has reported: 'Between pages 44 and 45 there is a brown guard and rough edges of a removed cream page; it could be MS paper, torn when fairly old.'

22, 23 [*Album pages 48 and 49*

Letter from a New Zealand chief to Mrs Hobson on leaving/for England

HOETE [RIRIKAKARA], Wiremu [William JOWETT]

Signed by copyist 'Na tou hoa aroha, Na Wiremu Hoete'/'From your affectionate friend, William Jowett'. Putiki Maehi 27 1843/Putiki March 27th 1843.
Brown ink 358 x 258 mm (each)
.16 mm cream wove paper, watermark 'J. WHATMAN TURKEY MILL 1837' on p.49 of Album
Text and translation inscribed in brown ink on Album page. Heading inscribed in black ink, above text, in another hand.

Considerable trade was carried on between Auckland and the kainga at Putiki on Waiheke Island where Hoete lived. 'Wiremu Hoete' was the baptismal name of the writer, a rangatira of Ngati Paoa, Waiheke, who was respected by and well known to the settlers (see also pp.26, 27, 160). Missionaries were fond of bestowing the transliterated names of prominent English church people on their converts: this name honours William Jowett, one of three secretaries of the Church Missionary Society.

The signature 'Wiremu Hoete Ririkakara' is on the deed of sale of the Kohimarama block, 28 May 1841 (APL). It is in Hoete's own hand. Some of his letters are preserved in the Grey collection (APL) so we can presume he wrote rather than dictated this letter.

As the copyist has not been fully accurate in transcription, we give here a corrected printing with a modern translation and notes.

Pūtiki, Maehe 27, 1843.

E kui, e Mata[1] Kāwana,

Tēnā koe, koutou ko [ō] tamariki.

E kui, e Mata, tēnā koe, te kanohi[2] o tō mātou hoa. Ahakoa kua mate ia, ko tōna āhua kei a koe. Koia taku reta aroha i tuhituhi atu ai ki a koe, no te mea kua rongo au ki a Te Karaka, e hoki ana koe ki tōu kāinga. Koia taku reta poroporoaki ki a koe, ki te ritenga o tō mātou kāwana tino pai, ahakoa mate noa ia. Kāhore ana whakaaro hē ki a mātou, koia ka nui ai tō mātou aroha ki a ia, ki a koe, ki āu tamariki hoki.

E kui, e Mata Kāwana, tēnā koe. Haere ra, e kui, ki tōu kāinga. Kāwhakina[3] atu ra

1. Wives of missionaries and other Europeans of standing were often called *Mata* (Mother) by the Maori. This is not the usual Maori word for mother, but a transliteration of the English word.
2. *Kanohi,* 'eye, face', i.e. the presence of the other person, his or her representative (cf. *māngai,* 'mouth', i.e. mouthpiece).
3. The original translator has interpreted this as *ka whākina,* 'will be acknowledged'. However, *kāwhakina,* 'taken away', balances very well with *waiho,* 'left behind'. Either reading would be possible here.

tō kōrua nei āhua pai ko tōu rangatira; waiho ra mātou i konei mihi kau ai ki ō kōrua nei haerenga.

Tēnei anō taku waiata aroha kei a koe, kei tō mātou nei hoa atawhai,

'Ō tahuritanga, he mihi kau iho'.[4]

E kui, te tikanga o tēnā kupu waiata aroha, mo kōrua ko tōu hoa: ngaro ana koe, ngaro ana a te kāwana, ko [tō] kōrua nei haerenga, waiho kau iho hei mihi ma mātou.

E kui, haere ra, e te hoa aroha o ngā rangatira o Niu Tīreni. Kāwhakina atu ra te kuru pounamu.[5] Heoi anō taku poroporoaki aroha ki a koe. Haere ra, e kui, ki tōu kāinga. Kāhore he kupu ki a koe; haere ra e taku reta aroha ki a Mata Kāwana.

Na tōu hoa aroha,

Na Wīremu Hoete.

Putiki, March 27th, 1843.

O Lady, Mother Governor,

Greetings to you and your children.

Lady, Mother, greetings to you, the representative of our friend. Although he is dead, his likeness lives in you. The reason I am writing my loving letter to you is because I have heard from Mr [George] Clarke that you are returning to your home. This is the reason for my farewell letter to you, because you are just like our good governor, even though he has died. He never bore us any ill will, and so we feel great love for him, for you, and for your children.

Lady, Mother Governor, greetings. We wish you well, lady, as you go to your home. Your kind presence and that of your husband is borne away, leaving us here alone to mourn your departure.

This is my song of love to you and to our kind friend:

'As you turn away, all I can do is grieve.'

Lady, the meaning of the words of this love song, which is for you and your husband, is that you are gone, the governor is gone, and your going leaves us behind with nothing but our grief.

Lady, farewell, loving friend of the chiefs of New Zealand. The greenstone ornament is borne away. So this is my loving farewell message to you. Good wishes, lady, as you go to your home. I have no more words to say to you, so go, my loving letter, to Mother Governor.

From your loving friend,

Wiremu Hoete.

4. It was quite usual to quote portions of waiata, often very long portions, in Maori letters. Frequently only the recipient of the letter recognised the hidden meaning behind the words. Wiremu Hoete here points out that he is quoting from a *waiata aroha*, and makes some attempt to explain its meaning to his Pakeha friend.

5. The original translator has obviously had difficulty with this sentence, which is translated as 'you will not be forgotten'. As in the sentence commented on in note 3, this could be interpreted in two ways, as *ka whākina* or *kāwhakina*. The words may well come from a *waiata tangi* (lament), as *kuru pounamu* is frequently used in such waiata as an honorific term for a person who has just died.

24, 25 [*Album page 55, top and bottom*

Ko te Waha o te Papa. Wakano (left) **Kino Kino. Ohuia** (right)

[?MERRETT, Joseph Jenner 1816-1854]

Unsigned [1843]
Pencil (top) 182 x 141 mm
(bottom) 183 x 143 mm
.20 mm cream wove paper, no visible watermark
Title inscribed in ink on l.l. of each drawing and place l.r.

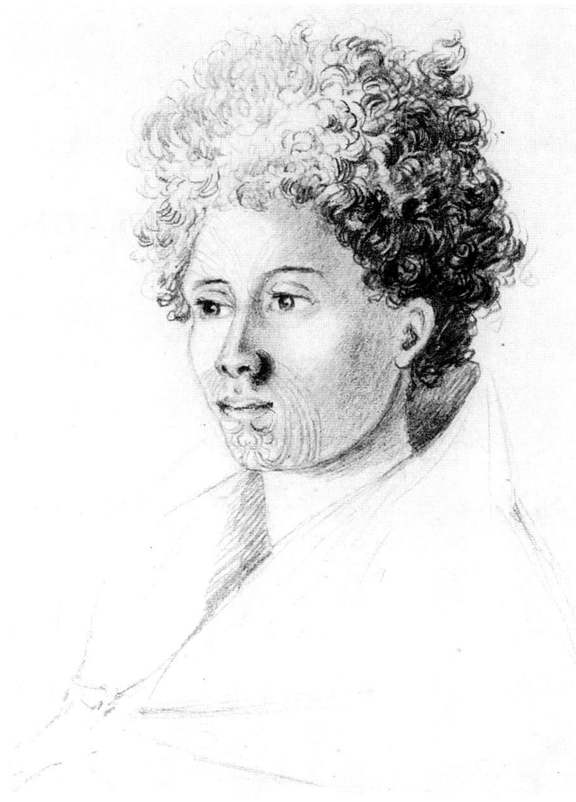

[MERRETT] *Ko te Waha te Papa* 1841, pencil, 170 x 120 mm
BL ADD. MS 19953. p.34 plate 90

These drawings, the most beautiful and sensitive portraits in the Album, are also two of its most puzzling. The well-constructed drawing of the heads and an assured elegance of style lifted these individual faces above the generalised prettiness of many figure paintings by Merrett. If they were done by Merrett it would seem that, for him, pencil was a more sensitive medium than watercolour and ink.

'Ko te Waha o te Papa' means 'the mouthpiece of the father', perhaps indicating that the son was representing him; 'Te Waha o te Papa' could also have been bestowed as his name. The Grey Album has a closely related drawing: p.34 plate 90, also inscribed l.r. 'Ko te Waha te Papa'. 'Wakano' is presumed to be a place name, but there was a chief of that name in the Wairarapa who could be referred to.

'Kino Kino' taken literally means 'Naughty or bad', a phrase which could have been used affectionately; or could have been given to a child to commemorate some disaster or misfortune occurring at the time of birth. A. D. Best reports that it was this phrase — 'the "Kino" of his Daughter' — that Te Waru used to describe the crime by which his daughter had avenged her brother's death (1966, p.298). It seems possible that Mrs Hobson was given this strong drawing as a reminder of the dramatic moment when a chief offered his daughter to be tried by British law. Best also reported, 'Mr Merrett got a sketch of the scene'. An ink drawing (page 41 plate 114) in the Grey Album is entitled 'Ewaru's accusation of his daughter before Captn. Symonds'. In this scene an old chief wearing huia feathers is lying watching another orate. In the lithograph by L. Haghe after J. J. Merrett, published as frontispiece to E. Dieffenbach's *Travels in New Zealand,* 1843, two European men stand listening on the left. The young daughter standing with head bent wears her hair cut in a mission-influenced hairstyle similar to that of 'Kino Kino', suggesting the possibility that she could be the same person.

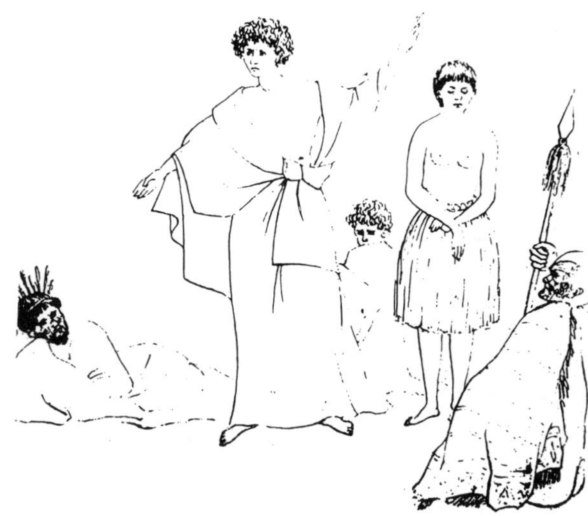

[MERRETT] *Erawu's* [*Te Waru's*] *accusation of his daughter before Captn. Symonds* 26 April 1841, ink, 170 x 140 mm
BL print from Micro MS 19953 p.41 plate 114

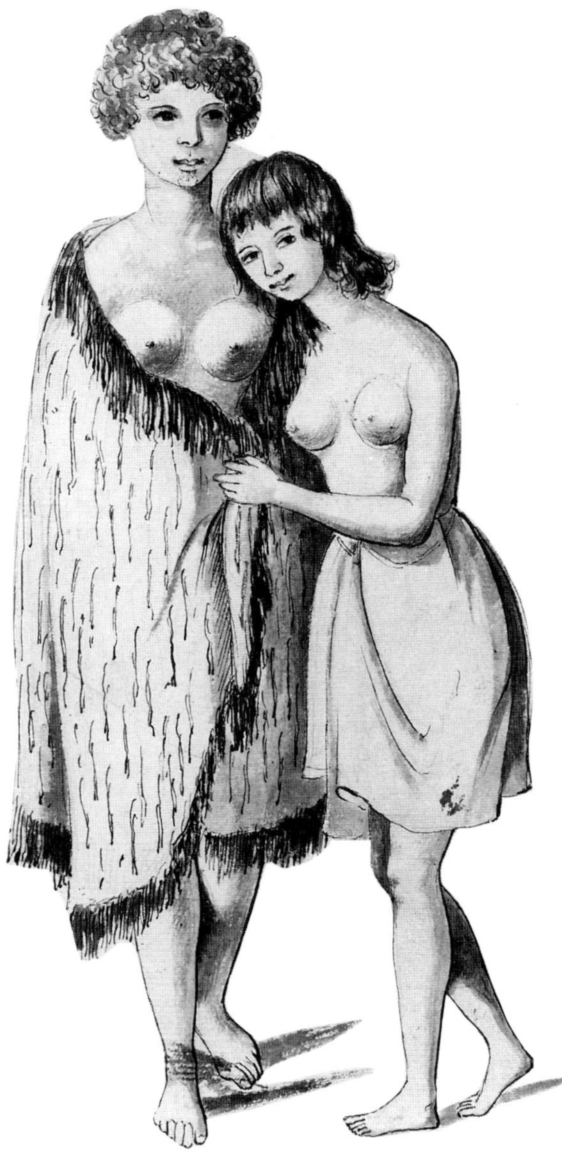

[MERRETT] [*Two Maori girls*], ink and wash, 240 x 110 mm
BL ADD. MS 19953 p.51 plate 152

26 [*Album page* 57

[Two Maori Girls]

[MERRETT, Joseph Jenner 1816-1854]

Unsigned [1842 or 1843 from an earlier drawing]
Pencil, watercolour 355 x 248 mm
.21 mm cream wove paper, no visible watermark

This warm and delightful painting has all the hallmarks of Merrett's style: his drawing of hands, feet, breasts, large expressive eyes, and tenderness of gesture which can be seen in 'A group of New Zealanders', Plate **11.** The original drawing for this painting is in the Grey Album (p.51 plate 152). Another drawing of the same two girls (p.62 plate 181) is entitled 'Two girls at Maraunui', and indicates a location. The taller girl wears the fringed and tagged cloak, the korowai-ngore, the smaller girl a waist kilt of European fabric.

27 [*Album page* 59

View on the lake of Rotorua. The island of/Mo Koia [Mokoia] in the Centre of the Lake

[MERRETT, Joseph Jenner 1816-1854]

Unsigned [*c.*1843 from an earlier drawing]
Black ink, grey wash 167 x 250 mm
.18 mm cream wove paper, no visible watermark
Inscribed in black ink on Album page

This view is from the east side of the lake where the Te Ngae mission was situated. Mokoia is the inhabited island on the right; behind lies Ngongotaha mountain. The original drawing suggests a low promontory where in the finished drawing there appears to be a small island. This is probably Kawaha Point.

Stylistically, this drawing had to be considered the work of either John Guise Mitford or Joseph Jenner Merrett. Comparison with the former's painting [Mokoia from Ohinemutu, Lake Rotorua], 1845, from a private collection shows the fundamental difference between Mitford's painterly, unoutlined, colour construction and this ink drawing. An on-the-spot outline drawing of 'the Lake of Rotorua' in the Grey Album (p.118 plate 288) confirms the attribution to Merrett.

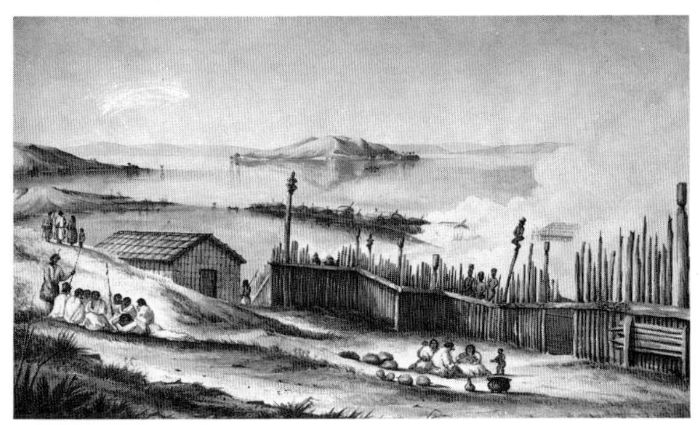

MITFORD [*Mokoia from Ohinemutu, Lake Rotorua*]
1845, watercolour
PRIVATE COLLECTION

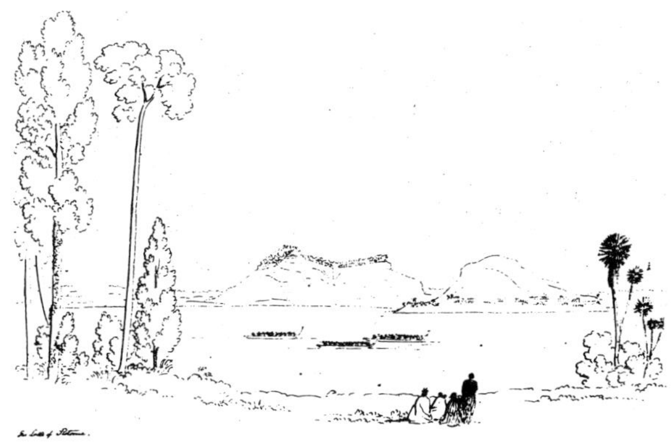

[MERRETT] *The Lake of Rotorua,* pen and wash,
200 x 300 mm
BL ADD. MS 19953 p.118 plate 288

The nature of Merrett's drawings in the Grey and Hobson Albums reveals his intention to make a record of Maori life. In this drawing, Merrett shows on the left foreground figures performing a powhiri, or welcome to visitors. Their leader is making his oration in a typical position, not facing the newcomers but with his shoulder turned towards them as he walks to and fro, a position ready for defence in case all is not as it should be. Those behind him are also sitting sideways. The standing figures in the centre, holding spears, are ready to reply. The artist has telescoped the different events so that some of the manuhiri (visitors) are sitting down, as they would do when the welcome was over. On the right, a meal is being prepared. (See also p.151.)

28 [*Album page 51*

"And the Wilderness shall become the fruitful Field"

JOHNSON, John 1794-1848

Signed l.r. 'J. J. 1843'
Sepia wash, brown ink 162 x 242 mm
.17 mm white wove paper, no visible watermark
Title inscribed in brown ink on Album page

John Johnson is one of only three contributors to sign his work. He was well known in Auckland for his delight in gardening and his hope for the horticultural future of Auckland; the quotation from Isaiah is appropriate from one of the founding members of the Church of Scotland in Auckland. In 1843 he was made the first President of the Auckland Agricultural and Horticultural Society. This drawing is of his own house and garden below Government House looking towards Official Bay. It shows grape vines on the slope below the house and other plants climbing up the verandah posts; fruit trees and weeping willow are established. The large-leaved plant in the foreground is a pumpkin or gourd.

Johnson's skill as a gardener is documented by a newspaper report only fifteen months after the first tents were pitched. 'A Looker On' wrote: 'Dr Johnson's and Mr Leach's gardens do certainly reflect much to the credit of their industrious proprietors, and fully demonstrate what our soil and climate can contribute to produce. It is the opinion of these gentlemen that the whole year round, vegetables of every description can be grown.' In 1843 Johnson harvested barley with a yield of 102 bushels to the acre, and in the last year of his life he gave lectures on cultivating the vine.

29 [*Album page* 73

"And the solitary places shall be made glad"

[JOHNSON, John 1794-1848]

Unsigned [1843]
Sepia watercolour, brown ink 199 x 278 mm
.17 mm cream wove paper, no visible watermark
Title inscribed in brown ink on Album page

The garden of this house runs down to Judges Bay, the only bay depicted in the Album which has not since been reclaimed.

Dr Johnson here records for Mrs Hobson the house of another close friend, the Attorney-General William Swainson. This view from the beach near to Parnell Point shows part of a post-and-rail garden fence and small shrubs on a lawn. Lady Martin, wife of Judge Martin from whom the bay takes its name, gave a charming description of her first impression of this bay: 'The blue water lay like a lake below. There was a strip of white shelly beach. The little bay was shut in by sandstone cliffs, and these were overhung by huge forest-trees. A high bank above our garden had one or two tall flax-bushes growing on it, and many ferns. The tall leaves of the flax glittered in the sunlight. To a Londoner born and bred this new home seemed like fairyland.' (Martin 1884, pp. 3-4.)

30 [*Album page* 69

Wellington from the 'London'

CONNELL, B. (unidentified)

Signed l.r. 'B. Connell' [1840]
Pencil 140 x 223 mm
.33 mm cream wove paper, no visible watermark
Title inscribed in black ink on Album page. On verso, in pencil, 'Wellington from the London'

With this picture we are given the name of the artist, but of his or her identity we are not sure. The ship *London* arrived in Wellington on 12 December 1840, and the shipping registers at the National Archives list among the cabin passengers 'Connell, William, wife, three children'. They may have spent some time in Wellington. In 1841 Connell was appointed Postmaster-General at Auckland and in October the same year became Registrar of Records in the Colonial Secretary's department. His signature on public documents is 'William Connell' and resembles in slope and fluency the signature 'B. Connell' on two of these drawings. But these drawings are signed in two different ways. This and Plate **38** have a flowing signature; 'Te Aro Flat', Plate **39**, has a more upright printed signature. It is not likely that William Connell would have used two different forms and styles. Perhaps William signed for drawings contributed by a relative. His wife, Isabella, may have been the artist, since that name was commonly shortened to 'Bella'.

31 [*Album page* 71

Entrance to the Harbour Manukao [Manukau] from Puponga Head

[?JOHNSON, John 1794-1848]

Unsigned [?1841]
Sepia watercolour, brown ink 196 x 282 mm
.17 mm cream wove paper, no visible watermark
Title inscribed in black ink on Album page. On verso, in pencil: 'View of the entrance to the Harbour of Manukao from Puponga Head' inscribed above a sketch map, in ink and pencil, of part of Manukau Harbour

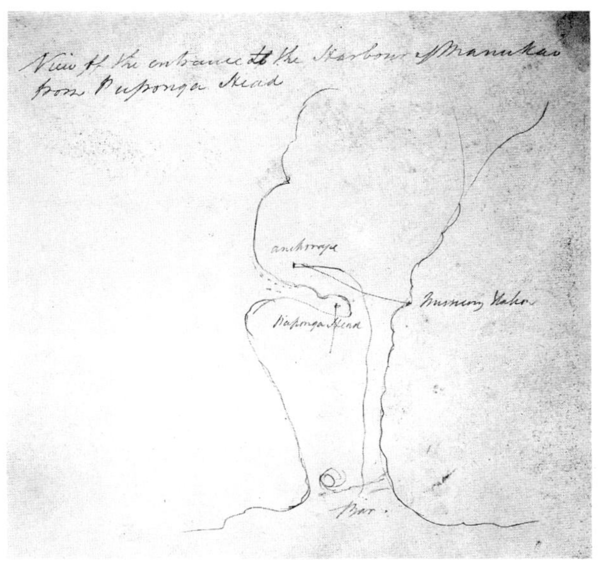

[?JOHNSON] *View of the entrance to the Harbour Manukao from Puponga Head* (showing Puponga Head, the position of the ship's anchorage and that of the Mission Station at Orua Bay), pencil, 196 x 282 mm

This drawing gives a wide view of the Manukau Harbour on Auckland's west coast where Captain William Cornwallis Symonds, a close friend of William and Eliza Hobson, was drowned. To the north of the entrance we are shown the prominent rock Paratutai and the peaks rising from it towards Mt Donald McLean. This harbour entrance is still considered dangerous. Edward Shortland described the harbour in his journal, [4] April 1842, as 'the fabled residence of a tanewha or sea god who is supposed by the natives to take great pleasure in upsetting their canoes. . . . The channel is about [a] mile in breadth. The north shore is very rugged and precipitous, the distant hills covered in timber . . . a bar of breakers very terrific in appearance extends quite across the mouth.'

While this drawing cannot be positively attributed, both style and medium resemble those of Plates **28** and **29**. The handwriting on the verso is like John Johnson's. It is not by Merrett nor is it like Ashworth's view of the Manukau. Neither Ashworth nor Mitford was in Auckland in 1841 when Captain Symonds was drowned. It was most likely to have been done by a mutual friend who wished to recall for Mrs Hobson the place where this tragedy happened on 23 November 1841 (see p.18). The pencil map on the verso shows this clearly, with the sand bar at the harbour entrance and the anchorage of the *Brilliant* behind Puponga Head. A line is drawn from this anchorage to the Mission Station at Orua Bay towards which Symonds's canoe was headed.

32 [*Album page* 78

Rangi Kawauw

[MERRETT, Joseph Jenner 1816-1854] poem;
[SHORTLAND, Edward 1812-1893] annotations

Unsigned [1842-1843]
Brown ink 360 x 260 mm, entire page adhered to guard
.19 mm cream wove paper, no visible watermark
Text of poem and annotations in same hand

Part of this poem (see Plate **17**) was written on the verso of Merrett's 'A Hot Spring in the Warm Lake of Rotomahana'. From other published poems under the pseudonym 'Crayon' we can identify the writer as Joseph Merrett; the annotations were written by Edward Shortland.

Although Merrett spoke Maori, his spelling of the language was eccentric. 'Kawauw' may well have been Merrett's attempt to spell 'Kōa', and the title, a shortening of his wife's name Rangitetaea Kōa, would be written to the woman whose charms these verses extol and whose portrait is on the following page (see also Plate **12**).

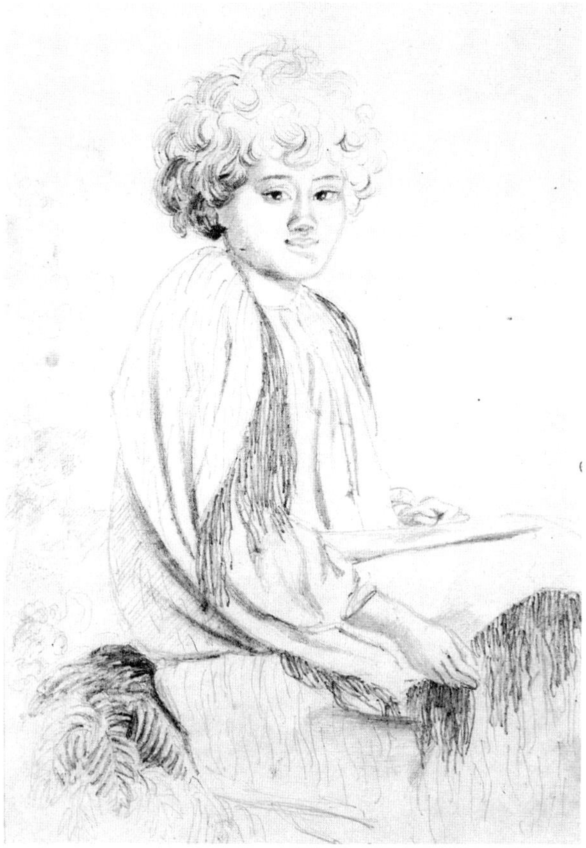

[MERRETT] *Original drawing for Rangi Kawauw*
[1842], pencil, 170 x 120 mm
BL ADD. MS 19953 p.65 plate 186

33 [*Album page* 79

[Rangi Kawauw]

[MERRETT, Joseph Jenner 1816-1854]

Unsigned [1842-1843]
Pencil, watercolour 171 x 129 mm
.70 mm cream wove paper
Title inscribed in brown ink on Album page above an embossed border

A letter from the Rev. Morgan to Archdeacon Brown, 1 May 1843 (A. N. Brown Papers ATL Micro MS 756), passes on a parishioner's problem. A Mr Merrett had been living with a young Maori woman: she had become pregnant. Should they marry? They did. The name of Joseph Merrett's wife is given in Land Court Records and on the death certificate of their daughter Ani Gage. It was Rangitetaea Kōa.

Shares in a small block of land at Te Akau, north of the Raglan Harbour, were held by descendants of Merrett under the name of 'Rangitetaea' until their sale in 1935 (Native Land Court records; Whangape block 75 B3).

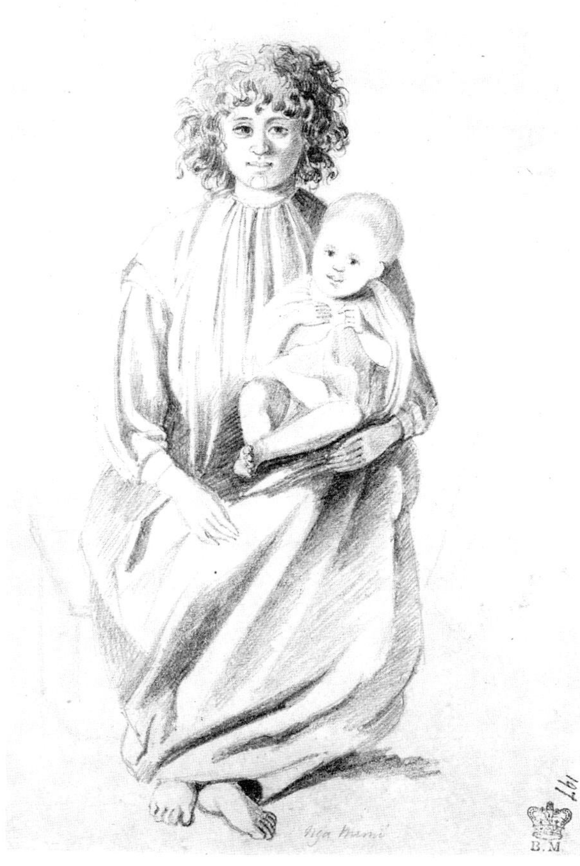

[MERRETT] [*Drawing of Merrett's wife and child, 1843*], pencil, 170 x 120 mm
BL ADD. MS 19953 p.69 plate 197

In Plate **12** we have seen a young woman reading while she nurses her baby; she could also be 'Rangi Kawauw', although the young woman here appears younger. She wears a similar korowai-ngore (pompom cloak). She has a book or paper on her knee and her loose cloak covers a long-sleeved European dress. Only her lips appear to be tattooed which may indicate that she is still very young: or her chin moko may simply have been omitted. The poem Merrett wrote to his wife refers to her facial decoration, and a watercolour in the British Library signed 'J. Merrett 1845' shows moko on lips and chin of an older standing figure (see previous page). It is inscribed 'Rangitetahi a young woman of the tribe of Ngati Koura' — this being one of the Waikato hapu located at Kihikihi and Whatawhata. (It can be assumed that 'Rangitetahi' should be 'Rangitetaea' and identifies a later portrait of Mrs Merrett.)

The Grey Album also holds the original pencil drawing for this Rangi Kawauw painting (p.65 plate 186): only a background of sky has been added. On p.69 plate 197 we see Merrett's wife again. She sits facing us wearing the same long-sleeved gown. There is a suggestion of moko on the chin. And the small child she holds shows the eccentricities of Merrett's style of figure drawing in a curious elongation of the head above the eyes. The inscription 'nga mimi' or 'little wet-bottom' might well be an exasperated endearment for Joseph and Rangitetaea Merrett's first child, Ani, who was born in 1843.

34, 35, 36, 37 [*Album pages 81-84*

"Maori Songs." [A collection of rurîruri, haka, puha, ngeri, and waiata, with comment and notes]

[SHORTLAND, Edward 1812-1893]

Unsigned [1842-1843]
Brown ink 360 x 260 mm
.20 mm ivory wove paper, no visible watermark
Inscribed on Album page

Ruriruri or Haka, corrected transcription:

Ko tō tinana ki Waitematā,
Ko tō wairua[1] i haere mai, i whakaoho i taku moe — ī.

E hoa mā, puritia mai taku huia,
Kia hoki mai te tau[2] o taku manawa kapakapa.

1. In Maori poetry the spirit is often said to wander away from the body as it lies asleep.
2. The idea that the heart has strings which vibrate under the influence of strong emotion is also found in English poetry. *Huia* and *tau* are just two of the many terms used in waiata to refer to the beloved.

Translation:

Your body is at Waitemata,
Your spirit came back here, and woke me from my sleep.

O friends, keep hold of my huia,
So that my beating heart-string may return to me.

Today we usually think of the haka as a war-dance, but in former times the term was used in a broader sense to mean a song accompanied by gestures, expressive of many different emotions. *Ruriruri* are also known as *pao,* and are often described as couplets, although they sometimes had more than two lines. Since in pre-European times Maori songs were never written down, the only way of ascertaining line division is through the music. Shortland's published version (1856, pp.170-2) has many more verses, of varying lengths. As these songs were usually composed extempore, standard verses such as these would be interspersed with verses giving a witty commentary on the events and personalities of the moment (see Markham 1963, pp.50-51).

Puha or Ngeri:

Kia kūtia, au, au,
Kia wherahia, au, au,
Kia rere[3] atu te kekeno ki tawhiti titiro mai [ai], āe, āe, āe.[4]

3. Comparison of Shortland's published translation of this *ngeri* (1856, p.172) with this version and his commentaries shows that *kia rere* both describes the seal's actions and gives the signal to the dancers to 'leap up'.

4. *Āe* means 'yes' but at the same time imitates the seal's bark, echoing the *au, au* of the previous two lines. The *ai* added in square brackets is found in published versions of the *ngeri,* and is required by the syntax of the sentence.

Translation:

Close up, *au, au,*
Open out, *au, au,*
So that the seal may flee far off and look back this way, aye, aye, aye.

As noted, the chant is very old and several variants are consequently found. An interesting one is quoted by Robin Winks (1953, p.244), where the word *kekeno* is replaced by *Kāwana,* meaning the government soldiers. Williams's *Dictionary* gives *kekeno* as a figurative word for a chief, in this case the enemy chief. Te Rangihiroa comments that 'the seal, which is rare in northern waters, was probably introduced to show how utter the flight of the enemy would be' (Buck 1970, p.392).

Detailed instructions on the performance of this *ngeri* are given in Buck (ibid.) and in Armstrong (1964, p.163).

Waiata:

Haere ra e koro — ē — i tōu tira, ko koe anake,
Kia whakairia koe ki runga i Waiwhetū.
Āe, kata ra, e koro — ē, kei hoki wawe ō koutou waewae.

Kore nei aku toto te inu mai ai koe,
Kua pakihi au i nui ōu rangi ra — ī.

Ma wai e ranga tōu mate i te ao?
Ma te pō tū mai i runga i Tirohanga?
Ma te pō taka mai i runga o Kaihinu?
Āe, engari rāia, tēnei, e hika — ē.

Tēnei ōu roro, ko te kōwhatu e tū ki te ahi kai,
Kia reka iho ai taku kainga iho — ī.

Translation:

Go, sir, alone on your journey,
So that you may be suspended above Waiwhetu.
Yes, laugh on, sir, and do not let your feet return too quickly.

I have no more blood for you to drink,
I have dried up over countless days because of you.

Who will avenge your death in this world?
Will it be the mist hanging over Tirohanga?
Will it be the mist settling over Kaihinu?
Yes, but this will be all there is, my friend.

Here are your brains, they are the stone beside the cooking fire,
And may they taste sweet as I eat them.

I tou tira, ko koe anake, literally 'with your travelling party, you alone', is a paradoxical expression, contrasting the warrior's expeditions while alive and surrounded by companions with the lonely journey he makes after death. According to traditional Maori thought, the soul travels to the far north to leap off the cliffs at Te Reinga and join the company of the dead in the underworld.

Whakairia, kata. According to Elsdon Best (1905, pp.183-4) the heads of either friends or enemies could be preserved and set up on a stake, but they were treated differently. The heads of friends and relatives were cried over and songs were sung in their honour, while those of enemies were subjected to taunts and indignities. As for the actual process of preservation, 'the Maori was very particular in preserving the heads of his relatives to render them sightly. . . . He liked to see the lips closed so that the teeth were not exposed. He was not so particular with the heads of his enemies.' (See also Angas 1847, p.48 and Robley 1896, pp.146-7.) As the head referred to in this waiata has been carried off by the enemy, the singer must be imagining the treatment it is receiving.

Pakihi, translated by Shortland as 'exhausted', literally means 'dried up'. The singer is said to have no blood left after so many days of letting it flow in grief. He or she is paying tribute to the dead person: the greater the flow of blood, the greater the mana of the person mourned.

I nui o rangi ra is a formulaic phrase often found in waiata, usually referring to the happier days now past (e.g. Ngata and Te Hurinui 1961, no. 118, line 12 and no. 130, line 2). By substituting the possessive pronoun *ōu* for the usual preposition *o*, the poet personalises the phrase, making it 'your days', that is, 'the days spent mourning for you'.

Ma wai. The copyist has confused the *ma* and *mo* forms: the first three lines in this section should all begin *ma*, and as the published version shows, all three are in the form of questions. Although Shortland has translated *ranga* as 'proclaim' here and as 'sing' in his published version (1856, p.182), his note to the latter reveals what the line really means: 'the speaker asks who will avenge the death of the chief referred to.' This call for vengeance is a very common theme in *waiata tangi* or laments for the dead. It may take the form of a direct exhortation to a particular person or group, or may be made indirectly, in words which shame or goad the hearers into action. Here the singer seems to be giving a subtle hint to the tribes who are living nearby (at Tirohanga and Kaihinu) that their aid is needed. The word used here for mist, *pō*, usually means night, but is found with the same meaning (mist as a symbol for avenging tribes) in a *waiata tangi* from a neighbouring area (McLean and Orbell 1975, song 22, line 3).

Āe, engari rāia, tenei, e hika — ē, 'Yes, but that will be all there is, my friend', is no doubt ironic in tone. The singer does not intend the matter to rest there, but expects vengeance to be taken.

Tēnei ōu roro, ko te kōwhatu. Shortland's translation 'May your brain be like the stone' ('O that this were your brain!' in his published version) does not quite mirror the directness of the expression in Maori, where the poet says that the brains actually *are* the cooking stone. Maori poetry often links ideas directly in this way, and in this case it makes the curse against Taraia even more forceful.

The incident Shortland refers to here is well described by Thomson (1859, v.2, pp.53-57). Ngati Tamatera of Thames and Ngai Te Rangi of Tauranga had been intermittently at war for generations. In 1842 Taraia, who lived at Pura near Thames, received fresh insults in a new form — by letter. With forty picked warriors he travelled up the Waihou River and over the Kaimai Ranges to take the small pa Engaro or Onare near Katikati by surprise; an easy task because most of the people were absent at a tangi. Those in the pa were killed or taken off as slaves. The bodies of the rangatira Whanake and Reko were cooked and eaten, and the uneaten portions, including the heads, were carried away. Whanake's people were Christians and as the survivors took refuge at the Te Papa Mission, Tauranga, the story quickly became known. It was Wiremu Hoete of Waiheke who responded to the Governor's request for information. Taraia however insisted that the Governor had no right to interfere in a purely Maori quarrel and won his point. In any case there was no force available to arrest him.

A slightly different version of this waiata has been published by Barry Mitcalfe (1961, pp.34-35, and 1974, pp.74-75), with his own translation and a note which states: 'This taunt was sung to the impaled head of one of the chiefs of Ngati Ira, the original tribe of Wellington-Hutt Valley, displaced by Ngati Tama in the 1820s.' The composer is given as Paenga-Huru of Ngati Tama (Port Nicholson) and the source as Hamiora Raumati of Urenui in Taranaki. When consulted, Mitcalfe had no additional information. It should be noted that the head chief of Ngati Ira in the 1820s was also called Whanake, and that he and Paenga-Huru took part in various battles at that time (*JPS*, v.10, pp.154-6; 18, pp.171-3; 19, pp.7-9). The place names in the waiata are associated with both the Hutt Valley (Waiwhetu) and the Bay of Plenty (Tirohanga and Kaihinu), although all three names are also found in other areas. Shortland was a member of the official party investigating the deaths of the two chiefs, and must have heard the waiata at that time. His title for the original version is 'Waiata mo Whanake, mo Te Paitui', the latter presumably being an alternative name for the chief called Reko by Thomson.

37 [*Album page* 84

Major Richmond's Cottage Auckland

ARTIST UNKNOWN [?MASON, William or JOHNSON, John]

Unsigned [1843]
Black ink 146 x 197 mm
.22 mm cream wove paper, no visible watermark
Title inscribed in brown ink on Album page

This timber cottage was brought, prefabricated, from the Bay of Islands by William Mason, the first Superintendent of Works. He and the interpreter Edward Marsh Williams claimed to be the first to sleep under a timber roof in Auckland. The cottage overlooked Official Bay.

On 10 October 1840 Mason reported to Hobson that he had 'the store ready for the reception of dry goods on the evening of Thursday 24th Sept and on the 25th the *Platina* and *Anna Watson* began discharging cases. . . . On Monday 26th commenced the 4 roomed house with 7 men, and having completed the framed sides on the evening of the 29th divided force and commenced Capt Symonds' house on morning of 29th, Dr Johnson's on Monday the 5th of October & Capt Rough's on the 7th inst all of which I hope to have completed as far as can be without boards tonight.' (See Stacpoole 1971, pp.30-31. The quotation is from the National Archives I.A.1, 40/589.)

The second occupant of the cottage was Dr William Davies, Medical Officer. Matthew Richmond (1801-1887) was the third occupant. Major Richmond was with his regiment in New South Wales when in June 1840 he was appointed by Governor Gipps to be one of three commissioners to examine land claims in New Zealand.

38, 39 [*Album page 87, top and bottom*

Kaiwarra Warra [Kaiwharawhara] from the Petoni [Petone] Road, Wellington (left)
'Te Aro' Flat, Wellington (right)

CONNELL, B.

Signed l.r. B. Connell [1840]
Pencil (top) 155 x 234 mm
(bottom) 153 x 237 mm
.22 mm cream wove paper, no visible watermark
Titles inscribed in brown ink on Album paper

This artist has a signature but no certain identity (see p. 31). The name of the place depicted in Plate **38** has been recorded as Kaiwharra, Kaiwarra and Kaiwarawara. Its form was eventually settled by the Geographic Board Act, 1946, when railway station, post office, village, stream and hill were all given the one name, Kaiwharawhara, meaning 'to eat the fruit of the *astelia,* a plant which grows in the forks of forest trees' (Cowan 1936, p.21). The name Petone also had a variety of forms which included Petoni, Pito o te one and Pito-one. Cowan (ibid.) gives the form Petone as a corruption of Pito-one, meaning 'the far end of a sandy beach', as originally referring to the village of the Ngati Awa at the western end of the long north beach of Wellington Harbour.

The Alexander Turnbull Library holds an unsigned watercolour showing Te Aro Flat and the grouped shipping, which must have been copied from, or painted from the same viewpoint as Plate **39.**

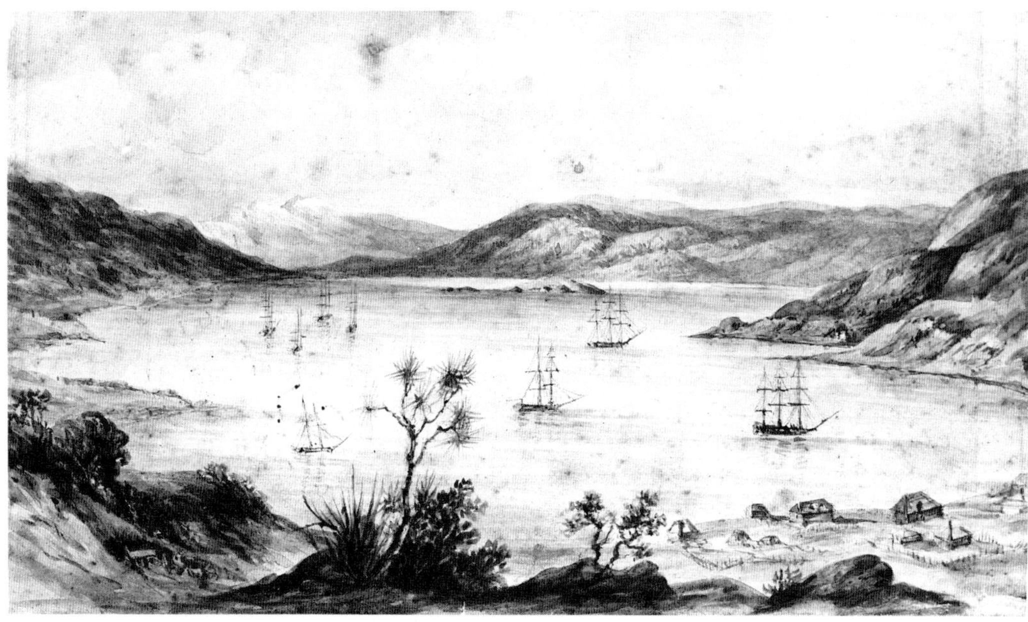

[CONNELL] [*Wellington harbour from hill behind Te Aro Flat.* 1842], watercolour, 138 x 220 mm
ATL A50/21

[Some Maori proverbs]

[SHORTLAND, Edward 1812-1893]

Unsigned [1843]
Brown ink, full page 358 x 256 mm
.20 mm ivory wove paper, no visible watermark
Text inscribed on two pages of the Album

Ruru [for *Rauru*] *kī tahi:* 'Rauru of a single word'. Proverbs connected with particular tribes can take on different shades of meaning depending on the speaker and the context. Shortland gives two possible interpretations of this saying, the explanation in the Album stressing Rauru's strong leadership and the other (1856, pp.31-32) his dependability: 'It is laudatory of their [his descendants'] good faith, signifying that they imitate the example of their ancestor Rauru, who had a reputation for doing always what he said he would do.' Although Rauru appears in many genealogies as either the son or the grandson of Toi, nothing much is known about him apart from the few shreds of information conveyed by proverbs, another of which (Grey 1857, p.75; see also p.55) connects him with the art of carving. There is also a tradition recorded by Hammond (1894, p.105) which relates that he commanded the Mataatua canoe and brought the taro plant from Hawaiki to Aotearoa.

Te uri o Te Matakapu (usually spelt *Tamatekapua*). The meaning of the proverb is made explicit in the expanded version quoted by Grey: 'Nga uri o Tama whanako roa ki te aha, ki te aha. The descendants of Tamate-kapua, have ever been stealing something or the other' (Grey 1857, p.78). Tamatekapua was the captain of the Arawa canoe, and his deeds included stealing fruit from Uenuku's tree, abducting the tohunga Ngatoroirangi, and seducing the latter's wife (Grey 1885, pp.76-81 and 85-93, English version; pp. 65-69 and 72-79, Maori version). As the context shows, these were not mere gratuitous acts but were performed to increase Tama's mana and advance the interests of his family and tribe. His descendants therefore take a justifiable pride in their famous ancestor.

He harihari kai:

He aha, he aha he kai ma tāua?
He pipi, he aruhe: ko te aka̧ o tūwhenua.
Ko te kai e ora ai te tangata.
Mātoetoe ana te arero i te mitikanga,
Me he arero kurī — au!

Translation (Food-bearing chant):

What, what will be our food?
Pipis, fernroot: the root that grows throughout the land.
This is the food which will keep a person alive.
The tongue grows rough from sucking it,
Like a dog's tongue — *au*!

Grey (1853, p.141) calls this 'He tau mo te kaikore', 'a song for when there is a lack of food'. It is true that fernroot, which grows everywhere and could serve where all else failed, does not seem particularly appropriate for a feast, but it would be only one of a great variety of dishes set before the guests, each dish being brought in to the accompaniment of its own special chant, as described by Potts (1882, p.17ff.). Songs such as these were often ironic in tone, the hosts teasing their guests by naming one type of food and providing another (see Best 1976, p.97, where the guests are told that they will be given only sandflies to eat, and McLean and Orbell 1975, pp.302 and 304). Williams says that *te aka o tūwhenua* is 'a proverbial expression for fernroot'. The word *au* at the end imitates the sound of a dog's bark. No doubt the singers also performed suitable dog-like actions as they brought in the food.

Proverbs

E mōkai tupunga rua, kawe ake, kawe iho. The translation chosen by Shortland for his published version of this proverb, 'O slave of two growths, shooting up, sinking down' (Shortland 1856, p.197), gives *mōkai* its primary meaning, which expresses better the idea of the inescapability of old age and death.

He hōhonu kakī, pāpaku uaua. Shortland (1856, p.201) gives the moral of this proverb as 'A word to a voracious, but lazy fellow'. Grey's translation (1857, p.31) is 'A fathomless throat, but no industry; a monster's appetite, but no perseverance in labour'.

Maori proverbs, like their English counterparts, often have a balanced structure, words of contrasting meaning being set in opposition to each other: *ake* and *iho* in the first proverb, *hōhonu* and *pāpaku* in the second. The unusual position of the adjectives (which usually follow their noun) also makes the second proverb memorable.

42 [*Album page* 85

The Raupo Cottage/of the Rev^{d} Mr Maunsell, Maratai [Maraetai], Waikato

JOHNSON, John 1794-1848

Signed l.l. 'J. J. 1845'
Black ink, grey wash image 54 x 102 mm on embossed paper 183 x 226 mm
.20 mm light mustard-coloured paper with embossed frame for watercolour
Title inscribed in black ink on coloured paper of item

The Rev. Dr Robert Maunsell, LL.D., missionary at Maraetai, Port Waikato, made his cottage a welcome resting place for travellers. The Maunsells lived in this raupo (bulrush) cottage from 1838 to 1843. It was superseded by a six-roomed weatherboard house which, after only three weeks' occupation, was burned down, and with it the extensive work the missionary had already done on his translation of the Old Testament. It all had to be done again.

Maunsell and his wife were hosts to Governor Hobson in March 1842. Hobson and Chief Justice Martin slept in the raupo house, while A. D. Best and Edward Shortland pitched their tents inside the unfinished wooden house.

Dr Johnson was away from New Zealand between November 1844 and November 1846. He must either have made this copy from an earlier drawing, or, more possibly, initialled and dated his work when he gave it to Mrs Hobson in England.

43 [*Album page* 115

The first Government Settlement on the Waitemata River. 1st October. 1840

[JOHNSON, John 1794-1848]

Unsigned 1 October 1840
Watercolour and pencil image 130 x 195 mm on paper 182 x 226 mm
Cream wove paper, no visible watermark
Inscribed in black ink under image, outside ruled margin

Dr Johnson made at least two known drawings on 1 October 1840: this present Album picture and another made earlier the same day. The earlier drawing, now lost, was copied by Elizabeth Hocken when she and Dr Hocken visited the Rendel family, the Hobsons' only descendants, in 1906. The group shown in this drawing, cheering the raising of the flag on 18 September 1840, includes Police Magistrate W. C. Symonds, Superintendent of Works William Mason, Surveyor-General Felton Mathew and his wife Sarah, the future harbourmaster, Captain Rough, the interpreter Edward Marsh Williams, and Dr Johnson himself. Presumably the Maori on the left include the four

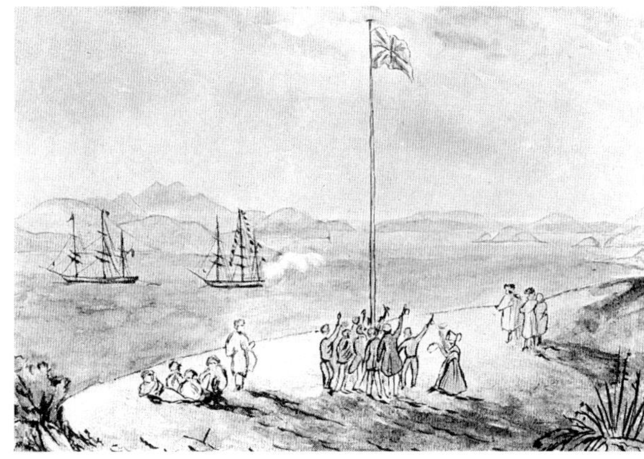

[JOHNSON, copy Elizabeth May Hocken (1848–1933)] [*Flag-raising ceremony when Captain William Symonds took possession of the site of Auckland,* 18 September 1840], watercolour, 150 x 200 mm
HOCKEN LIBRARY

signatories to the sale of the land that same day (Te Rereti, Te Tinana, Te Kawau and Horo) and the uniformed men would be officers from the ships. Mechanics and workers who witnessed the scene are not recorded here. The ships are the *Anna Watson* and the *Platina*; one of them is firing its guns in salute.

Only a fortnight elapsed between this taking possession and Dr Johnson's drawing of the 'first Government settlement'. By then the Surveyor-General had set up his marquee to serve as an office. The tent nearest the beach was Captain Rough's. On the skyline appear more tents, and the Union Jack flying on Point Britomart. The ships *Anna Watson* and *Platina* are oddly shown in full sail. In the foreground, some building timber has already been off-loaded.

44 [*Album page* 107

Auckland looking NW

[ASHWORTH, Edward 1814-1896]

Unsigned [1843 or January 1844]
Watercolour, pencil 242 x 365 mm
.19 mm cream wove paper, no visible watermark
Inscribed in pencil on image l.l. 'Auckland looking NW'.

This is one of the pictures which can be positively attributed. It is closely related to the drawing 'Auckland looking NW' in Edward Ashworth's pencil sketch in the ATL collection, A208/18. The foreground stream and flax are in both. Ashworth has added a small group of spectators on the left of this painting. Government House is shown inside its fence in both. In the drawings, St Paul's is shown without its tower (which was finished by July 1844) but in the painting a completed tower is silhouetted against Mt Victoria across the harbour. The painting could have been made as late as January 1844, just before Ashworth left for Hong Kong, when possibly the tower could sufficiently have taken shape.

ASHWORTH *Auckland looking NW* [1843], ink, 237 x 390 mm
ATL A208/18

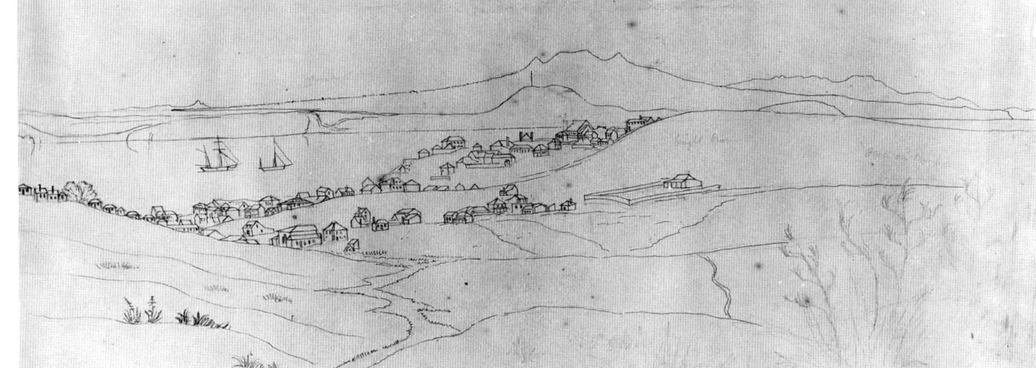

45 [*Album page* 111

[View from above Grafton Gully, showing graveyard and Government House]

[?ASHWORTH, Edward 1814-1896]

Unsigned [1843]
Watercolour 195 x 301 mm
Heavy cream wove paper, no visible watermark
Untitled

This watercolour is taken from a viewpoint almost identical with that of Plate **19**, 'Entrance to the Harbour, Auckland', attributed to John Guise Mitford. A little more of the land is shown on the left and the road running past the graveyard towards Government House. It is not likely that Mrs Hobson would have been given two similar views from the same hand, but she could well have received with interest two renderings of the same view by different artists. The attribution then has to rest entirely on stylistic difference.

This version is much colder in colour. Prussian blue and cold green rather than cobalt and mauve come nearer to the colour range in Ashworth's 'Auckland looking NW', Plate **44**. This artist also uses tone to render the rounded forms of trees and the slope of the hills, rather than colour contrast, and white highlights have been scratched into the paper with a sharp blade. The minute scale of the detail in the distant cliffs suggests that this may be the work of an architect. But one leaves a query in front of this suggested attribution.

46 [*Album page* 120

West Front/1st Church at Auckland/1844

[MASON, William 1810-1897]

Unsigned 1844
Black and brown ink 228 x 149 mm
Lightweight wove paper, 'J. WHATMAN 1840' watermark
Title printed under image and '1st church at Auckland 1844' handwritten in ink on drawing

The Metropolitan Church of St Paul's was designed and built by the architect William Mason, using as an almost exact pattern his earlier design for the Church of St James, Brightlingsea, Essex. The foundation stone was laid with due ceremony in Emily Place on 28 July 1841. On 17 July, the *New Zealand Herald and Auckland Gazette* published a subscription list and also Mason's call for tenders for limeburners, bricklayers and builders, excavators, fencers and brickmakers. Nearly two years passed before it was ready for construction. The steeple, surmounted by a ball and cross, was not completed until July 1844, which is the date inscribed on this drawing.

The church retained this form until 1863, when it was ingeniously enlarged to the designs of Col. T. R. Mould, R.E., by building a new nave across the existing structure, which then formed transepts to the whole. In 1885 the building was demolished to make way for the reduction of Point Britomart and the improvement of the roading pattern about Emily Place (see Stacpoole 1971).

47 [*Album page 122*

East Front [St Paul's Church, Auckland] (top)
Side Elevation (bottom)

[MASON, William 1810-1897]

Unsigned [1840-1841]
Black ink (top) 152 x 137 mm
(bottom) 150 x 209 mm
Lightweight wove paper. Watermark (bottom drawing) 'J. WHATMAN 1840'

St Paul's Anglican Church was designed by William Mason, architect and first Superintendent of Works. The first stone was laid by Governor Hobson on 28 July 1841. The Rev. J. F. Churton reported in a letter of 17 March 1842, printed in the *Ecclesiastical Times* and reprinted in the *Auckland Times,* 13 September 1843: 'The building is in rapid progress; the foundation and walls are several feet high; 120,000 bricks are now on the ground; several bricklayers are actively at work and we are in hopes of having it roofed in . . . in the course of a few months. It will contain 600 sittings of which one third will be free. Our own contributions (actually paid) about £600, whereby we are entitled to an equal grant from the Colonial treasury. . . . For the present Divine Service is in the Court house.'

Other contemporary opinion was not uncritical. W. C. Cotton wrote (Journal, v.8, p.31): 'The brick walls are rough inside and not well built. . . . Outside one or two pieces of mud coloured stone (wrought) inserted here and there among the honest red brick has a most unhappy appearance.' Edward Ashworth was also critical of the work:

> This structure belonged to the lancet or Early English style of Gothic architecture & is of rather pretty design the labels, corbels, and buttress caps being formed of moulded brick. They seemed however not to be in the secret of baking clay properly, for long before this church was completed, the facing bricks were corroded to the depth of nearly an inch; another defect was there being no proper coping on the gable ends, for want of freestone or Roman cement. In rainy weather the upper part of these unprotected walls was soaked through & the exposed situation in which the building stood caused the rain to drift in under the shingles. (Journal, 1843, typescript p.29)

A meeting of visitors/Mounganui [Mt Maunganui] Tauraga [Tauranga] in the distance.

[MERRETT, Joseph Jenner 1816-1854]

Unsigned [1843 or 1844, from earlier drawings]
Black ink, grey wash, pencil 166 x 246 mm
Cream wove paper, no visible watermark
Title inscribed in brown ink on Album page

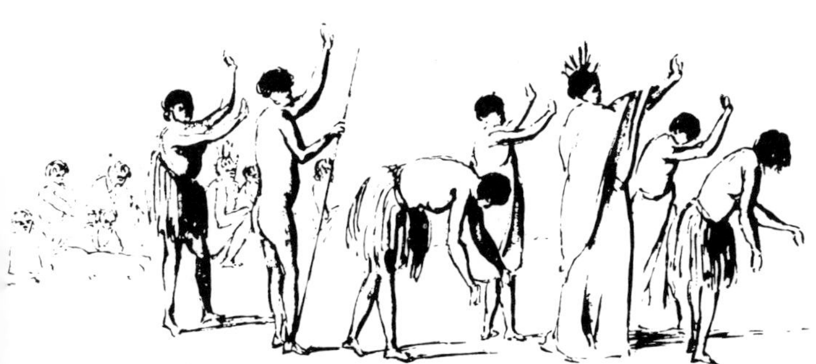

[MERRETT] [*Powhiri — welcome*], ink and wash, 120 x 170 mm
BL ADD. MS 19953 p.58 plate 170

Merrett here documents an important Maori ceremony: the powhiri or welcome. It is a time when those who welcome, and those who accept their hosts' greeting, are united in remembering the dead. In this ceremony people who are strangers, or those who have been apart, are brought together in their common humanity. The powhiri moves through invitation to reply. The dead, called up by women in the karanga, are remembered — hosts and guests standing with bowed heads.

The place is specific. The welcome occurs on an East Coast beach, outside the palisades of the Otumoetai Pa. In the background is the outline of Mauao ('grab the clouds'), the steep hill now known as Mt Maunganui, at the east entrance to Tauranga Harbour. It was seen in the distance by Captain Cook and recorded in his *Journal,* 3 November 1769: 'At 2 pass'd a small high Island Mayor Island lying 4 miles from a high round head in the Main.'

When we look at this drawing we need to remember that an artist is not a camera, people move as he draws. In this picture Merrett has compressed a series of events so that what looks like a single happening is, in fact, two groups of people, each drawn at a slightly different time as the ceremony progressed. (The pre-Renaissance painters used a similar device if, say, they showed three wise men approaching Bethlehem from a distance, shepherds hearing the angels' good tidings, and all again, in the foreground, bringing presents to the infant Jesus.)

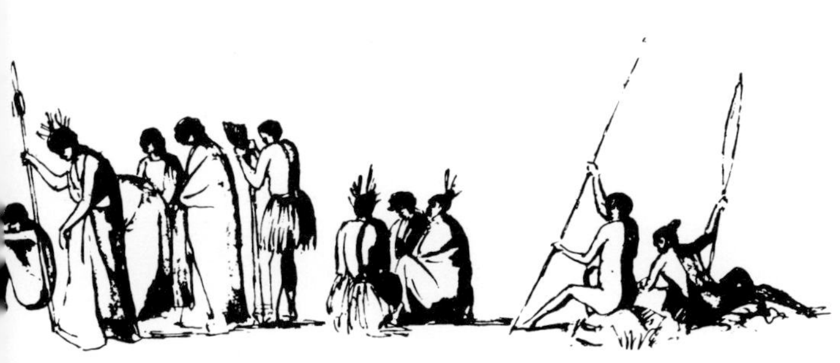

[MERRETT] [*Visitors reply*], ink and wash, 120 x 170 mm
BL ADD. MS 19953 p.43 plate 124

Two drawings in the Grey Album also telescope events. On p.58 plate 170 some figures have arms raised in greeting while others, by gesture and position, indicate deep mourning; they are probably crying 'aue, taupiri e'. Those on p.43 plate 124 and on the right in this picture are responding appropriately to the later sequence.

An alternative interpretation has been suggested that those on the right are from a related hapu or sub-tribe and soon all will be combined as tangata whenua to welcome the visitors in the canoes. Surprise has also been expressed that a man wearing the common rapaki (waist garment) should be holding a tewhatewha, a weapon appropriate to a chief.

49 [*Album page* 127

The Banks of the Waiho [Waihou]/near 'MataMata'

[MERRETT, Joseph Jenner 1816-1854]

Unsigned [1843 or 1844, from an earlier drawing]
Pencil, black ink, grey watercolour 167 x 259 mm
Mediumweight white wove paper, no visible watermark
Title inscribed in brown ink on Album page

Here the Waihou river winds past bush-covered hills which are part of the Kaimai Ranges. 'MataMata' refers to the much-visited pa of Te Waharoa on the Waitoa, a tributary of the Piako river, about six kilometres north of the present town of Matamata.

Edward Shortland wrote in his Journal on 16 October 1842: 'Towards the afternoon we moved on to Matamata. . . .The swamps were numerous, and some small lakes which could easily be drained. . . . From the swamps to the river were the remnants of canals, which we were told had been dug for the sake of eel fishing — nets being placed in different parts of them and the water turned off so as to make its bed dry. Many of them are in a state of repair and are at present used for the same purpose.'

William Colenso gave this account in his 'Excursion in the Northern Island of New Zealand, in the Summer of 1840-41', reprinted in *Early Travellers in New Zealand:*

> We crossed the river Waiho which at the ford was breast-high, and proceeded on, over the plain and through the extensive swamps, towards Matamata. . . . The chapel at this village, being wholly of native execution. . . . Length, breadth and height included, I suppose it to be the largest native-built house in New Zealand. It measures 95 feet by 40, and is nearly 18 feet to wall-plate. It has fine large slabs of totara for posts, some of which were nearly 3 feet in width. The interior was very neatly constructed of a kind of chequer-work, composed of stalks of the common fern (*Pteris esculenta*), placed laterally on each other, interlaced with strips of the fibrous kiekie (*Freycinetia banksii*): the grave colour of the fern stalks agreeing well with the purpose for which the house was built.

This drawing is by the same artist as the confirmed Merrett in Plate **50**. The Grey Album drawing (p.81 plate 233) appears to be a view from the same position; entitled 'The Waiho Source of the Thames', it has no trees on the promontory. Merrett appears to have made this ink and wash version more lively for Mrs Hobson. He has added trees, two war canoes and sculptural figures on the foreground rocks.

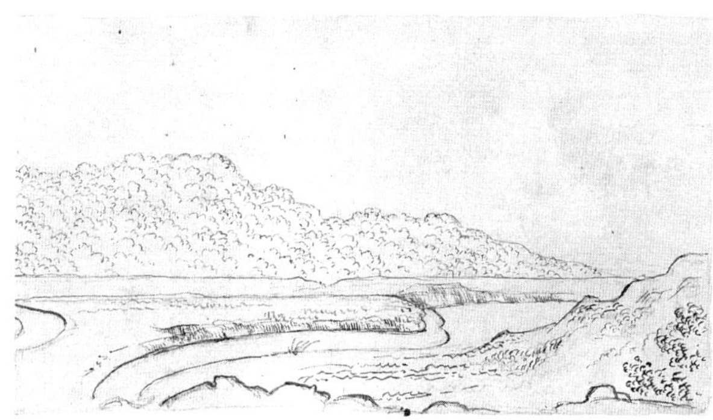

[MERRETT] *The Waiho, source of the Thames,* ink and wash, 70 x 140 mm
BL ADD. MS 19953 p.81 plate 233

"Wake, warriors, wake! there's danger in your sleep;
Unnumbered forms are moving in the fern,
Creeping like swine through every wind and turn;
Rise chiefs! arise! and strike the hatchet deep,
Man the defences and the portal keep,
The shout of blood, ring loud in every ear,
for ruthless foes are fast approaching near."
An aged warrior raised the battle cry;
Watchful was he when all were slumbering by,
His practised ear detected soon the sound,
Listening he stood, till near him human heads
Arose with caution, from their ferny beds;
He knew the foe, and starting from the ground,
Shouted the battle cry, which echoed round,
Th' alarm was heard, the gathering bands arise
And quickly arm, to meet the dread surprise.
Mothers with haste, their children quickly lead
To cells and ruas overgrown with weed,
There should success attend th' assailing blow,
These secret holes might shelter from the foe.
Near to the trenches, fierce the warriors rage
The pah was scaled, each hand to hand engage;
The tu meri, and taia's sweeping blow
Strike through the scull, and lay the warrior low,
The long timata urged with furious thrust,
Pierces the foe, who falling, bites the dust;
Vain his attempt to wrest the pointed wood
Transfixed to earth, he welters in his blood.
Th' assaulted tribe, give way on every side
And slaughter sweeps their ranks with giant stride;
The shrieks of wounded, and the dying groan,
The children's scream; their mother's wailing moan
The savage curse, the muskets' rattling peal
Fierce crackling flames, and blows on ringing steel
Complete the horrors that the victors feel,
The chieftain leader of th' assailing foe
Towering in height deals death in every blow,
His hatchet quivering o'er his feathered head,
with eyes distorted make his presence dread;
The blazing fortress, lights him on his way
A demon savage rushing on his prey;
With bloodstain'd hands and gory weapon flew,
A vulture preying on the foes he slew;
Tore out their hearts, gazed on the crimson flood
Shouted his victory, and drank their blood.

Signed J. J. Merrett

Transcription of Merrett's handwritten poem.

The Pah of "Maketu"/at Otawao/in the Waipa [The pa of Otawhao with the meeting house Maketu]

[MERRETT, Joseph Jenner 1816-1854]

Signed l.r. 'J. Merrett' on holograph poem on verso and dated l.l. 'Decr. 1843'
Black ink, grey wash 163 x 247 mm
Mediumweight cream wove paper, no visible watermark
Title inscribed in brown ink on Album page. On verso, part of a handwritten poem by the artist

The style of this drawing is the same as in landscape drawings, Plates **16** and **27**, already attributed to Merrett, and in further landscapes in Plates **49**, **57**, **58**, **59**, **61**, **62**, and **63**. The presence of part of a poem on the back of this drawing not only confirms Merrett as the artist who contributes most to the Hobson Album, but also establishes those related drawings which bear his handwritten inscriptions in the Grey Album. This crucial connection could only be made when the conservator of works on paper at the National Library lifted this drawing and had the verso photographed. 'Wake, warriors, wake! there's danger in your sleep. . .' is typical of the overblown romantic verse published under Merrett's pseudonym 'Crayon' (see also p.16, n.22).

Dieffenbach (1843, p.316) described his visit on 24 April 1842:

> The mission station of Otawao was established about a year ago. . . . It is situated on the banks of a small tributary of the Waipa: opposite to it, on an eminence, the Christian natives have constructed their pa, as at the first introduction of Christianity a sort of separation always takes place between the Christian converts and the Heathen without, however, materially affecting the general harmony of the tribe. . . . At this place . . . the pa of Te Puata, the principal chief and warrior, which stood at a little distance on rising ground, was almost uninhabited, although the native houses in it were by far the best I had yet seen in New Zealand, and the carvings on them were executed with much ingenuity.

The artist George French Angas painted buildings in this pa in 1846, and in *Savage Life and Scenes* (p.149) wrote that 'Maketu House in the old and ruined pah of Otawhao . . . is one of the finest remains of Maori ornamental architecture still extant. . . . This house was erected by Puata in commemoration of the taking of Maketu on the east coast by the people of his tribe; and the carved figures are intended to represent the various warriors . . . all have their tongues protruding as a mark of the extreme defiance with which they regarded their enemies.'

The missionary A. N. Brown, however, was less appreciative: 'There is a very large house built there and called Maketu in order to keep alive a spirit of revenge against Rotorua. I have never seen a building so fully and elaborately carved with huge indecent figures, all named after the different chiefs who have fallen in the war with Rotorua' (Brown, Journal, 2 July 1839). Mokorou, principal chief of Ngati Ruru with wide

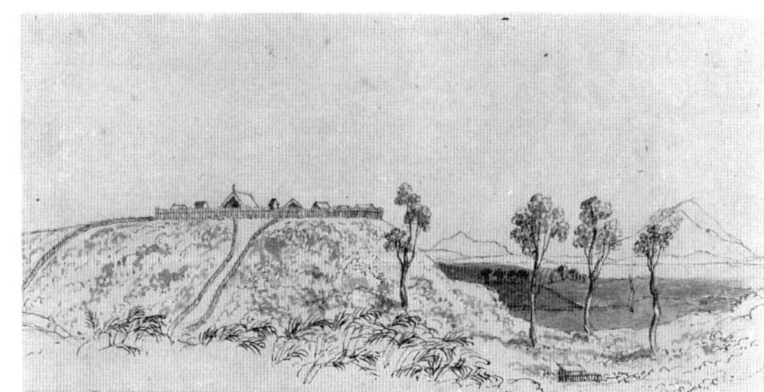

[MERRETT] *A pah at Otawao Waipa,* ink and wash, 150 x 175 mm
BL ADD. MS 19953 p.20 plate 46

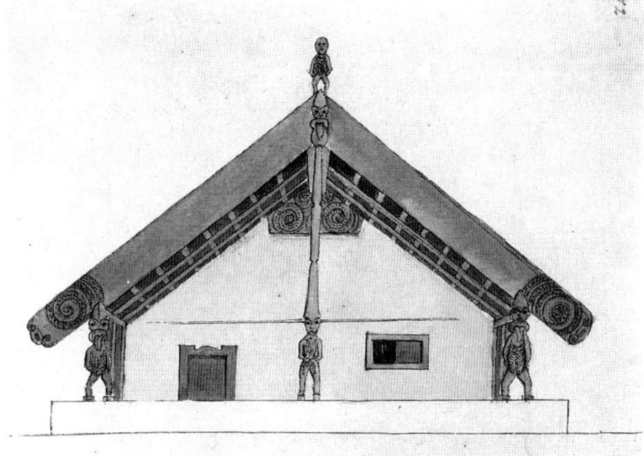

[MERRETT] *Native house at the pah Maketu,* ink and watercolour, 125 x 140 mm
BL ADD. MS 19953 p.28 plate 72

[MERRETT] *Otawao pah,* ink, 75 x 130 mm
BL ADD. MS 19953 p.28 plate 73

influence, was a leading warrior in the fighting between Waikato and Te Arawa which followed the murder of a Ngati Haua man in 1835. He was baptised in 1835, taking the name Riwai (Levi). Maketu was successfully attacked in March 1836. A Maori version of the building of the house Maketu appears in the Maori Land Court Minute Book Otorohanga 1, evidence of Hauauru Poutama, 15 September 1896. The names of the chiefs engaged in the work include Te Mokorou (Tumukuru) but not Te Puata.

In the Grey Album is one directly related drawing, 'A pah at Otawao Waipa' (p.20 plate 46), and a watercolour entitled 'Native house at the pah Maketu' (p.28 plate 72). (In this Hobson Album drawing the house Maketu would be the tallest roof showing in the centre above the palisade.) A third drawing in the Grey Album (p.28 plate 73) shows the distant pa against a background of Pirongia Mountain with burned trees in the foreground. (Art historians will have to give Merrett the credit for being the first New Zealand artist to use the dead tree as a motif.)

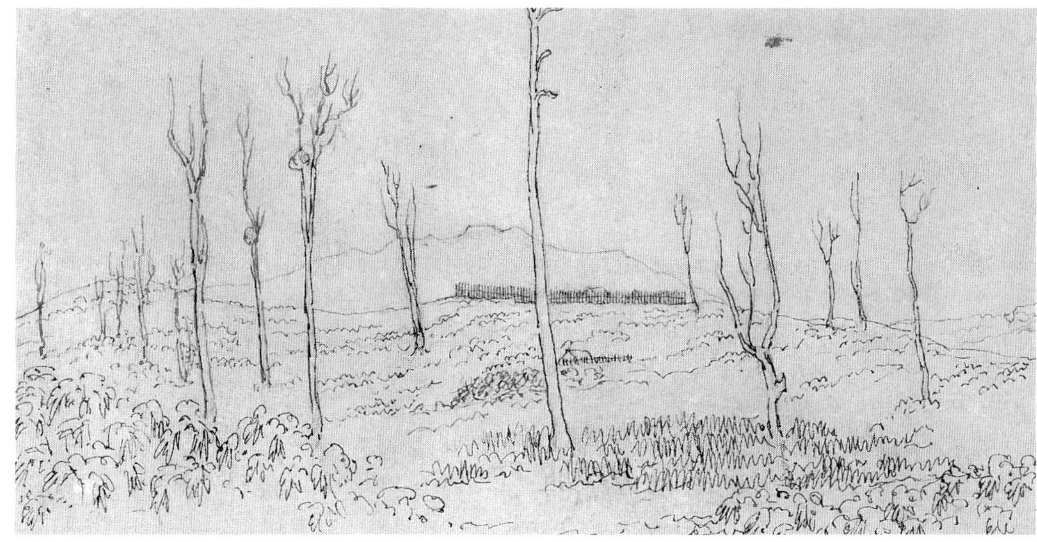

52 [*Album page 101*

[Maketu Waretotara — copy]

Signed by copyist, March 1842
Brown ink 358 x 256 mm
.18 mm ivory wove paper. Watermark 'J. WHATMAN TURKEY MILL 1837'
Item inscribed directly on Album page

This moving and dignified message from a condemned man expresses Maori pride but uses Christian terms. From the tone of the sentiments expressed, and the language, one seems to be listening to a missionary voice, probably that of the chaplain Rev. J. F. Churton, who attended Maketu during his imprisonment in Auckland. Maketu's repentance was published in Maori in the newspaper *Te Karere o Niu Tireni* (The Maori Messenger) in March 1842.

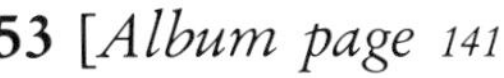

53 [*Album page* 141

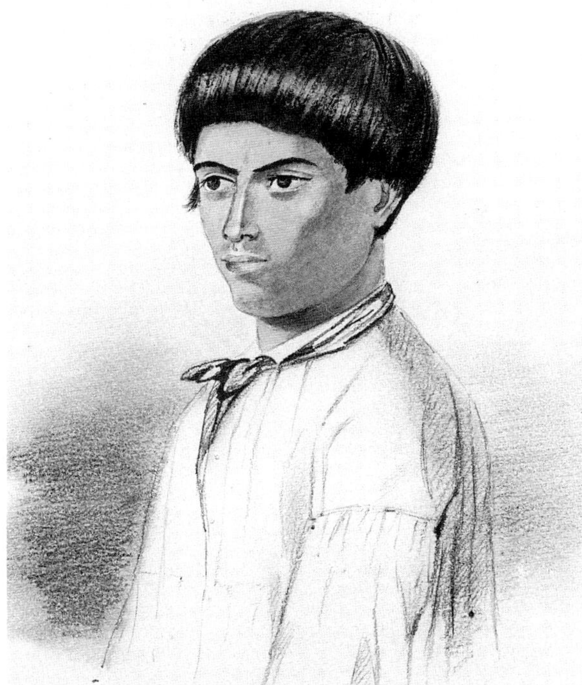

Maketu, a young NZ chief of the Nga Puhi tribe ca 1841, inscribed on mount in Dr T. M. Hocken's hand 'Painted by Dr Shortland', watercolour and pencil, 254 x 178 mm
HOCKEN LIBRARY

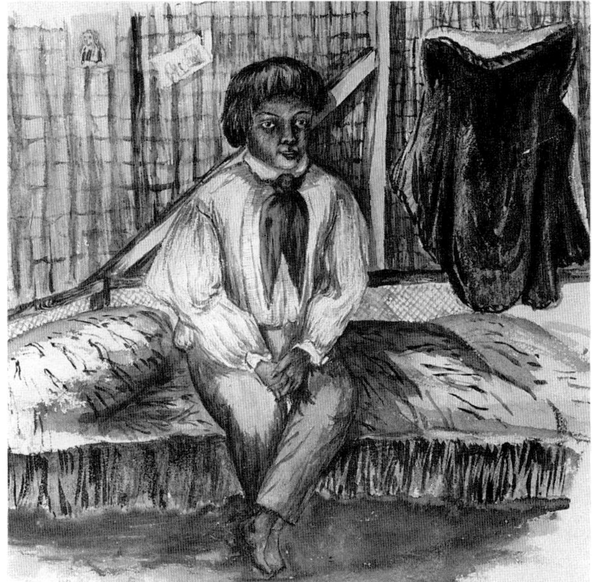

HUTTON (1824-1886), *Ko Himiona Tu* [?1845], watercolour and pencil, 180 x 200 mm
ATL

Maketu

[MERRETT, Joseph Jenner 1816-1854]

Unsigned [1842]
Pencil, watercolour 191 x 147 mm
Mediumweight cream wove paper, no visible watermark
Watercolour done to fit within embossed 'frame' on Album page

Here we are given a second portrait of Maketu. This differs, both in dress and in intensity of anger expressed on the young face, from the more skilful watercolour in Plate **6**. It is much closer to the drawing held in the Grey Album. It seems likely that Merrett, the only professional artist working in Auckland in 1842, made various portraits of Maketu for sale and here copied his original to fit the embossed space in Mrs Hobson's Album. Another close copy of this version is held in the Hocken Library inscribed by T. M. Hocken 'Painted by Dr Shortland' and shown here.

Maketu's haircut and clothing suggest missionary care. The chaplain, Rev. J. F. Churton, may have provided both. A watercolour by Thomas Biddulph Hutton of a schoolboy at St John's College School, Auckland (Hutton, E137, 14) shows in more detail the mission school shirt and haircut as worn in 1845. A painting in oil of Maketu held in the National Library of Australia (NK10763) is attributed to 'W. Duke'. The angle of the head and the drawing of shirt and cloak suggest that this artist also may have used the drawings from the Grey Album as a source material for a more elaborate painting.

Merrett's original drawing (p. 115) may have been made at the preliminary hearing, 1 December 1841, and this moving portrait recorded during the Supreme Court trial of 2 March. The *New Zealand Gazette and Wellington Spectator* (26 March 1842, pp.2-3) reported: 'The prisoner a fine young man whose stature was upwards of six feet, was brought from the condemned cell soon after 12 o'clock to the press-room. Here the precept was read to him and interpreted by Mr Mourant. He was dressed in a blue blanket, of native manufacture, and exhibited the peculiarly dignified demeanour and appearance for which the native chiefs are so peculiarly distinguished.'

54, 55 [*Album pages 157 and 158*

To Mrs Hobson/From her friends on the day/of her departure from New Zealand.

[?JOHNSON, John 1794-1848]

Unsigned [June 1843]
Brown ink 369 x 260 mm
Mediumweight cream wove paper, no visible watermark
Title inscribed directly on Album page

This poem from her friends may have been composed by a committee, but the handwriting, with distinctive 'th' and medial 's', resembles John Johnson's. Its content and its title indicate that it was written into the Album just as Mrs Hobson was about to leave New Zealand.

56 [*Album page 165*

Government House — Russell — Bay of Islands, New Zealand

MATHEW, Felton 1801-1847

Signed 'Felton Mathew 6 Apl. 1840'
Pencil 241 x 358 mm
Heavyweight cream wove paper, no visible watermark
Title inscribed in pencil l.r. of drawing using a medial 's' in Russell

The full history of this first place of government at Okiato was given by Ruth Ross in *New Zealand's First Capital,* from which the quotation and map on p.125 have been taken. To support his recommendation to purchase 300 acres from James Reddy Clendon, the Surveyor-General Felton Mathew reported: 'I have most carefully examined every part of [Clendon's property] . . . . There is a much larger portion of it level than I have yet seen in the Bay, and fully sufficient to afford space for a very pretty and convenient town. There are on the land a very comfortable [eight-roomed] cottage with suitable Out Buildings, an Extensive and substantial Store, Office, Smith's Shop, Boatbuilders Shed &c, the whole of which are in good repair, and would be immediately available for the purposes of the Government.' (p.33.) Preliminary arrangements to purchase were made by Mathew and endorsed by Hobson, 23 April 1840: 'Approved subject to the decision of the Commissioners as to the title to the land. Buildings are valued at Thirteen Thousand Pounds sterling, and the Land at Two Thousand Pounds.' (p.44.)

The site selected at Okiato, renamed Russell, was five miles up-harbour from Kororareka. 'Clendon's storehouses and cottages appear to have met the main needs of government; the only other buildings put up of which there is any record were the gaol at the back of Goverment House toward Pipiroa Bay . . . a messhouse . . . and later some partially erected barracks. . . . It is possible that some enlargements were made by adding to existing buildings, and no doubt Mrs Hobson carried out such improvements to the garden as her fancy dictated and circumstances allowed, but for the rest everything was left as it was.' (p.47.)

A pencil drawing on p.124 shows a close view of Mrs Hobson's first home in New Zealand done by the young governess who accompanied her, Ellery Short, who later married Captain David Rough in Auckland on 22 October 1841. After the Hobsons moved to Auckland, it was occupied by the local police magistrate until it was burned down in 1842.

57 [*Album page 167*

[?Mount Eden or Mount St John or Mount Hobson]

[MERRETT, Joseph Jenner 1816-1854]

Unsigned [1843 or 1844]
Black and brown ink, grey wash 205 x 321 mm
Mediumweight cream wove paper, no visible watermark

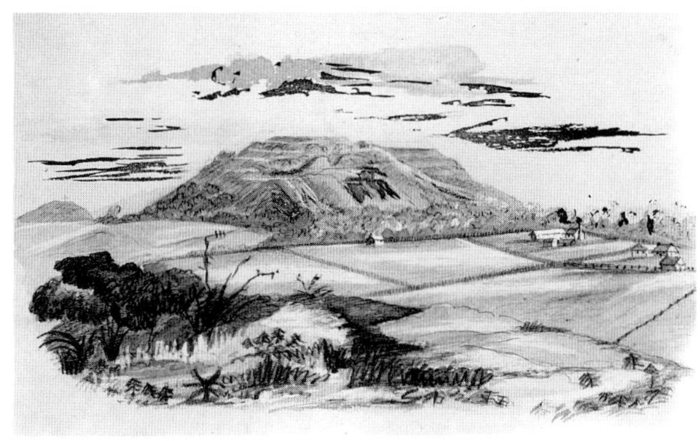

[MITFORD] *Mount St John, an extinct Volcano near Auckland, and the village of Epsom in the year 1842,* copy by Alexander 8.4.1846, watercolour, 225 x 270 mm APL

The mountain in this untitled drawing is now difficult to place with certainty, since many of the Auckland volcanoes have been excavated and their profiles altered. This drawing, previously titled in the ATL pictures catalogue 'Mt Wellington', shows a relationship of mountain background, harbour and hills more consistent with the view of Mt Eden seen from One Tree Hill, or of Mt Hobson seen from near Grafton Road. Small farms and houses in the middle distance would, in either view, be of settlement along the Epsom Road. A copy by Alexander of John Guise Mitford's 'Mount St John', 1842, also includes the terraced earthworks, bush at the base of the mountain, and in the foreground fenced paddocks and small farm buildings, but no distant water or bush-covered background hills. Lack of settlement in 1843-1844 rules out Mt Albert and leaves Mt Eden as the most likely subject — a conclusion upheld by Ron Brownson of the Auckland City Art Gallery.

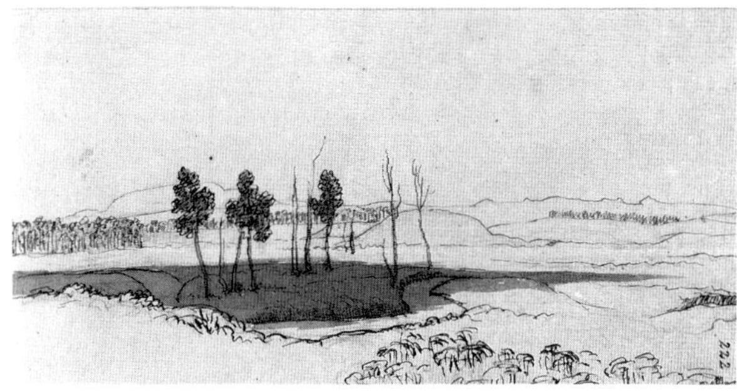

[MERRETT] *Waipa,* ink and wash, 90 x 150 mm
BL ADD. MS 19953 p.79 plate 222

58 [*Album page* 129

The Waipa/near its source/at 'Rangitoto'

[MERRETT, Joseph Jenner 1816-1854]

Unsigned [1843 or 1844]
Black ink, grey wash 163 x 259 mm
Mediumweight white wove paper, no visible watermark
Title inscribed in brown ink on Album page

The headwaters of the river Waipa lie within the Rangitoto Range, from which it flows north, along the western margins of the Hamilton lowlands, to join the Waikato at Ngaruawahia. At the time of this drawing the Waipa (the river of fortified villages) was an important access route and from its many Maori settlements grain, corn, flax and dairy products were sent to early Auckland.

Merrett was staying at Rarowera with his friend John Edwards when he joined Dieffenbach's party in 1841. Many drawings of the Waipa area in the Grey Album are by Merrett. He may have pictured Edwards's huts and fenced ground in 'Pirongia from Waipa' (p.41 plate 116) and in another (p.79 plate 222) he shows the Waipa as a narrow stream. The stands of trees appear to be kahikatea.

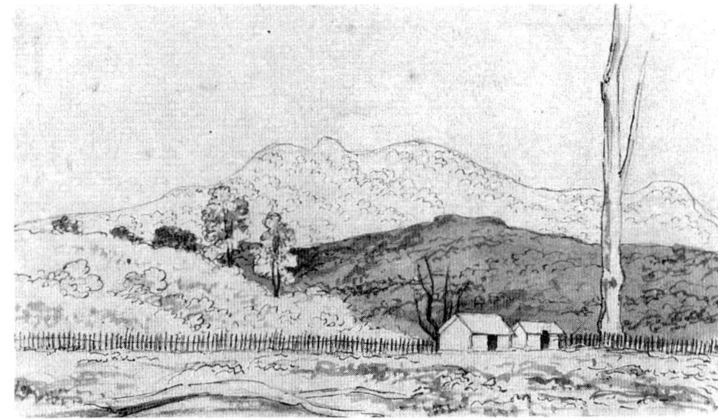

[MERRETT] *Pirongia from Waipa,* ink and wash, 75 x 125 mm
BL ADD. MS 19953 p.41 plate 116

The focus of interest in this drawing is the river-crossing with a pole, a method used both by the Maori and by modern trampers. Here one man goes ahead to test the depth with his long rod. The technique is to link arms with one another and wrap them round the horizontal pole; the strongest man fronts the current, the next strongest takes the other end, and the lightweights come between.

59 [*Album page* 171

'Perongia' [Pirongia] from 'Maungatauturi' [Maungatautari]

[MERRETT, Joseph Jenner 1816-1854]

Unsigned [1843, from an earlier drawing]
Pencil, black ink, grey wash 162 x 250 mm
Mediumweight cream wove paper, no visible watermark
Title inscribed in brown ink on Album page

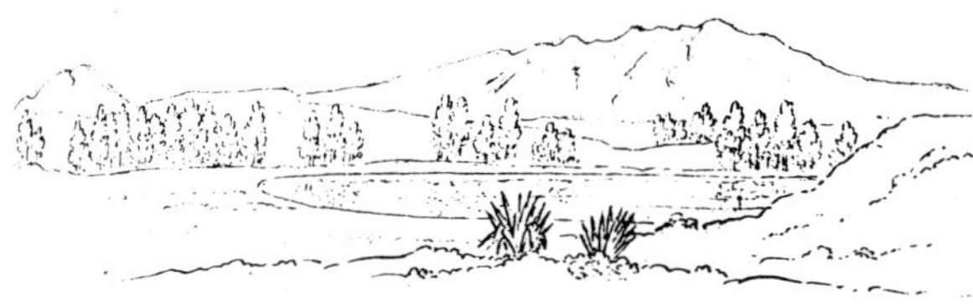

[MERRETT] *The Mountain of Pirongia from Rarewera,* ink and pencil, 155 x 260 mm
BL ADD. MS 19953 p.36 plate 95

In his drawings Merrett shares a Maori respect for the land, for its rivers and its sacred mountains. Pirongia is the centre of this painting. The smaller mound of Kakepuku stands between tree trunks on the left.

The mountain was named Pirongia-te-aroaro-o-Kahu by the first Maori explorer of this area, Rakataura, one of the leaders of the Tainui canoe (see Kelly 1949, p.69, for the traditional account of the naming). This extinct volcano forms the summit of a range dividing the west coast harbours of Kawhia and Aotea from the Waipa and inland Waikato. A number of Merrett's drawings in the Grey Album relate to views of, and from, both these mountains; in particular 'The Mountain of Pirongia from Rarewera' (p.36 plate 95) and 'Pirongia from Waipa' (p.41 plate 116), the latter showing small European buildings in the landscape (see also Plate **61** of this Album).

This picture is one of Merrett's most beautiful, and illustrates well his fine sense of composition and his individual use of trees as space-formers.

60 [*Album page 174*

The Waré of Te Whero Whero, Chief of the Waikato/Onahonga. (top)
The Waré of Weremu Hoete Chief of the Ngatepaua [Ngati Paoa] Putiki (bottom)

[JOHNSON, John 1794-1848]

Unsigned [?1845, from drawings done in 1841]
Brown ink, watercolour wash (top) 73 x 108 mm
(bottom) 73 x 109 mm
Mediumweight ivory wove paper, no visible watermark
Titles inscribed in brown ink under each image, below embossed 'frames'

John Johnson described this house in 1846, having visited it earlier in 1841: 'The road slopes gently down to Oneonga [Onehunga], a landing place on the Manukau, to which small vessels can ascend. It may be about five miles distant from Auckland. The aspect of this place had also undergone a favourable change . . . a somewhat superior ware [whare] occupied by the great chief Te Wero Wero [Te Wherowhero], on his occasional visits to this part of the country, was now represented by a public-house. I remember to have spent a cold comfortless night under its porch . . . the interior being tapu, so as not to be desecrated by a pakeha.' (Taylor 1966, p.118.)

This Onehunga house has a side entrance under an ornamented porch and is similar in design to a house painted by G. F. Angas in 1846, Plate 38 in *The New Zealanders Illustrated,* entitled 'Entrance to a dwelling house at Raroera Pa (ruined and deserted) not far from the tomb of Te Wherowhero's daughter'. Angas does not say this house is Te Wherowhero's, but the connection was made by Alan and W. A. Taylor in *The Maori Builds* (pp.34-35): 'A distinctive feature of early Waikato architecture was the side entrance found in larger buildings. Notable in this respect was Urutomokia, one of Chief Te Wherowhero's houses at Raroera pa. . . . The house had an exceptionally long frontal beam that served as a maihi above a wide but undecorated verandah.'

Bishop G. A. Selwyn wrote in his Visitation Journal on 16 July 1842:

> Went in one of Tomatin's boats to Putiki, in the Island of Waihekeh, to the house of a most valuable native chief, Wirimu Howeti (William Jowett). He has just built a house, divided into rooms: one for dining, one for sleeping, one for cooking, and one for a study! From this study he wrote me a very polite invitation, which led to my visit. Mr Maunsell, of the Church Missionary Society, accompanied me. On Sunday I read, preached, catechized, and baptized some infants. The school classes were admirable: fine tall men, chiefly in English clothes, reading the new Testament, verse by verse, with great accuracy; and afterwards repeating a whole chapter by heart, without missing many words. William Jowett himself has the natural good breeding of a true gentleman. (*Letters from New Zealand*, London, 1847.)

The excellent anchorage of Putiki Bay, where Ostend is now situated, was often used by visitors to the Maraetai mission, who then crossed the narrow strait by rowboat.

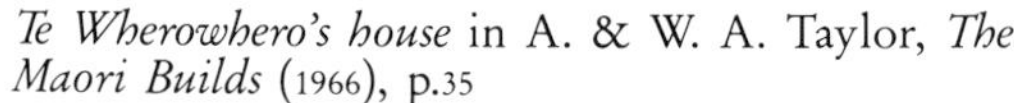

Te Wherowhero's house in A. & W. A. Taylor, *The Maori Builds* (1966), p.35

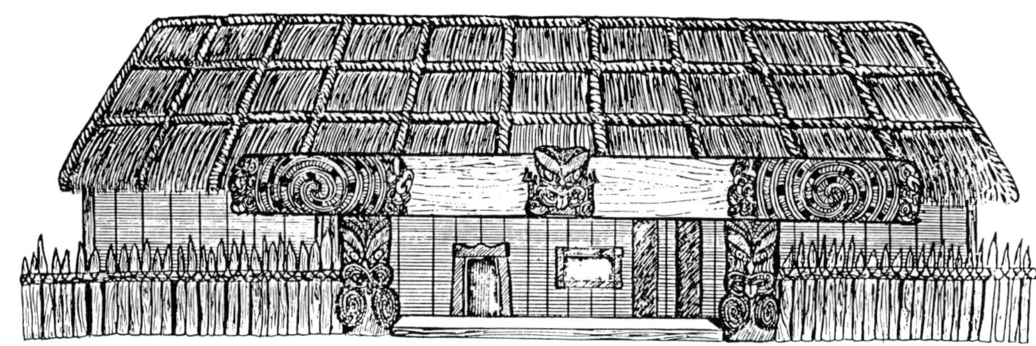

61 [*Album page 177*

View of 'Perongia' [Pirongia] and 'Koka Puka' [Kakepuku]/from 'Rarowera'

[MERRETT, Joseph Jenner 1816-1854]

Unsigned [1843, from an earlier drawing]
Pencil, black ink, grey wash 164 x 255 mm
Mediumweight cream wove paper, no visible watermark
Title inscribed in brown ink on Album page

Pirongia Mountain (see Plate **59**) lies to the right and the volcanic cone Kakepuku to the far left. The rounded mountain rising directly from the flat was named 'Kakepuku-te-aroaro-o-Kahu', referring to Kahukeke, the wife of Rakataura (see Kelly 1949, p.65).

In the Grey Album the drawing entitled 'The Mountain of Pirongia from Rarewera' (see p.158) shows a small lake in the foreground. In 1840-1841 Merrett is said to have lived

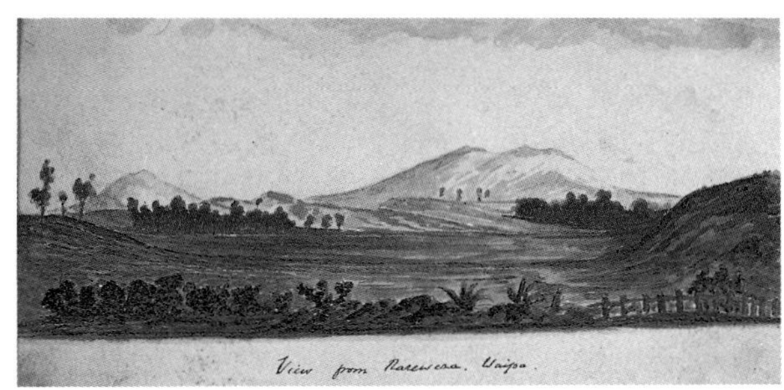

[MERRETT] *View from Rarewera* [*Rarowera*] *Waipa,* watercolour
ANL RNK 9945

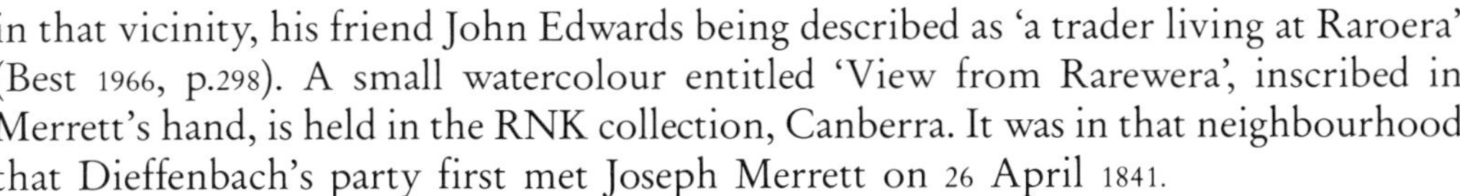

in that vicinity, his friend John Edwards being described as 'a trader living at Raroera' (Best 1966, p.298). A small watercolour entitled 'View from Rarewera', inscribed in Merrett's hand, is held in the RNK collection, Canberra. It was in that neighbourhood that Dieffenbach's party first met Joseph Merrett on 26 April 1841.

John Guise Mitford's watercolour entitled 'Kakapuku and Pirongia Mountains at Maungatawiri on the River Waipa, from Rarawera December 1844' points up the stylistic differences between Mitford and Merrett, differences noticeable even in the copy by Alexander, dated 4 April 1846 (Alexander Sketchbook, APL).

Rarowera Pa was on what is now Wallace Terrace, about a mile from the centre of Te Awamutu. Palisading of the pa appears on the right foreground of this drawing. G. F. Angas described Rarowera Pa as having 'some of the finest Maori works of art still extant'. His detailed watercolour 'Ancient Carvings at Raroera Pa' (Angas 1972, plate 40) shows two huge figures 'carved by one individual, a lame man, named Parinui . . . his only tool was the head of an old bayonet'.

62 [*Album page 179*

The Pah of Okatina on the Lake of [the same] Name/(taken by Pomare from the Bay of Islands) in the Taua [war party] of Hungi [Hongi]/16 years ago [1825?]

[MERRETT, Joseph Jenner 1816-1854]

Unsigned [1841]
Pencil, black ink 163 x 250 mm
Mediumweight cream wove paper, no visible watermark
Title inscribed in brown ink on Album page

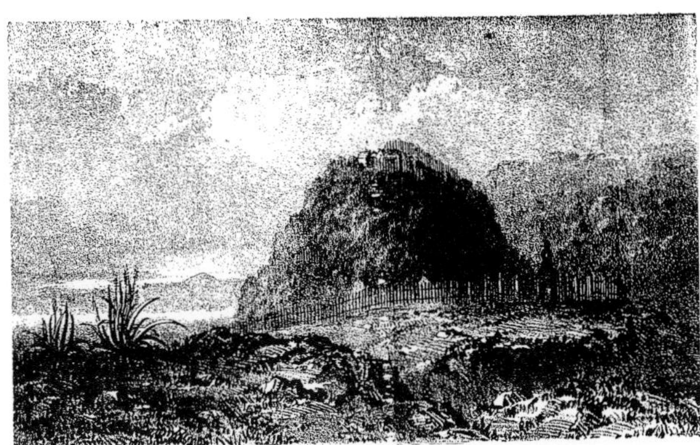

[MERRETT] *Fortified Native Village,* lithograph, 105 x 170 mm, in C. Terry, *New Zealand . . . as a British Colony* (1842), p.71

The Te Koutu pa was built on a peninsula on the east side of Lake Okataina, which lies east of Lake Rotorua and to the north of Lake Tarawera. This drawing shows the palisade at the foot of the hill and a famous carved waharoa (entrance to a fortified village), Ngati Tarawhai, which is now in the Maori Court of the Auckland War Memorial Museum.

A version of this drawing, but without human figures, was published as one of twelve illustrations to Charles Terry's *New Zealand, its Advantages and Prospects, as a British Colony,* 1842. Merrett must have made the prototype drawing no later than 1841, if we are to allow sufficient time for the work to be sent to England, lithographed and printed by 1842.

In this drawing, Merrett has added a powhiri, and the visitors are seen on the right. The central challenging figure carries a spear. The hilltop palisades are more clearly visible in this than in the 1842 lithograph.

63 [*Album page* 181

View of Koka Puka [Kakepuku]/from Waipa and Otawau [Otawhao]

[MERRETT, Joseph Jenner 1816-1854]

Unsigned [?1841]
Pencil, black ink, grey wash 170 x 257 mm
Mediumweight cream wove paper, no visible watermark
Title inscribed in brown ink on album page

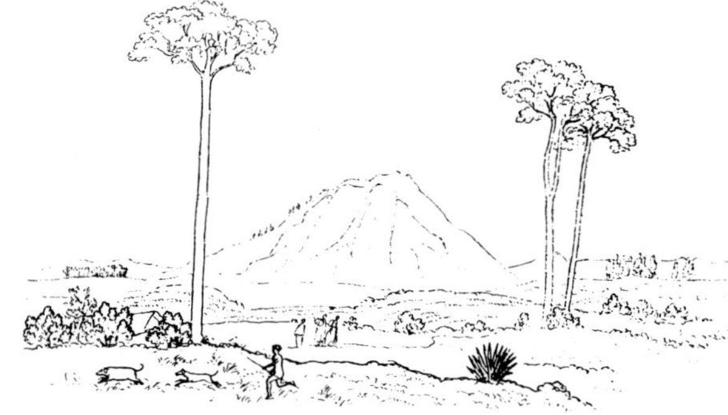

[MERRETT] *Koka Puka at the head of the Waipa,* ink and pencil, 150 x 250 mm
BL ADD. MS 19953 p.17 plate 41

Otawhao is on the tributary of the Waipa. The accompanying map shows the relationship of Kakepuku to the river and to the mission station at Te Kopua, considered by the Te Awamutu Museum to be the probable viewpoint. (Compare the view in Hochstetter 1867, p.317.)

Three Grey Album drawings relate closely to this one. 'Waipa' (p.28 plate 69) shows the mountain with toetoe and palisades in the foreground. 'The Waipa' (p.21 plate 48) is a more distant view from the south-east, showing canoes on the river and two houses on the far left. 'Koka Puka at the head of the Waipa' (p.17 plate 41) also views Kakepuku between tall trees and has the roof of a house on the left. It is likely that in this last-named work, Merrett has drawn the house which he helped to build and the view most familiar to him.

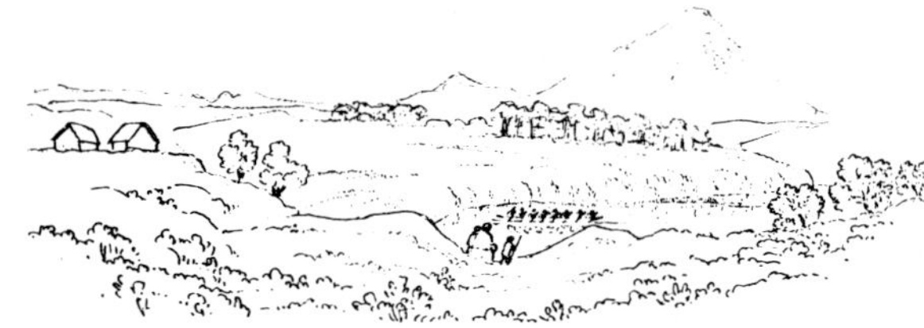

[MERRETT] *The Waipa,* pencil and ink, 150 x 250 mm
BL ADD. MS 19953 p.21 plate 48

Hobson and his party ascended Kakepuku on 16 May 1842 as Shortland recorded in his Journal:

> Ascended Kakepuku about 8 miles from Otawhao, a lofty conical hill — soil of the finest description — with stones basalt. I considered the hill about 800 feet, the Governor put it at 1000. [The correct height is 1472ft or 448.6m.] Towards the summit rather steep and overgrown with fern. Natives lit a fire by rubbing and made a smoke in order that it might be seen we had reached the summit. The greater part of this hill has at no distant time been cultivated. The natives resorted to it for the greater security from their enemies. . . . We looked down on Kakepuku's wife Kawa. A swamp is now between them. Native tradition that they once lived together, side by side. They quarrelled one morning and Kawa marched slowly through the swamp to her present place.

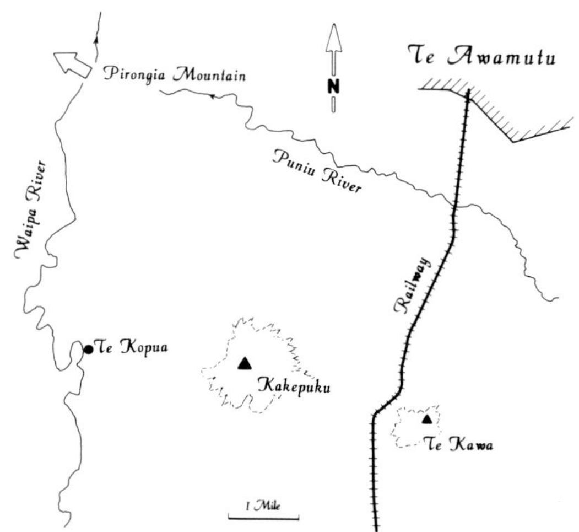

Map showing relationship of Kakepuku to mission station on Waipa River (1 inch to 1 mile)

S. M. Mead (*Te Maori,* p.20) writes of a mountain as a reference point, a known landmark to which is attached some cultural meaning. Mountains 'together with other named features of the land — rivers, lakes, blocks of land, promontories, holes in the ground, fishing grounds, trees, burial places, and islands — they form a cultural grid over the land which provides meaning, order and stability to human existence'. The Maori have clothed the mountains with words, with stories, have made them male or female symbols, potent in the spiritual history of different tribes. In Merrett's landscape we sense the mountain as a noble presence.

Glossary of Maori Words

The macron indicates a long vowel. The English 's' is not added in the plural. Plant names in common use are not included.

ariki	paramount chief
haka	posture dance
hapū	sub-tribe
hui	gathering, assembly
kāinga	village
kaumātua	elder
koha	gift
korowai	cloak of woven flax fibre
korowai-ngore	same, decorated with pompoms
kūmara, kūmera	sweet potato
mana	prestige, authority
mere	hand weapon of stone
moko	tattoo
pā	fortified village
Pākehā	non-Maori, usually white-skinned
pātaka	elevated storehouse
poi	ball swung on a cord
ponga	type of tree-fern
poroporoaki	leave-taking speech or message
pōwhiri	welcome ceremony
rangatira	chief, leader
raupo	bulrush
rāpaki	waist garment, kilt
runanga	important assembly, council
tāngata whenua	local people, people of the land
tangi	mourning
taonga	valuable possession
tapu	sacred, under special restriction
tikanga	custom
tiki	carved, stylised human figure
tipuna, tupuna	ancestor
waiata	song or chant
whare	house
wharepuni	most substantial house of settlement

Select Bibliography

Abbreviations

AIML	Auckland Institute and Museum Library
ANL	Australian National Library
APL	Auckland Public Library
ATL	Alexander Turnbull Library
AUP	Auckland University Press
BL	British Library
Hocken	Hocken Library, Dunedin
JPS	*Journal of the Polynesian Society*
ML	Mitchell Library, Sydney
OUP	Oxford University Press
VUP	Victoria University Press
MS	manuscript
TS	typescript
MF	microfilm
GBPP	*Great Britain, Parliamentary Papers relating to New Zealand*

Newspapers

(Publication of early newspapers was often brief or intermittent. Surviving copies are mainly found at APL, AIML, ATL, General Assembly Library and Hocken.)

Auckland Chronicle and New Zealand Colonist, 1841-45.
Auckland Standard, 1842.
Auckland Times, 1842-46.
New Zealand Colonist and Port Nicholson Advertiser, 1842-43.
New Zealand Gazette and Wellington [originally *Britannia*] *Spectator,* 1839-44.
New Zealand Herald and Auckland Gazette, 1841-42.
New Zealand Journal [London], 1840-52. Complete file, ATL.
New Zealander, 1845-66.
Southern Cross [later *Daily Southern Cross*], 1843-62.
Sydney Morning Herald, Index 1831-42, Mitchell Library, Sydney.

Official Papers

Great Britain: Parliamentary Papers relating to New Zealand (*GBPP*). (Old series. The same material appears in the Irish University Press series of British Parliamentary Papers, Colonies: New Zealand, 3. Shannon, IUP, 1968-71.)
Great Britain. Parliament. House of Commons Select Committee on Aboriginal Tribes. Report from the Select Committee on Aborigines (British Settlements). 2v. London, 1836-37. v.2. House of Commons 1837, 425. ATL.
Lands and Deeds Office records, Auckland.
New Zealand Government Gazette, 1840-46.
National Archives: Colonial Secretary's papers (I.A.), Governor's papers (G).

Books and Articles

Adams, Peter. *Fatal Necessity: British Intervention in New Zealand, 1830–1847.* Auckland, AUP, 1977.
Alexander, [Hood] John. *Historic Auckland.* [Christchurch], Whitcombe & Tombs, [?1961].
Alexander, K. Staples. Sketchbook. APL, NZP 134.
Alexander Turnbull Library Art Correspondence, TL 3/1/1.
Andersen, Johannes C. *Maori Place Names.* Wellington, Polynesian Society, 1942.
Angas, G. F. *Savage Life and Scenes in Australia and New Zealand.* 2v. London, Smith, Elder & Co., 1847; repr. 1969.
—*The New Zealanders Illustrated.* London, Thomas McLean, 1847.
—*Portraits of the New Zealand Maori,* with a modern text by G. C. Petersen and S. M. Mead. Wellington, Reed, 1972.
Armstrong, Alan. *Maori Games and Hakas.* Wellington, Reed, 1964.
Ashwell, B. Y. Letters and Journals of Kaitotehe, 1834-1836. TS, MS9, AIML.
Ashworth, Edward. Journals, 1841-45. MS, ATL.
—Sketchbook. ATL.
Beaglehole, J. C. *Captain Hobson and the New Zealand Company.* Northampton, Mass., Smith College Dept. of History, 1928.

Bell, Kenneth N. and W. P. Morrell (eds). *Select Documents on British Colonial Policy, 1830-1860.* Oxford, Clarendon Press, 1928.
Best, Abel Dottin. *The Journal of Ensign Best,* ed. Nancy M. Taylor. Wellington, Govt. Printer, 1966.
Best, Elsdon. *Games and Pastimes of the Maori.* Wellington, Dominion Museum, 1925.
—*The Maori.* 2v. Wellington, H. Tombs, 1924.
—'Maori eschatology'. *Trans. of the NZ Inst.,* v.38, 1905.
—'Te Whanga-nui-o-tara'. *JPS,* v.10, 1901.
Blackley, Roger. 'John Guise Mitford, a topographical painter of the 1840s.' *Art New Zealand,* 27, 1983, pp.40-45.
Brodie, Walter. *Remarks on the Past and Present State of New Zealand.* London, Whittaker & Co., 1845.
Brown, Alfred Nesbitt. Papers. MSS and MF 756, ATL.
Brown, William. Extracts from Journal, 1840-45. MS, AIML.
—*New Zealand and its Aborigines.* London, Smith, Elder & Co., 1845.
Buck, Peter (Te Rangihiroa). *The Coming of the Maori,* 2nd ed. Wellington, Maori Purposes Fund Board, 1970.
Buick, T. Lindsay. *The Treaty of Waitangi.* Wellington, S. and W. Mackay, 1914.
Bunbury, Thomas. *Reminiscences of a Veteran.* 3v. London, Charles J. Skeet, 1861.
Burns, Patricia. *Te Rauparaha, a new perspective.* Wellington, Reed, 1980.
Bush, G. W. A. *The Centennial History of the Auckland City Council.* Auckland, Collins, 1971.
Campbell, G. H. 'Dr Edward Shortland and his work in Northern New Zealand, 1841-47.' M.A. thesis, University of Otago, 1935, Hocken.
Campbell, John Logan. *Poenamo.* London, Williams & Norgate, 1881.
—Reminiscences. TS, MS51, AIML.
Carleton, Hugh. *The Life of Henry Williams,* 2v. Auckland, Upton & Co., 1877.
'Catalogue of Pictures in the Hocken Library.' Dunedin, Otago University Library, 1948.
Chapman, Thomas. Letters and Journals, v.1, 1830-1869. TS, ATL.
Clarke, George (senior). *Extract from the final report of the Chief Protector of Aborigines in New Zealand.* Auckland, privately published, 1846.
Clarke, George (junior). *Notes on Early Life in New Zealand.* Hobart, J. Walch & Sons, 1903.
Cotton, W. C. Journal of a residence in New Zealand, 21 Aug. 1842–25 Aug. 1844. MS, Dixson Library, Sydney, NSW.
Cowan, James. *The Maoris of New Zealand.* Christchurch, Whitcombe & Tombs, 1910.
Davidson, J. W. 'New Zealand 1820–70, an essay in re-interpretation.' *Historical Studies, Australia and New Zealand,* v.5 no. 20, May 1953.
Davis, C. O. B. *The Life and Times of Patuone.* Auckland, J. H. Field, 1876.
—*Maori Mementoes,* Auckland, Williamson & Wilson, 1855.
Dieffenbach, Ernst. *Travels in New Zealand,* 2v., London, John Murray, 1843.
Dyer, Bob. 'The Price of Auckland.' *Rimu,* no.1, 1984.
Early Epsom. Compiled by the staff of the Epsom Branch Library, Auckland, 1972.
Esler, A. E. 'The Living Landscape. Auckland Yesterday and Tomorrow.' Scrapbook, AIML, 1971.
'A Farewell for an Enemy.' *Te Ao Hou,* no. 34, March 1961. (Anon.)
Fenton, F. D. *Important judgments delivered in the Compensation Court and Native Land Court, 1866-79.* Auckland, Henry Brett, 1879.
—*Observations on the state of the Aboriginal Inhabitants of New Zealand.* Auckland, NZ Govt., 1859.
Fletcher, H. J. Index of Maori names. TS, ATL.
George, James George. 'A few odds and ends of Remembrances from 1823 to 1876.' MS, APL. TS, ATL.
Gluckman, L. K. *Medical History of New Zealand prior to 1860.* Auckland, the author, 1976.

Grey, Sir George. *Ko nga Whakapepeha me nga Whakaahuareka a nga Tipuna o Aotea-roa.* Capetown, Solomon, 1857.

—*Nga Mahi a nga Tupuna.* 3rd ed., ed. H. W. Williams. New Plymouth, Thomas Avery, 1928.

—*Nga Moteatea me nga Hakirara o nga Maori.* Wellington, Stokes, 1853.

—*Polynesian Mythology,* 2nd ed. (English and Maori), Auckland, Brett, 1885.

Gudgeon, Lt.-Col. William. 'Maori Wars.' *JPS,* v.16, 1907, pp.13-42.

Hall, T. D. H. *Captain Joseph Nias and the Treaty of Waitangi; a vindication.* Wellington, L. T. Watkins Ltd, 1938.

Hammond, T. G. 'The Taro'. *JPS,* v.3, 1894, pp.105-6.

Hobson, Eliza and William. Papers. MS, ATL. TS, APL.

Hobson, William. Extracts from letters written to his wife, 15 March to 4 April 1840, while convalescing at Waimate. TS, APL.

Hochstetter, Ferdinand von. *New Zealand.* Stuttgart, J. G. Cotta, 1867.

Hocken, T. M. Historical Notes. MSS 37 and 37B, Hocken.

Hutton, Thomas Biddulph. Book of New Zealand sketches. Purewa, 1845. ATL.

Johnson, John. Journal 17 March–28 April 1840. (Occassional [*sic*] Diary in New Zealand.) MZMS 154, APL. MF, ATL.

—'Notes from a Journal 1846-47.' In Taylor, Nancy (ed.), *Early Travellers in New Zealand.* Oxford, Clarendon Press, 1959.

Jones, Pei te Hurinui. *King Potatau.* Wellington, Polynesian Society, 1960.

Kelly, Leslie, *Tainui.* Wellington, Polynesian Society, 1949.

Lennard, Maurice. *Motuarohia.* Auckland, Pelorus Press, 1959.

Mackaness, G. (ed.). *Some Private Correspondence of Sir John and Lady Jane Franklin.* Sydney, privately published, 1947.

McLean, M. and M. Orbell. *Traditional Songs of the Maori.* Wellington, Reed, 1975.

McLintock, A. H. *Crown Colony Government in New Zealand.* Wellington, Govt. Printer, 1958.

Markham, Edward. *New Zealand or Recollections of it.* Wellington, Govt. Printer, 1963.

Martin, Lady Mary Ann. *Our Maoris.* London, Society for Promoting Christian Knowledge, 1884.

Mathew, Felton and Sarah Mathew. *The Founding of New Zealand; the journals of Felton Mathew and his wife, 1840–47,* ed. J. Rutherford. Wellington and Dunedin, Auckland University College/Reed, 1940.

—Letters of Felton Mathew and his wife, 1840–47. TS, APL.

—Letters, 1833. MS, Mitchell Library, Sydney, NSW.

Mead, S. M. *The Costume Styles of the Classical Maori in New Zealand, 1642–1800.* London, Costume Society, 1969.

Mead, S. M. (ed.). *Te Maori: Maori art from New Zealand Collections.* Auckland, Heinemann/American Federation of Arts, 1984.

Meiklejohn, G. M. *Early Conflicts of Press and Government.* Auckland, Wilson & Horton, 1953.

Merrett, Joseph Jenner. 'An Account of a Visit to the New Zealand Chiefs Heki and Kawiti.' *Simmonds' Colonial Magazine,* v.9, 1846, p.427.

Meurant, Edward. Diary, 1842-1848. TS, ATL.

Mitcalfe, Barry 'Poetry of the Maori'. *Te Ao Hou,* no. 34, March 1961, pp.31-40.

—*Maori Poetry: The Singing Word.* Wellington, VUP, 1974.

Mitford Family Records 1066-1959. MS, MF 689, ATL.

Morgan, John. Letters and Journals of the Rev. John Morgan, missionary at Otawhao 1833-1865. TS, APL. MF, ATL.

New Zealand Pictorial Scrapbook, Drawings and Sketches illustrative of New Zealand 1845-1854, Album presented by Sir George Grey, 13 Sept. 1854. (Grey Album.) British Library, London, Add. MSS 19953 and 19954.

Ngata, Sir Apirana and P. Te Hurinui. *Nga Moteatea,* Part I. Wellington, Polynesian Society, 1928; Part II, 1961; Part III, 1980.

Orange, Claudia. *The Treaty of Waitangi.* Wellington, Allen & Unwin, 1987.

Paul, Janet. 'Artists of the Hobson Album: Edward Ashworth, 1814-1896'. *TL Record,* v.18, no.1, May 1985, pp.22-32.

Phillips, J. R. 'A Social History of Auckland, 1840-53.' M.A. thesis, University of Auckland, 1966.

Platts, Una. *Colonial Auckland: a collection of paintings, drawings and prints by early artists. Catalogue of exhibition at Auckland City Art Gallery.* Auckland, ACAG, 1959.

—*The Lively Capital.* Christchurch, Avon Fine Prints, 1971.

—*Nineteenth-Century New Zealand Artists.* Christchurch, Avon Fine Prints, 1980.

Potts, T. H. *Out in the Open.* Christchurch, Lyttelton Times, 1882.

Pendergrast, M. *Te Aho Tapu/The Sacred Thread: Traditional Maori Weaving.* Auckland Institute and Museum, 1987.

Roberts, Vernon. *Kohikohinga; Reminiscences and Reflections of 'Rapata'.* Auckland and Wellington, Whitcombe & Tombs, 1939.

Robley, H. G. *Moko; or Maori Tattooing.* London, Chapman & Hall, 1896.

Ross, Ruth. *New Zealand's First Capital.* Wellington, Dept. of Internal Affairs, 1946.

Rough, David. 'The Early Days of Auckland.' Supplement to the *New Zealand Herald,* 11, 18 and 25 Jan. 1896. Pasted into book, APL.

Scholefield, Guy H. *Captain William Hobson, R.N.* London, OUP, 1934.

Selwyn, G. A. *Letters from the Bishop to the Society for the Propagation of the Gospel; together with extracts from his Visitation Journal from July 1842 to January 1843.* London, Society for the Propagation of the Gospel, 3rd ed., 1847.

Servant, C. *Customs and Habits of the New Zealanders.* Trans. J. Glasgow, ed. D. Simmons. Wellington, Reed, 1973.

Sherrin, R. A. A., and J. H. Wallace. *Early History of New Zealand.* Auckland, H. Brett, 1890.

Shortland, Edward. Journals of an expedition through the Waikato with Governor Hobson in April 1842 and of an expedition with Mr Clarke, Protector of the Aborigines, to Coromandel from Auckland via Maraetai, 2 July 1842 *et seq.* MS 21, Hocken.

—Journal of a journey to Matamata, Tauranga and Waikato, 8 October 1842 *et seq.* MS 22, Hocken.

—Journal of journeys, 29 Nov. 1842–Aug. 1843. MS 20, Hocken.

—Journal notes kept while in the Middle Island 1843-44. MS 24, Hocken.

—'A gentleman of the Governor's party.' *Auckland Standard,* 9 May 1842.

—Letterbooks, 1842-50. MSS 86/A and 86/B, Hocken.

—Letterbook, miscellaneous notes, and Waiata book. MS 489, Hocken.

—*Traditions and Superstitions of the New Zealanders,* 2nd ed. London, Longman, Brown, Green, Longman & Roberts, 1856.

Smith, S. Percy. 'History and Traditions of the Taranaki Coast.' *JPS,* v.16, 1907, pp.120-73, 175-219; v.17, 1908, pp.1-47; v.18, 1909, pp.157-204; v.19, 1910, pp.1-38.

—*Maori Wars of the Nineteenth Century.* Wellington, Whitcombe & Tombs, 1910.

Sorrenson, M. P. K. 'The Maori People and the City of Auckland.' *Te Ao Hou,* June 1959.

Stacpoole, John M. *William Mason, First New Zealand Architect.* Auckland, AUP, 1971.

Stone, R. C. J. *Young Logan Campbell.* Auckland, AUP, 1982.

Swainson, William. *Auckland, the Capital of New Zealand, and the Country Adjacent.* London, Smith, Elder & Co., 1853.

Symonds, W. C. Copy of Journal. MS, Hocken.

Taylor, Alan and W. A. Taylor. *The Maori Builds.* Christchurch, Whitcombe & Tombs, 1966.

Taylor, Nancy (ed.). *Early Travellers in New Zealand.* Oxford, Clarendon Press, 1959.

Taylor, Richard. *Te Ika a Maui.* London, Wertheim & MacIntosh, 1855; Wellington, Reed, 1974.

—Sketchbook. AIML.

Terry, Charles. *New Zealand, its Advantages and Prospects, as a British Colony.* London, T. & W. Boone, 1842.

Thomson, A. S. *The Story of New Zealand.* 2v. London, John Murray, 1859.

Wade, W. R. *A Journey into the Northern Island of New Zealand.* Hobart Town, George Rolwegan, 1842.

Waititi, John. 'An Outline of Auckland's Maori History.' *Journal of the Auckland Historical Society,* v.2 no. 1, Oct. 1963.

Wake, C. H. 'George Clarke and the government of the Maoris.' *Historical Studies, Australia and New Zealand,* v.10 no.39, Nov. 1962.

Ward, Alan. *A Show of Justice; Racial 'Amalgamation' in Nineteenth-Century New Zealand.* Auckland, AUP, 1973.

Whiteley, John. Correspondence. Methodist Archives, Christchurch.

Williams, H. H. *A Dictionary of the Maori Language.* Wellington, Govt. Printer, 1971.

Williams, John B. *The New Zealand Journal, 1842–1844, of John B. Williams of Salem, Massachusetts,* ed. Robert W. Kenny, Salem, Peabody Museum, 1956.

Winks, Robin. 'The Doctrine of Hauhauism.' *JPS,* v.62, 1953, pp.199ff.

Yate, William. *An Account of New Zealand.* London, Sealey & Burnside, 1853; Wellington, Reed, 1970.